One Foot In The Grave

One Foot In The Grave

David Renwick

BBC BOOKS

With love to Win and Jim
for having me

Published by BBC Books,
a division of BBC Enterprises Limited,
Woodlands, 80 Wood Lane, London W12 0TT

First Published 1992

Reprinted 1992

© DAVID RENWICK 1992

ISBN 0 563 36428 9

Photoset in Sabon by Redwood Press, Melksham, Wiltshire
Printed and bound in Great Britain by Redwood Press, Melksham, Wiltshire

Contents

CHAPTER ONE

Trouble in the Air

A s usual the weather was wet.

Not wet in the sense of damp or good for the garden, but wet in the sense of a train-spotter wearing open-toed sandals.

The sky was the colour of a history essay, and the dulling clouds of a late March morning reeked coldly of indifference. Outside, the East wind rose, fell away, rose again, dithered about the rooftops for a while in a pretty tentative fashion, took a huge breath, and then, changing its mind just at the last minute, scuttled for cover down the drainpipes like some form of baroque organ toccata in reverse.

It was 5.55 a.m.

And by tradition Victor Meldrew would not splutter to life for another hour and a half with, as ever, one nostril horribly blocked up and a mouth as dry as dust; as if some midnight prowler had decided to sand down his tongue during the night with a piece of emery cloth and then shoved it up his nose.

Alongside him his wife Margaret emitted hardly a murmur. Her slumbering form was at peace with the world, her batteries of endurance still on overnight charge, readying her for the Herculean challenge of another day's marriage. The ghost of a smile played softly on her lips, as behind her eyelids she gazed into a serene oblivion of nameless pleasures that had little to do with the drudgery of a fifty-five-year-old suburban house-wife.

Victor twitched suddenly in his sleep. Something had just tickled the side of his face: something small, flickering and hairy. Without actually rousing him to a state of consciousness, his brain at once analysed the neurological stimuli and issued a reflex response via his autonomic nervous system.

'Bugger off.'

A few seconds passed. And then, there it was again. The undeniable sensation of a moist, bristling something exploring his right cheek, its comb-like filaments brushing across his skin.

1

Slowly, rhythmically, up and down ... something spiky and disagreeably slimy. Yes, there was no mistaking it this time.

It could only be an estate agent.

Victor's eyes snapped sharply open as he heaved the young man's sticky, gelled head off his shoulder and jammed it indignantly into the small recessed window of the aeroplane.

Aside from a momentary tacit in his snore the man did not appear to react, but, with property pamphlets clutched to his chest like a teddy bear, snuggled cosily into his new position and snoozed merrily on.

Victor, on the other hand, was now un-merrily wide awake. Sweeping the cabin from stem to stern with a searchlight-scowl he settled back and tried to get comfortable in his seat.

He was, of course, mindful of the fact that comfort and travelling Pauper Class on a crowded 707 charter flight were not exactly synonymous. But he tried anyway. At one point earlier on he had attempted to cross his legs, and the domino effect had woken up people thirteen rows ahead and knocked over the drinks trolley. So he settled for the semi-bearable agony of one knee squashed against the arm-rest with a foot wedged down the magazine pocket on the back of the seat in front of him.

His stomach was only slightly scrunched up now, dramatically reducing the acute sensation of nausea from which he had been suffering since his airline lunch. For this he had only himself to blame: through lack of concentration he had, in a ghastly blunder, thrown away the cellophane wrapping and eaten the chicken risotto instead. A foolish mistake for which he was now paying dearly.

'Ohhhhhh *Goddddd*.'

Sleep had, at least, afforded him a brief respite. He had been dreaming – he remembered now – and it had been a quite wonderful dream.

He had dreamt that the world was a decent place to live, and the people in it rather friendly; that he had not in fact been made redundant two months earlier, and after forty-five years of full-time employment callously tossed aside onto the scrap-heap of life.

He had dreamt that the last fortnight had not been spent on a package holiday of ineffable misery in rain-sodden Greece, from which he was now returning with all the optimism of an arthritic cart-horse bound for a glue factory.

He had dreamt that though no longer young he was yet young in spirit, with a valid role still to play in society; that age and experience were recognised and revered by the generations that followed his, and that, when it came down to it, Life at Sixty really wasn't as odious and hopeless as it was cracked up to be, and there was still plenty left to be cheerful about.

But of course it was just a dream.

Athens! Well, it had seemed like a bad idea at the time, and the reality had more than lived up to the prospect.

The accommodation had been predictably pokey. Crammed into a tiny attic room where you had to open the fanlight to take your vest off, the two of them had been awoken every morning at five by a racket in the square below of voices and car horns almost certainly orchestrated by the late Jacques Tati.

In-house breakfast had been a complimentary glass of water-flavoured orange juice, washed down by a slab of arid Madeira cake that was like chewing the paperback edition of *Little Dorrit*. So by Day Four Margaret had suggested they eat out.

On Day Five Victor had had an argument with a waiter over the tip, and had spent most of the afternoon tweezering pieces of crumbled baklava out of his left ear. In the evening he had strolled down to Syntagma Square for a souvlaki and come back with an unpleasant anal infection, sparking a frantic search in the phrase-book for a Greek word that meant 'fungicidal jelly'.

By the end of the first week the novelty of trudging round grimy streets inhaling a fragrant cocktail of carbon monoxide and fetid fetta had, oddly enough, begun to fade. Nevertheless, even Victor had recognised the advantages of being away from home, like not having to talk to the boring man up the road whose only topic of conversation was the price of lawn-mowers. An advantage which terminated abruptly when they found that, by a hideous coincidence, he was staying in the hotel room next to theirs. As a result, they had been forced to spend the rest of the holiday dodging hastily out of sight round corners whenever they heard the approaching rustle of a Qualcast brochure.

And it would be some time to come before Victor recovered from the joyless experience of ascending the ancient Hill of the Muses, to discover on its crumbling marble columns the scrawled legend 'Meldrew is a Wanker' in green aerosol paint.

An inscription, he was informed by a local Greek student, that had been there at least five years now to his certain knowledge, although he was unable to shed any light on the identity of its original author.

Victor sighed a deep sigh that began somewhere in the furthest extremity of his complimentary airline slipperettes and emerged expressively at the other end, filtered through every molecule of his weary being.

Life and those who were blessed with it had long been one great unfathomable mystery as far as Victor was concerned. Far from conforming to a set of universal laws, the world and everything in it appeared to function in a totally arbitrary fashion devoid of any rational order whatsoever. It stood to reason there was no actual *point* to any of it: why, otherwise, when he was bound for Athens two weeks ago would he have found a dead snake in his flight bag? *That*, for certain, was beyond any law of logic *he* could think of.

With three score years behind him now Victor's tolerance of the gallery of grotesques who made up mankind had worn pretty threadbare. Like that reptile he had found coiled around his bag of Opal Fruits he seemed, with advancing age, to shed more and more layers of skin to a point where his powers of resilience had all but deserted him.

Who was it who once said we weave a noose of ill-humour to hang ourselves from the gallows of our own bad grace?

It was Mrs Skimpson at Number 45 if memory served, and *she* was as mad as a hatter. And not the sort of person to get stuck next to when you were queuing up in the post office of a Monday morning, as Victor had often learned to his cost.

Victor was, of course, a loser.

True, the snags and flaws in the fabric of life that were the cause of his constant rage are familiar to most of us in one form or another. But Victor, assuredly, came in for more than his fair share of them: seismic eruptions of adversity, of which Victor Thomas Meldrew was the inevitable epicentre. It was a simple enough philosophy, and one he found reliably to have stood the test of time: that just when you are convinced things are never, ever going to get better, they suddenly get worse.

'*Ping*,' said the small illuminated rectangle above his head, and obediently he coupled his seat-belt and prepared himself for descent. All around him bodies were half-stirring, faces crumpled like old socks, blinking in the milky dawn of a bright new day.

It would not be such a bright one for Victor Meldrew.

CHAPTER TWO

Retire and
Light Blue Touch Paper

Mrs Inglis rose from her snowy leather chair, closed the door to her office and sat down again.

No, she could still hear it loud and clear. The worst of it was wafting up from the entrance downstairs and in through her window. Rising again she pulled the double-glazed panel to, sealing out the chunter of the car-clogged one-way system below with a seductive '*phhhutt*', and once again sat down.

But still she could hear it. If she was not mistaken it was coming up through the floor, rising from the cavernous lobby, which was acting as a rather efficient amplifier unit, and then being conducted with digital accuracy along the steelwork frame of the building into a form of high-fidelity THX sound right in the middle of her ashwood-and-chrome fourth-floor suite.

Easing the foam-rubber pads delicately over her ears she rolled the volume wheel to maximum and slid the switch to Play. Strangely, the rap beat that now thundered through the bone of her skull enabled her to resume work on her presentation to Mr Mycroft. Some sounds you could work around, others you couldn't. And *that* sound in particular was one she would rather not have playing on her conscience this bleak January morning.

It was the sound of Victor Meldrew's desk being systematically dismantled and broken up for firewood.

He had taken it very well, considering. Considering he had failed to propel the personnel manager through a plate glass window to her certain death, he really had taken it far better than expected.

He did not remember driving back to his house that morning. Which was pretty scary in itself. In fact it had all been over so quickly, like the swift wringing of a chicken's neck, that he could scarce believe it had happened at all. Already the gory details were becoming sketchily indistinct: she had asked him to step into her office and not to sit down as the chair had just been re-upholstered, but as to what happened next, he couldn't confidently say.

He had emerged, zombie-fashion, into the employees' car park like some staring pod-creature from *The Invasion of the Body Snatchers*, apologising profusely to a litter bin when he stubbed his foot on its concrete base. Fortuitously, his Hillman Avenger, after some five years of travelling to the office and back, was by now feeling pretty confident about the route and managed to ferry its dazed passenger back to 37 Wingate Crescent safe and sound.

Early retirement.

She had said it with a nervous chuckle ... or was it a witch's cackle?

Productivity downturn across the board ... manufacturing output squeezed by the recession ... inevitable process of integrational streamlining ... little black box ... desperately sorry to see you go ... almost part of the furniture ... we all shed a tear or two ... buy yourself a fishing rod ... traumatic time for you, I appreciate that ... Ginny! I've been trying to call you all week, how were the Alps?

The words darted to and fro on motes of memory, tauntingly, like demons inside his head. Meaningless euphemisms that added up to one thing: his job as security officer on the front desk at Watson-Mycroft was, after twenty-six years, no more. He, Victor Meldrew, had been as good as told to go away and stick his head down a waste-disposal system. He was an unwanted item, a piece of ballast being cruelly heaved over the side, with nothing left to look forward to but a few brief years of plummeting and then thunk.

Just a minute ... what was that again?

He spooled back mentally until it re-appeared in crisper focus....

Little black box!

Yes, that had been the ultimate insult.

They had kicked him out so as to install, in his place, a small programmable keyboard unit on the wall of the entrance lobby. Sleekly superior in its matt-black casing it sat speciously inside the main doors like a rather condescending giant slug. Future visitors would simply feed in an assigned personal security code and a pre-recorded voice of talking treacle would invite them to take a seat while their arrival was duly announced in the appropriate quarters. Infinitely cheaper than Victor to run, and with the added benefit that it didn't keep moaning about the air-conditioning.

Twenty-six years! Of painstaking dedication and loyalty, and now here he was making way for a glorified bread bin stuffed with wires and micro-chips.

It was a sad fact, but inescapable: Victor Meldrew had become a lower form of life than a Duracell battery.

A t first Margaret refused to believe it, it was just Victor's idea of a sick joke. But then when Fat Agnes who kept the celery stall in the market rang up to offer her condolences, she had to accept it as incontrovertible fact.

As she replaced the phone in its cradle the deep furrow in her brow gradually receded.

'So that was what he was talking about, it all makes sense now....'

'What who was talking about?' said Victor.

'That man at the bus stop yesterday morning. Came up to me and said he was very sorry to hear the tragic news, but said it was nothing to get suicidal about, you should look on it as a new chapter in your life, and on no account to go home and stick your head in a gas oven. I just put him down for a weirdo at the time, but of course now I see what he was on about.'

Victor gazed at her in bafflement.

'W—. How is it all these people know everything that's about to happen before I do? I suppose when the CIA decide to invade Nicaragua the first thing they'll do is ring up Fat Agnes and convene a top-level briefing with the man at the bus stop! I mean I'm nobody – I'm only the one they're firing!'

Margaret sank into the armchair with a philosophical shrug.

'Seems to be happening to everybody just lately. It was exactly the same with poor old Arthur, d'you remember? A lifetime of loyal service and commitment, and then all of a sudden, one morning, that was it. They said he was past it. And *he* was only fifty-seven.'

'He was an elephant.'

'I know he was an elephant. I'm well aware he was an elephant. He was giving the children elephant rides, so it's obvious he was an elephant. I'm just making the point, how quickly you can become dispensable.'

Victor bristled, turning the page of his newspaper, beadily.

'Already the beginning of the end,' he grumbled, bitterly. 'Young boy down the corner tried to help me across the road this afternoon. Till I gave him a swift cuff round the ear. Only be a matter of time before they're forcing me at gunpoint to go on a day trip to Eastbourne. Replaced by a box? It won't be long now before they're sticking me inside one . . . . '

Margaret heaved a grave sigh, inwardly. Today was the first day of the rest of her life. Why did she get the strange feeling she had just become a mother?

It was a foolish thing, but Margaret couldn't suppress a certain feeling of guilt. After all, her job at the florist's had never been so secure. With the economic climate grim beyond belief and the health service in tatters the shop was enjoying an unprecedented upturn in suicides and natural deaths. In the ten years she'd worked there she'd never known such a run on lilies. *A cornucopia of corpses*, Mrs Treby had called it, as she merrily bowled another wreath into the stock room with a bamboo cane. For certain, after thirteen years of Conservative government the future of the floral tributes industry had never looked rosier.

No, his wife was not at all without sympathy. For there was a deep well of compassion in Margaret Meldrew, belied by her often stoic exterior. The slightness of her feathery frame masked formidable reserves of character that were founded on a constitution of high-tensile steel. And thirty-five years spent with a man as volatile as phosphorus had equipped her with an elastic tolerance equal to most of life's routine insanities.

There were, however, lurking round the corner, insanities that were very far from routine . . . .

Buying the camera was a mistake.

Like most things it had seemed a good idea at the time: photography was, after all, 'a uniquely exciting leisure pursuit guaranteed to afford any recently retired senior citizen hours of rewarding fun by unlocking his creative instincts and encouraging him to explore the natural wonders of the world around us'.

9

And so it was that Victor set out for Bluebell Hill with his tripod to take a timed exposure of the sunset and was mugged by a gang of Arsenal supporters.

Unaware of their presence until, squinting through the lens, he observed the top of a gruesome shaved head rise up like Chad in the view-finder, he was powerless to fend them off. And a minute later, as he ricocheted from tree to tree in an orgy of mindless violence – desperately trying to recall a judo move he had once seen Valerie Singleton demonstrate on *Blue Peter* – he was obliged to concede that he would, after all, have been better off buying a stamp album.

As it happened he had been carrying little of value besides the camera and his wallet containing a small amount of cash. In addition they had made off with his brown tweed jacket, prompting Margaret to speculate that the thieves were either blind or planning to line a dog basket.

'Bloody thugs,' cursed Victor, as he and Margaret returned that night after three hours of untrammelled misery in the hospital's accident wing. 'I mean, what is it with kids today? If they're not cracking your skull open with a Mackeson's bottle for pleasure and profit they're daubing obscenities all down your street and shoving jars of urine through the bloody letter-box.'

'They're doing *what*?' said Margaret, putting her keys away.

'You saw that on our front doormat this morning!'

'That was a free sample of Lucozade!'

'Yes, well. They're just as bad, the crap they keep trying to sell you all the while these d— Ohhhhh I don't *believe* it!' He broke off, clawing at his ears in despair as a deafening symphony of clangs and rattles suddenly woke every echo in the house – rather as if a colony of mice had constructed a high-speed rail network inside the hot water pipes and it was just coming up to rush hour.

'That bloody central heating! Two weeks of this we've had to put up with, you can't tell me that's just an airlock. Driving me round the bloody bend – clang! clang! clang! morning, noon and night!'

'Will you watch your stitches!' shouted Margaret. 'Keep jerking your head up and down like that your forehead'll *never* knit back together. I'll ring for a plumber first thing in the morning.'

'Well just make sure it's not that one with the glass eye again. That lavatory's still a death-trap to this day. Trying to make out he knew exactly what he was doing – even I know a ball-cock goes on the *inside*.'

Victor paused, then glared balefully up at the ceiling with a pacified grunt.

'Stopped now. For the time being, anyway.'

And jamming his cap over the end of the bannister he tramped sourly through into the kitchen, while Margaret disappeared upstairs. What he needed now, without question, was a stiff drink. An escape hatch through which he could, if only for a few hours, gain relief from headaches temporal and spiritual. Ah, the heart-warming glow as that first slug of whisky flows across the rocks and kicks the palate, the burning clash of fire and ice. Victor was already mentally salivating as he uncapped the bottle and set down a tumbler on top of the freezer.

He opened the cabinet to slide out the ice tray and then stopped, gobsmacked, in his tracks.

No....

No, no, it couldn't be.

He slammed the door shut again, closing out the horror of it. Obviously the concussion was worse than he'd thought. This was one after effect of a Dr Martens scalp massage he had not been warned about. For a fleeting moment just then he thought he had seen....

But no, *that* would be ridiculous.

Having paused while his pulse settled back down into the high hundreds, he dared to try again....

And immediately wished he hadn't.

He was still standing there, motionless, as if in a state of perpendicular *rigor mortis*, when Margaret reappeared, flicking through a copy of *Yellow Pages*.

'There was a plumbing firm Mrs Althorp used last year to sort out *her* central heating. You remember? When she found those tomato pips had taken root in the carpet...?'

'Margaret....'

'What is it?'

'Did you put a cat in our freezer?'

'What?'

'The freezer cabinet, for God's sake – look! There's a *cat* in it!'

'W ... a dead one?'

'Well it's not playing with a bloody ball of wool, woman! Look at it, it's frozen solid!'

11

Margaret ventured to look now, and almost passed out on the spot.

Curled up on the second shelf, nestling forlornly between a packet of faggots and two large bags of oven chips, it stared out at them sheepishly. Rock hard from its tail to its whiskers, it had once been a rather sweet, long-haired marmalade tom. Now it was an ice sculpture. Its thick, fluffy coat had taken on the permafrost of an Electrolux frozen food compartment, and, inevitably, lost. Its fur, looking for all the world as if it had been liberally dusted with caster sugar, resembled something more commonly seen wrapped around an Eskimo.

'How many times have I told you about leaving that bloody door open?' Victor seethed as, gingerly donning a pair of oven mitts, he prepared to slide the shelf, complete with its deep-frozen passenger, out into the open.

'You're not going to take it *out*!' Margaret positively shrieked with sudden terror.

'Well I'm not going to leave it in there, am I?' Victor rounded on her. 'So its little eyes light up every time we open the door? God almighty, I just don't believe this is happening....'

'Are you sure it's dead....'

Victor paused to stare in disbelief. 'Well I should think it's a pretty safe bet, wouldn't you? I mean it's a bit parky in there at the best of times!' Brusquely, he rapped the creature hard up and down on the side of the table to prove the point. Unsurprisingly, there was not so much as a shivery miaow. 'I mean how's it supposed to have kept warm? Rubbed two fish fingers together to start a fire?'

Margaret backed off, squeamishly, as Victor snapped a black refuse bag off a roll and slid the hapless animal inside.

'Hohhhh my Godddd ... I've come over all cold....'

'*You've* come over all cold!'

'I think I feel sick.... How long do you think it had been in there?'

'I don't know, I'll look for its sell-by date! I mean this was all I needed, the end to a perfect day! It's lucky we haven't got a chest-freezer, we might be standing here with a frozen mammoth!'

Margaret crossed her arms around herself, weakly, and clutched her sides. 'It's that stray. It's been sniffing around here for the last two or three days....'

'Well I think it's safe to say it won't be sniffing around any more!'

With which Victor knotted the bag, slung it over his shoulder like a burglar's swag, and stalked off with it to the wheely-bin down by the garden gate. Margaret shuddered as she took a last quivering look inside the freezer and then pushed the door to.

'I've gone right off those Lean Cuisines.'

K er-clank! Ker-clank! Ker-clank!

On the radio a politician in a mind-numbingly expensive suit was talking about something of vital importance to every man, woman and child in the United Kingdom in an extremely patronising manner. Because he was in a BBC radio car that was parked next to some road works it was impossible to make out any actual words as such, but the extremely patronising manner was coming over loud and clear, and that was the main thing. And oddly enough, despite the fact that it was only radio, you could make out his mind-numbingly expensive suit just as clearly as if he were on television.

Ker-clank! Ker-clank! Ker-clank!

Margaret, already late for work and in something of a fluster, jabbed the off button, causing both the politician and the woman who was interviewing him – if, philosophically, you were that way inclined – to cease to exist, and scurried back into the kitchen in search of some tissues.

Ker-clank! Ker-clank! Ker-clank!

The plumbing was in skittish mood again this morning, that was readily apparent. What had begun a fortnight ago as a gentle mating coo from one radiator to another downstairs had blossomed now into a rampant animal relationship with copper pipes thumping lustily away at each other in the ceiling into the early hours and beyond. It would have been tempting to throw a bucket of cold water over them had this not involved turning on the tap and triggering still further eruptions.

Ker-clank! Ker-Clank! Ker-cl—

Nothing.

Thank God. It had stopped.

Not so Margaret who was about to fly out the back door when she almost collided with a small pudgy mass reminiscent of a bacon dumpling with a hearing-aid.

'Morning, Mrs Meldrew!'

'Ohhh! Morning, Mrs Burkett, I forgot you were coming round this morning – for the jumble is it?'

'If it's not convenient I can always call back . . . . '

'No, no, no, I've got to dash but, look, there's a big black bag of stuff in the loft. I meant to get it down last night only erm, one or two things cropped up, and . . . . In any case, Victor'll be back any second, he's just popped out to get his prescriptions.'

'If you're sure you can trust me alone in the house, Mrs Meldrew?'

'Oh don't be daft!'

'Well, these days. We've just had some money gone missing at the Institute you know, someone fiddling the funds somewhere. We've had to freeze the kitty and everything.'

'*What!*'

The words sent a thrill of horror through the marrow of Margaret's spine as the events of the previous evening returned to haunt her. It was bad enough that she had spent the night, in her dreams, attempting to thaw the poor thing out with a blow-torch before dashing off to attend a charity premiere of 'Puss In Boots on Ice'. Now the whole hideous episode was one she was keen to expunge from her mind forever.

'I said we've had to freeze the k—'

'Yes! Right! Well. I really have got to rush Mrs Burkett, so I'll leave you to it – OK? And I'll talk to you later – bye!'

'Bye, Mrs Meldrew!'

But Mrs Meldrew had ceased to exist. So to speak.

Mrs Burkett blinked after her through her little round spectacles, and then, revolving on her axis into the hall, proceeded to plod lumpily up the stairs like a snail ascending a lamp post. No stranger to the Meldrew household, she quickly located the hooked rod which unlatched the trap-door into the loft, slid the ladder down, and disappeared into the blackness beyond. The bag would be here somewhere – it was a pity, really, that she hadn't thought to bring up a torch.

Slam!

Victor tossed his cap down on the kitchen table and fumbled feverishly with the packet of goodies he had brought back from the chemist. He had never been able to explain his ghoulish fascination for pharmaceutical preparations, but it was a fact. To Victor, the assembled bottles of pain-killers, eye-lotions and mouthwashes in Superdrug were so many vintage wines, to be lovingly laid down in his medicine cabinet and uncorked years later on the occasion of some special affliction; while the prospect of lighting upon an untried remedy for gum disorders or an exciting new concept in cough syrups caused him to drool at the mouth in anticipation.

Tenderly, he drew the slim white tube of ointment from its cardboard sheath and ran his eye over the small print on the side with growing trepidation.

'Warning! May cause skin to turn dark red and flake off. May bleach dyed fabrics. Avoid contact with mucous membranes. Apply to back of neck with extreme caution. If vomiting occurs discontinue use. Use only as a topical desquamative . . . . Fine! What's in this next one, a nasal spray filled with mustard gas?'

It was just as he began picking at the flaps of his other purchase that a sudden two-tone chime summoned him from his chair into the hall to open the front door.

'Plumber?'

It was one word and yet it was sixty-three words. The text in full ran as follows: 'Look, don't imagine I get any pleasure out of this job, but the mortgage doesn't pay itself and I'm afraid I'm an O level short of becoming a brain surgeon. I've already had it up to here this morning with sodding burst mains and blocked soakaways, so the last thing I need is for *you* to start giving me a hard time, all right?'

'Oh! Yes – right,' said Victor. 'Come in.'

They came in.

Two of them, but one and a half really: the one who had spoken, and his assistant who carried a cloth bag full of rattling noises. The one who had spoken was about thirty with a face of bronzed parchment, a floppy military-style tee-shirt and a pair of grubby khaki shorts. Judging from his acetic manner he probably had veins full of vinegar. His colleague, still convalescing from the shock of puberty, was dressed in shreds with a small silver ring through one ear and probably boxed for the Hitler Youth.

'It's the central heating. The pipes keep clanking,' said Victor. 'It's absolutely deafening, you can't even hear yourself think.'

For two minutes they all stood in the hall listening to complete and utter silence.

'Yes ... well, they've stopped *now* – obviously,' said Victor lamely. 'But you never know when they're going to start up again.'

'Where's your pump?'

Victor led them upstairs to the airing-cupboard on the landing. To open out the louvred pine door he first had to slide the ladder back into the loft and re-lock the hatch, mentally cursing his wife as he did so for continuing to leave things open all over the house.

'I think you'll find it's in there.'

The plumber reached inside to start feeling around the back of the tank, and promptly snapped back out again as if on elastic, with an anguished yelp.

'Bloody *Hellfire!!* That's red-hot, that pipe, what've you been doing, testing nuclear war-heads in there? Look at that, that's burnt me all down the side there, look at that!'

In between dancing about the landing in a jig of agony he indicated a long scorched laceration down the inside of his thigh.

'Yes well I'm sorry about that,' grunted Victor. 'Perhaps we'd better get some sort of dressing for it....'

'Don't tell *him* that, he'll come back with a bottle of vinaigrette! Bloody bollocks for brains, him. I'd be better off with a trained chimp but you think you can get decent labour these days?'

A pause as he squeezed back inside, more gingerly this time, and tinkered about with various spanners for a minute or two. Then....

'That's as I thought, your thermostat's knackered, you could fry an egg on that tank. I mean bugger me, look at that,' he crooked his leg round again by way of hard evidence. 'Look at that, all down there, that's coming up in ruddy blisters now. I mean you must have noticed it was as bad as that for God's sake!'

Victor's patience was now gradually dribbling away down the bannisters. 'Well no, strangely enough I'm not in the habit of crouching about my own airing cupboard dressed as Alec Guinness from *The Bridge on the River Kwai!*' he retorted. 'I thought it was *supposed* to be hot, I thought that was the whole point.'

'I'll have to order you a new one up.' Turning to his assistant he jerked his thumb at the bag on the floor. 'Pack that up and take it back to the van. That's the big white thing on wheels parked outside.' And then to Victor, 'You got a pen for me to do the paperwork?'

Victor and the plumber having disappeared downstairs to the

kitchen, the boy with the pierced ear now began to gather up all the rattling noises and return them to the cloth bag.

At which point he became aware of a faint, ghostly whimper wafting down from somewhere above his head....

'Hello? ... Hello down there! ... Mr Meldrew?? Hello! Somebody! Somebody down there let me out!! Please!! Undo this door!!'

Was it his imagination playing silly bleeders, or the desperate sound of a little old lady calling for help ... a frantic, pitiful cry from another human being in acute distress?

And? What if it was?

He was a plumber, not a bloody social worker. And besides, let's face it, you were better off leaving well alone these days. Go sticking your nose in where it didn't concern you and there was no telling what sort of trouble you could land yourself in.

Ker-clank! Ker-clank! Ker-clank!

And then ... it was almost as if, her croaking voice having failed her, she had begun desperately whacking a rusty old vacuum-cleaner pipe against the cold water tank, in order to gain attention....

Ker-clank! Ker-clank! Ker-clank!

Having packed up the bag and anxious not to linger, the young apprentice scuttled hurriedly downstairs in time to join his gaffer who was just bidding Victor good day at the front door.

Ker-clank! Ker-clank! Ker-clank!

'Ohh for God's sake – will you shut the Hell *uppp!!*' bawled Victor, craning his neck up towards the heavens. 'Just *shuttt uppppp!!*'

The boy looked back up the stairs and then nodded to himself sagely. Of course, that was it. As usual there was a perfectly simple explanation for everything....

The man was a psychopath. A deranged, lunatic goofball who kept an old madwoman locked up in the attic for his own sadistic ends. Fair enough. He made a mental note to leave the van's engine running next time they called back, to be on the safe side.

'We'll let you know as soon as it comes in,' said the plumber as they departed.

'Yes. Right. I suppose so,' said Victor. 'Thanks.' And he closed the door with a clouded brow.

Ker-clank! Ker-clank! Ker-clank!

'Will you for God's sake shutt the bloody H— Ohhh, right, that's it!! I'm not staying here to put up with this all day long!'

And pausing only to snatch his cap from the kitchen table, Victor stormed off down the garden path, slamming the front door grimly behind him.

V ictor had said it would be a complete and utter waste of time. Margaret had argued otherwise. How could you ever expect the police to curb crimes if they weren't informed about them? Failure to report was tantamount to issuing a Muggers' Charter. It was like sending out nice cards with pink deckled edges to every villain in the Home Counties: 'You are hereby cordially invited, on the 18th January next, to viciously kick in the head of Victor Thomas Meldrew and make off down the road with his wallet a bit sharpish. Dress optional, please bring a broken bottle'. No, his course was quite clear: he *had* to go and tell the police.

But Victor said it would be a complete and utter waste of time.

Margaret persisted. That kind of stodgy, apathetic thinking was food and drink to the criminal fraternity. Implicitly you were acknowledging their right to pillage and plunder without fear of redress. And it was his bounden duty to notify the authorities as expeditiously as possible.

But Victor said it would be a complete and utter waste of time.

That, however, was in bed last night. Since when he had paused to reconsider the matter. After all, why *should* they get away with it, the callous bastards? With all the facts at their disposal the police might yet apprehend those responsible, and who knows, he might even get his camera back. Besides which he had no intention whatever of staying inside the house all day long with that bloody pile-driving racket going on in the loft. No, he would, after all, pay a call on his local constabulary and place before them the details of the whole dreadful affair.

It was a complete and utter waste of time.

For an hour and a half he was kept waiting in front of the inquiry desk, flanked on one side by a young mother shaking a wailing baby up and down as if it were a bottle of ketchup, and on the other by a man with a nose shaped like a steam iron who was grappling with the collars of two pit bull terriers he had evidently brought in to be destroyed. At one point the girl quite baldly hauled out her left bosom and offered it to the grizzling homunculus to slurp on, which action appeared to have the effect of a dinner gong on the two dogs. Their jaws grinding away like metal plates behind their muzzles to the accompaniment of a Satanic snarl, they began terrifyingly to shower Victor's trouser leg with foaming spittle, prompting the ever-comforting assurance from their owner, 'It's all right, they won't harm you.'

It was long gone midday when a wild, staring man with claw-like hands who Victor assumed to be some sort of serial killer came over and said 'I'm Detective Constable Lawrence, would you like to come through now please?'

Two hours of testimony followed, during which Victor did his best to reconstruct the incident. Then, having asked him to remain seated for a moment, DC Lawrence left the interview room and was presently replaced by a slender woman in her thirties carrying a floppy leather briefcase and a tin of biscuits. She wore a smart woollen suit in French mustard, little material of which had been wasted on the skirt, and her dark, smoky hair billowed uncontrollably behind her as if her head was on fire.

She said her name was Monica, but she said it as if she was addressing the back row of the Dress Circle at the Apollo Astoria.

'Mr *Meldrew* isn't it!! *Lovely* to meet you, please don't get up!!'

Victor didn't.

'I'm actually from the Social Services!' she shouted. 'But the Detective Constable thought it might be a good idea if I came by and just had a little *chat* with you! About this horrid business you've been through, would that be all right d'you think!!'

Victor stared at her, then turned round and peered pointedly out of the window.

'I'm sorry? I thought perhaps the Hunchback of Notre Dame was swinging about outside on a bell-rope. Are you talking to me? I'm not deaf, thank you very much. I can hear you perfectly well without you having to shout.'

'Of course you can!' shouted Monica, and sat down in front of him, linking her legs with a silken whisper of black nylon beneath the table. 'Basically I'm working alongside the police here at the moment in a kind of experimental liaison interface, to provide counselling for persons such as yourself where we feel it might be helpful. Would you like a biscuit?'

She levered off the lid of the tin and, as if to prove there was no trickery involved, plucked out a single Nice wafer and nibbled at the corner before referring back to her document folder.

'Now then, Mr Meldrew ... it's *Victor* isn't it ....'

'Yes.'

'And I gather it was a rather vicious and totally unprovoked attack ...'

'Yes.'

'... involving a group of young boys ...'

'Yes.'

'... which occurred while you were out last night.'

'Yes.'

'Tch tch tch .... Rrrrright.'

She tossed her hair about sadly and scribbled something on a yellow legal pad before looking up to fix him through her deeply compassionate tawny eyes.

'And you've no idea what it was that made you beat them up.'

'None at all. One minute I was j— what do you mean?' Victor suddenly jerked upright in his seat. 'What do you mean, made *me* beat them up?? *They* beat *me* up, for God's sake! I was the bloody victim! I don't go around leaping on innocent people and battering them half to death for my own idle amusement!!'

'Oh.' Monica paused, suddenly thrown off course, it seemed. 'Oh you don't.'

'Well of course I don't!'

'Ah, right. Well, in that case let's just go back over the main details again then, shall we ...'

And, pausing to put down her pen for the moment, she replaced the lid on the biscuit tin.

K er-clank. Pause. Ker-clank. Pause. Ker .... Clerrr. The racket in the attic, whatever it was, seemed to be running out of steam somewhat.

And small wonder. It was, after all, now gone six o'clock in the evening. Unbridled and full-throated much earlier on in the day, the plangent distress signal of hoover-pipe upon water-tank had gradually ground to a halt rather like an old vinyl record winding down. For the sad but simple truth had finally and inevitably dawned: there was no one in the house to hear. And, after some nine and a half hours of furious clanking and clunking, it would be a very fit racket indeed with the stamina to maintain such a level of metallic stridency.

It was, therefore, to a house recently fallen silent that Victor returned, grudgingly, after his unhappy ordeal at the police station.

He hadn't, of course, come directly home. There had been a bit of shopping to get in, notably that pair of wax ear plugs he had noticed on sale in Boots, and a small starting pistol from the sports shop with which he intended to deter any future would-be assailants. Later on in the pub he had shown this to Mr Prout who quipped that it would certainly come in handy if he was attacked in an alleyway by Chris Akabusi. Over a pint they had both bemoaned the rising tide of violent behaviour among the young, with Mr Prout citing in evidence his trip to the corporation rubbish tip that very afternoon, where to his horror he had found wedged down one of the skips a dead cat that some monster had suffocated inside a plastic bin liner. For sick people like that birching was, in his opinion, too lenient. Personally he would have them all flayed alive.

'Margaret? I'm back! ... Margaret?'

Silence.

Which was a little strange, since it was her half day at the florist's. Obviously she had been detained somewhere on some routine errand or other.

But then, as he was about to fill the kettle, the phone went, and it was his wife's consternated voice at the other end.

'Victor! I've been ringing all afternoon, where the Hell've you been to!'

'Don't!' rasped Victor. 'I've been stuck waiting half the day down the bloody police station, squashed next to naked nipples and horrific Hell-hounds and God knows what-not ... and then got precious little sympathy in the end when I *did* finally get in to see someone. Seem to care more about the bloody criminals these days than the victims. They end up catching the thugs that did it they'll probably give them the Queen's Award for Industry. Anyway, where are you?'

A huge sigh gusted back down the earpiece.

'I haven't had a chance to get back at all yet, I'm at Mr Burkett's. His wife hasn't come home, and no one seems to have the faintest idea where she's got to.'

'What – you mean she's just disappeared?'

'There's nobody seen hide nor hair of her since she left our place this morning. And now of course Mr Burkett's got one of his nasty trembling fits coming on, and he's j—'

There was a sudden sound of rattling and crashing crockery in the background, like afternoon tea being served on a scenic railway.

'Leave it, Mr Burkett!' called Margaret. 'I'll sweep it up later!'

'Tchh, that's a mystery and a half then,' said Victor. 'I wonder where she could have g—. Ohhhh I don't *believe* it!!'

Ker-clank! Ker-clank! Ker-clank!

Suddenly it had started up all over again. That bloody clanking in the loft!

Somewhere, too, amid all the weary pounding there was a muffled, barely discernible voice, like some half-felt presence at a seance, trying to make itself heard through a pair of ceilings. But Victor hadn't detected it, and was, in any case, already stripping the plastic bubble pack off his new ear-plugs.

'Shutttt uppp! You hear that, Margaret? Bloody worse than ever now! Anyway, yes I suppose you'd better just stay there with him till she shows up. No, no, I'll be fine here – yes all right, bye.'

Ker-clank! Ker-clank! Ker-clank!

Replacing the receiver on its wall-mounting he stuffed the two little vermiculate plugs deep inside each ear cavity, listened, opened the door into the hall and listened again at the foot of the stairs, and finally sighed a deep sigh of unutterable relief.

Perhaps he would get some peace for the rest of the evening now after all.

'Any joy?' asked Victor, looking up from his newspaper as Margaret trudged through the back door the following morning.

Happily he, for once in his life, had had a good night. The ear plugs, he soon discovered, were an absolute hit. Not since the invention of the rubber prophylactic had such a successful barrier been devised against undesirable incursions. Not only had they shielded him from that ruddy din of percussive pipes in the roof, they had also proved gloriously effective in muting his own voice, with the result that he was able to moan and groan out loud for much of the night about rising crime and early retirement and dead cats and many other related topics without ever once having to listen to himself. Add to this the fact that he afterwards learnt he had failed to hear two Jehovah's Witnesses ringing his doorbell at seven o'clock, and it was clear there was a lot to be said for a policy of self-inflicted deafness.

Margaret, on the other hand, was looking rather less triumphant after a long and sleepless night of nervous jitters at the Burkett residence.

'He's started fretting now that she may have been abducted to grant sexual favours to various sultans in the United Arab Emirates. I'm afraid he always did tend to live in a bit of a fantasy world.'

'Well she must be *somewhere*, for goodness sake.'

Margaret flopped down beside him at the kitchen table letting her bag droop to the floor. She looked as if every last drop of energy had been sucked out of her body with a giant drinking straw. 'Did she say anything to you before she left here yesterday morning?'

'I didn't see anything of her. What time did she come round?'

'Well. I left her to go up into the loft for that jumble, must have been round about nine-forty-five, which would mean she must have l—'

Ker-clank! Ker-clank! Ker-clank!

'Hallo! First of the morning,' said Victor, apparently inserting a small piece of solidified chewing-gum into his ear. 'I suggest you get yourself a pair of these, they're more effective than I thought they'd be. Don't know what I'd have done without them all last night, to be honest, they were an absolute Godsend....'

But Margaret was no longer listening.

Ker-clank! Ker-clank! Ker-clank!

She was gazing, dumbly, up towards the roof of the house with an expression of dawning, apocalyptic dread....

Ker-clank! Ker-clank!

Surely there was no man alive who would be capable of such an atrocity? No human being in his right mind who could have perpetrated such a truly awful, unthinkingly barbaric act as *that*?

Ker-clank!

She took one look at the man beside her spreading lemon curd on his Weetabix and knew she had her answer.

'Ohhhh *Godddd*, Victor, nohhhhh....!'

'Sorry?'

'You *haven't!!*'

Like an arrow she was out of her seat and up the stairs, leaving Victor still gazing after her blankly at the table.

'What is it? Margaret...?'

It would remain, in all probability, indelibly branded on her conscience for the rest of her days: that crushed, hollow-eyed face that gazed down as she unlatched, finally, the loft-door in the landing ceiling.

It was a face etched with a misery that knows no name. A face impoverished of spirit and gutted of all hope. It was a being of humankind in outward physiognomy only. For her soul had long past ebbed with the shapeless passage of hours, ultimately to melt as dust and flee upon the wind.

And if there were any certainty left in this world, where chaos and turmoil and the capricious hand of fate are all the order by which we may try to live our lives, it was just this. That never, ever, again would Mrs Burkett call round to the Meldrews' house to collect a bag of jumble.

CHAPTER THREE

Danger on the Stairs

There were no snows that winter, merely a Cabinet re-shuffle. And since the latter had very much the same effect of snarling up the country and bringing misery to millions, the snows were hardly missed.

The worldly-wise among us said, in any case, that it was too cold for snow. And indeed it was hard to remember a February that had been more bitingly brutal. The rivers froze into landing-strips for skidding seagulls. Children skated on the Serpentine, and Madonna, to no one's great surprise, jogged on water. Buckled branches of leaf-lorn trees, rimed white in the night, clawed at the early morning sky in cheerless supplication: the bare, blanched fingers of the dead.

Margaret had not spoken to him for a week.

The fall-out from unwittingly jailing an eighty-year-old claustrophobic with one kidney inside a benighted garret for twenty-four hours was not swift to subside. Mostly she communicated in a form of primitive morse code that involved messily slamming plates of soup down in front of him and drumming her fingers on the arms of the chair; or, as on one occasion, beating a tattoo with his head on the door of the wardrobe when he asked what the Hell was the matter.

Overnight, since they pensioned him off, Victor felt as if he had become a magnet for hostility.

Little things irked him, like the crumpled crisp packets that flapped around the plant borders on his front lawn. The fist-mangled Heineken cans that turned up inside his little stone wishing-well. The Twix wrappers he found jagged on the honey-suckle. Like the Statue of Liberty the Meldrew garden seemed to beckon to it the wretched refuse of teeming shores.

Or in a word, crap.

Of all descriptions, in every stage of putrid decomposition known to man. In fact there were days when Victor was tempted to wonder whether such events as a simple funeral would soon become a thing of the past: 'Aunty Norma's dead, shall we bury her? No, I can't be buggered, just sling her over that bloke's fence.'

What was it, some chromosomal deficiency that produced the kind of mental mutant that was capable of tossing a KP Discos wrapper onto the pavement? Presumably these were people who regarded a lavatory in their toilet as an optional extra; neo-Neanderthals whose social conscience had been amputated by the junk-life values of an ad-agency culture.

Try as he might, Victor could see little sign of light at the end of the sewer. On his more desolate days he had come dangerously close to ending it all with a tin of ozone-unfriendly furniture polish.

Memory is a flexible friend, editing our lives and experiences to make the recollections more bearable. But nowhere in his remembrance of things past could Victor point to an age of such civic complacency as this: an age where a wall of repression had come down in Eastern Europe only to be reconstituted outside the local polytechnic from empty tins of Diet Lilt.

Like most of us, Victor had always found the Past an interesting place to visit, though he wouldn't want to live there. On the other hand, with the Present and the Future currently looking so unaccountably grim there were days when it had its attractions.

In the aftermath of the Mrs Burkett affair he had, unknown to Margaret, been spending more and more time on his own in the attic. Initially he had begun nosing about up there out of simple morbid curiosity, like a group of Americans touring the death cells at Sing Sing. But then his torch-beam had illuminated a peeling old leather trunk which, when opened, had disgorged such treasures as his very first school report and his earliest, original teddy bear. Stacked tea-chests and dilapidated suitcases had yielded even more wonders: an old chemistry set he had been given for his tenth birthday, a collection of albums of mounted cigarette cards, a plastic model of a flying Superman that you fired from a catapult, the *Radio Fun* annual of 1943 containing a comic-strip of Tommy Handley with trousers flapping like circus tents, the remains of a box of indoor fireworks, the Boys Book of Magic which had been his favourite Christmas present ever, from his Nanna and Grampy Meldrew in Dundee ... and enough dust-encrusted icons from a time of his life now gone forever to stock a fair-sized family museum.

Why?

Why *did* people cling on to a collection of creaky old relics that had served no useful purpose for more than half a century? What conceivable point was there in keeping a half-eviscerated teddy bear with crayoned-on eyes and one ear made crudely from plasticine? It was hard to imagine any child waking up next to it without screaming the house down.

Useless, musty clutter, all of it, that should have been turfed out years ago. Granted it was idly diverting to peruse and ponder here and there – briefly re-living moments and memories that flooded forth like genies released from a bottle – but in the final analysis nothing was sacred. The minute he had finished sorting through it all, he vowed, this lot was going straight on the bonfire.

To this innocent pledge, in due course, could be traced the seeds of his direst nightmare.

On the twenty-fifth day of the month there arrived on Victor's doormat a number of threatening messages.

It wasn't the first time he had received unsolicited mail of this kind. Exactly the same thing had happened at exactly the same time last year. And the year before that. But Victor simply dismissed the messages as the work of cranks, and chose studiously to ignore the rather warped suggestion they all kept making to him.

In short, he was totally determined *not* to have a Happy Birthday.

Once, a long while ago in the brunch-time of his life, before he began to feel quite so threatened by them, birthday cards had been a thing of joy. Nowadays what were they, but successive exit-markers leading off the motorway of Life?

There had been a time, he remembered ruefully, when his young cousin Gladys used to buy him a five-year diary as a Christmas present. Now, he couldn't help noticing, she had switched to the ones with only twelve months in. Presumably it wouldn't be long before she cut her losses altogether and just sent him a week's worth. Clearly no one believed he was long for this earth.

Death was at the top of the agenda these days, there was no getting away from it. And as one who was prone to browsing

through the medical dictionary as if it were a Freeman's catalogue Victor was never short of worrying symptoms.

'I've got two big lumps on the back of my head now!' he
ejaculated in alarm when he and Margaret were out in the car
that morning. 'They weren't there this morning, *I* know! Ohhh
God! Do you know what it said in that book under Stomach
Tumour – "often no symptoms in early stages" .... Well that's
exactly what I've got!'

'Will you give over grizzling, it's just glands!' snapped Margaret, bringing them to a halt beside a big house with a guttering
sprouting sparrows' nests. 'Now then. I wonder what he wants to
see us for?'

Composing himself with heavy reluctance, Victor unfolded the
birthday card he had received that morning from his friend
Beetroot George. It simply said: 'Pop round about twelve, I've
got a little surprise for you'.

'Huhh. What do you *think* he wants to see us for! More
sodding beetroot! Same every time we come here! There's neither
of us ever eats the stuff, it goes straight in the bin. Well I'm sorry,
but I've had enough. I'm finally going to put him out of his misery
today, once and for all.'

'Have you gone totally insane!' hissed Margaret. 'He's been
giving it to us for the last thirteen years! We're the only reason he
grows the bloody things!'

'It stains as well, and you can't get it out for love nor money.'

'In any case, if he said a *little surprise* it might not *be* beetroot
this time. It might be something else, it might b——. Oh! Morning
George!'

They had taken the side path round to the back of the house,
where serried ranks of claret-coloured leaves spanned the garden
from fence to fence in contiguous clusters.

Bestriding them like a Colossus in wellingtons was a gentleman whose face had to all intents and purposes been painted by
Hieronymus Bosch. Delicately extricating himself from the plot
he strode over to pump Victor's hand and then slap him repeat-
edly on the back as if trying to dislodge a hamster from his
windpipe.

'Victor! Happy birthday, boy! Here, come round the back, I've
got a little something for you. You'll never guess what it is in a
million years!'

Exchanging doleful glances, Victor and Margaret followed

him down the muddy pathway to the rear of an old Anderson shelter built from bowed corrugated iron.

And there Beetroot George came to a halt, throwing his hand out in a triumphant gesture of pride.

'Happy Sixty-first, boy!'

That was when they saw it.

As grim and ghastly a vision as Victor could ever have hoped to lay eyes on. Had it been conjured from the drear pen of Edgar Allan Poe it could hardly have aroused in his breast such a sense of insufferable, melancholy woe.

'Be honest, I bet this was the last present you were expecting today!'

'Yes,' croaked Victor. 'Yes, it was. It's ermmm....'

'It's a gravestone.'

'Yes.'

And indeed there was no denying it. More precisely, it was Victor's gravestone. And, if anyone doubted it, there, writ large across the gleaming marble face in an appropriately Gothic type-face was the professionally inscribed legend:

VICTOR THOMAS MELDREW
'OLD VIC'
1930 –
A DEAR OLD FRIEND, SADLY MISSED
HIS SOUL LIVETH ON IN PARADISE

'You haven't already got one?' said Beetroot George, with a sudden wave of concern.

'Nnnnno,' spluttered Victor. 'No, I erm....'

An exhalation of immense relief wafted out across Beetroot George's crooked teeth, like a breeze whistling through Stonehenge.

'Yes, six months I've been working on that. I'm quite pleased with the scroll-work up the top here. Very tricky business. One slip with the chisel and you've bollocksed up your whole slab. And I mean that's a top quality piece of stone as well, that'd cost you a fortune. You see – well, as that always used to be my trade, stonemasonry, I thought he'll appreciate that. It'll make his birthday for him.'

'Mmm? Yes ... yes, right....'

'Obviously I haven't filled in the second date there yet, Margaret, but if and when – just give me a shout. I can soon knock that off. That won't take me a second.'

'Rrrright ... fine,' said Margaret, hoarsely. 'Thanks very much, George.'

Five minutes later, as they were both struggling to heave the tombstone onto the roof-rack, Beetroot George came racing out again clutching a lumpy, wine-stained paper bag which he had very nearly forgotten to give them before they left. They thanked him profusely, asking if he was sure he could spare it, and he assured them there was still much, much more where *that* came from.

M rs Berenger said her husband had been just the same in the early stages, but you had to give it time.

'Forty years down the abattoir and suddenly they give you your cards, it would be a blow to anybody,' she said when she popped into the shop that afternoon to ask Margaret a slightly sneaky favour. 'Ripping pigs to pieces was the only life he knew, and of course suddenly it left the most terrible vacuum. I came downstairs once in the middle of the night and found him kneeling astride the leather pouffe with a carving knife. Hacking away to his heart's content in his sleep. Took about two years before he finally managed to adjust.'

Margaret came back to the counter with six long-stemmed roses and fanned them across a sheet of cellophane paper with a shudder.

'If it takes that long I'll be the one reaching for the carving knife,' she groaned. 'Friend of his gave him a gravestone for his birthday this morning, you can imagine how that went down. I'd just told him to stop thinking about death. Every little thing sets him off just lately. Last night it was that programme about spontaneous combustion – you know, where people suddenly burst into flames for no reason of any kind. You think I could get him out of the shower afterwards? Spends most of the day while I'm at work stuck up in the attic, rummaging through all his old toys. He thinks I don't know anything about it, but I do. Mind you, if it wasn't for that I hate to think what he'd be up to. Slitting his wrists with the letter-opener by now probably.'

'Job to know what to do for the best, isn't it?'

'Yes – well, as a matter of fact I've devised a plan,' said

Margaret, enigmatically. 'I don't want to say too much just yet because it's not confirmed, and in any case he'd only worry himself sick. But it might just turn out to be the answer to all our problems.'

Needless to say, it would turn out to be nothing of the kind.

Friday morning Margaret baked a cake, lovingly folding in the chopped fruit, raisins and mixed nuts with a large wooden spoon. Seven hours later, a team of doctors were removing these same ingredients from the stomach of Mrs Jean Warboys with a rather unpleasant piece of plastic tubing.

Somewhere in between, Mrs Warboys and Margaret had enjoyed a cosy pot of tea together on the sofa in Victor's sitting room. The plate of cakes had been wheeled on by way of a small celebration, to mark their next-door neighbour's first day out of bed following a nasty attack of trichinosis. For two months previously her chief interests in life had been nausea, vomiting, diarrhoea and the novels of Catherine Cookson. In addition, her eyes had become so massively puffed up that people passing her house had been shocked by the apparent sight of a giant frog in heated rollers peering down from the bedroom window.

Being Jewish was, for Mrs Warboys, less an act of faith and more a taste in wallpaper. Which explained how parasitic larvae on a piece of infested pork managed to find their way into her digestive system. Of course there were those who had observed that the parasites were the ones to be pitied in this case, and that if the drugs didn't get them the stories about her childhood in Stanmore would. But these were just the voices of an unkind majority.

'How does it feel now, not quite so bad?' inquired Margaret, having watched a succession of macaroons and chocolate éclairs rapidly disappear past her friend's lips like spacecraft drifting too near a black hole.

'Well it comes and goes when it thinks it will,' said a mouthful of churning meringue. 'The doctor said he thought it had passed its peak now, so I'm all right going back onto solids. I'm so sorry I wasn't able to call round earlier in the week. I felt terrible about not coming to see Victor on his birthday.'

Margaret refrained from pointing out that this had been the one ray of sunshine in her husband's otherwise deeply clouded day, and instead looked up as the man in question trudged in from upstairs wearing a sombre grey trilby hat that would have looked boring even with a flashing fluorescent dildo strapped to the top of it.

'Oh! How was it?'

'Yes very nice thank you,' replied Victor dutifully but with little pretence at enthusiasm. 'Very nice with my best grey coat.'

'It was my Uncle Edwin's,' said a mouthful of grinding cherry cake, as Victor was relieving his head of the belated birthday present. 'They were originally going to bury him in it, but I said no, don't waste it on a corpse. Give it to Victor Meldrew.'

'How very thoughtful of you, Mrs Warboys,' said Victor, while thinking 'How incredibly thoughtless of you, Mrs Warboys,' and then returned to the hall where, before the arrival of the hat, he had been in the process of hoovering the stairs.

Bloody woman.

Bloody birthdays.

Bloody everything.

Bloody Hell . . . .

Bloody footmark on the carpet now.

Bloody people coming in with wet shoes . . . .

Victor padded irritably into the kitchen and began burrowing inside the cupboard beneath the sink. Where had that bottle of carpet shampoo gone to? No wonder they called it Vanish.

In the front room, behind closed doors, Margaret confided to Mrs Warboys her secret plan to lift Victor's spirits and Mrs Warboys thought it sounded an excellent idea.

'I've never been on a holiday to Athens myself,' she said, cheerfully, 'but I'm told it's absolutely horrible. For pollution and congestion and what-have-you.'

'Oh.'

'Filth . . . squalor . . . litter in the streets . . . noise from the traffic. No, it'll be a terrific break for you both, and about time too if you ask me.'

'Yes. Well, I hope so. As I say, the travel agent had these two last-minute cancellations for next week – and incredibly reasonable prices really – so I just took the plunge. I thought it might be the tonic we both need, after all our recent upsets.'

'Oh, and raw sewage. That's another one. They say the stench from the drains sometimes is so disgusting it's enough to knock you clean off your feet. Still, I'm sure you'll both have the time of your lives there, it'll be absolutely marvellous.'

At that point the doorbell rang and Victor, who was now whipping up carpet-cleaning fluid in an old cracked mug, said he would see to it.

His first impression, looking through the frosted glass, was that some bastard had decided to erect an office block on his front doorstep. Then he opened the door to find that the office block was wearing a raincoat and clutching an extremely damp clipboard.

'Electricity?' said a voice like a sonic boom from somewhere high up around cruising altitude.

'Sorry?'

'I need to read your meter. You've had four estimates in a row according to our figures. Can I come in?'

Victor doubted this, as his ceiling was only eight feet high. But more importantly he didn't want this mountain of a man treading muddy splashes all the way down his hall. The rain was pouring off the roof of his porch now like a waterfall, and the overall scene was eerily reminiscent of something out of *Psycho*: it only needed Bernard Herrmann's shrieking strings.

'All right but would you please mind taking your shoes off first – please!'

The small peppery moustache that all meter-readers are issued with upon recruitment twitched grudgingly, as if it were a caterpillar clinging on to his nostrils for dear life.

He grunted, demurred, and then complied.

'Is that the girl from Oxfam?' Margaret shouted through the sitting room door.

'Electricity!'

'Oh right . . . . Yes, so I thought I'd probably break the news to him tonight in bed, when he's half asleep,' she said, returning to Mrs Warboys. 'It's a bit like waiting till someone's under anaesthetic before you actually cut them open, you know? W . . . what is it? You feeling sick again?'

Her friend, who had now turned a rather alarming pasty colour, managed a frail nod, and nursed her stomach. At which Margaret, preparing for the worst, slid Victor's new trilby hat further along the coffee table.

In the hallway a bottom the size of a hippopotamus was projecting from the tiny stair cupboard as the electricity man,

now on all fours, struggled to direct his flashlight at Victor's
meter. Emerging with great difficulty he fixed Victor with an odd
look before putting pen to paper.

'Do you know there's a gravestone inside that cupboard?'

'I do know that, yes,' said Victor. 'I'm well aware of that fact,
thank you very much.'

'It's got an inscription on it.'

'Yes! Thank you, Indiana Jones, I don't need you to tell me
that! It's actually my great uncle. Forty-five years in service to the
gentry, it was his last wish to be buried below stairs. Now have
you quite finished buggering about or what?'

The doorbell sounded again, distracting him.

This time it was the girl from Oxfam.

In the kitchen Margaret sat Mrs Warboys down delicately at
the table and placed a plastic bucket under her nose.

'Just sit still there and try to relax. I'll be back in a second,' she
said, and then raced into the hall and up the stairs, passing, as she
did so, Victor who was just closing the front door.

'What's the matter? What's happened?' he said.

'It's all right, Jean's just feeling a bit jippy in the stomach
again!'

'Too much cake,' was Victor's verdict, but he trudged through
into the kitchen to ask if there was anything he could do.

'It'll probably pass in a minute,' said Mrs Warboys, queasily.
'I'm sure I'll be fine.'

'You want to try some Andrews Liver Salts,' said Victor.
'Always works for me, but you have to drink it right back while
it's still fizzing.'

Having said which he set down, for the time being, the cracked
mug of frothing carpet cleaner which he had been stirring with a
spoon, and left to go upstairs to the bathroom.

'Oh. Right. Thank you,' said Mrs Warboys.

Down by the front door the Electricity Man was ferreting
strangely around the foot of Victor's coat-stand. Slowly, he
straightened, with a glow of danger in his eyes.

'Where's my shoes?'

'Sorry?'

'My shoes!'

'Shoes?'

'Yes, the things I was wearing on my feet when I called at your
house!'

'Well I don't know, I mean you j—' Victor broke off with an anxious eyeline towards the front porch. 'You didn't put them on top of that cardboard box that was out there?'

'I might have done – why?'

'Well that was bloody bright, wasn't it? That's just gone off to Oxfam.'

'Ohh you're winding me up!'

'Why didn't you look where you were putting them, for God's sake?'

'Well I didn't think I was putting them on the next sodding flight to Mozambique, did I!! Whisked away to be air-dropped to famine victims! How am I supposed to go back out there in that lot now with no shoes on? Slop up and down the gutter like Gene Kelly?'

Victor groaned in despair.

'All right! All right! I'll lend you a pair of mine. Wait there one second.'

Tramping back into the kitchen he was, momentarily, surprised to note that Mrs Warboys and her thick fluffy coat which had been draped over the chair were now both gone. He peered out of the window, but through the wall of rain could make out nothing more than an old stray sheepdog lurching uncertainly towards the garden gate on all fours.

'Bloody things,' he rasped, and then fished a pair of his black shoes out from the ironing-board cupboard and offered them to the Electricity Man, who was barely able to squeeze more than a big toe inside each one.

'W— what size of feet d'you call these?' said Victor, blinking down in disbelief.

'Thirteens if it's any business of yours.'

'*Thirteens?* These are eight-and-a-halfs! No wonder Oxfam took them, they'll get a couple of food parcels inside those two. Just tie a parachute to the laces. And look at these socks! What on earth do you need to wear socks as thick as this for? There's no necessity for that, I know!'

'Have you quite finished?' said the Yeti with the clipboard, glaring at him with a beady eye. 'I didn't come here to have the size of my feet ridiculed and the calibre of my socks debated! This is all your doing, this! I should have known better than set foot inside this house in the first place! They warned me about you down at head office. They told me you were a strange piece of work – gravestones in the bloody stair-cupboards. Well I am not leaving here this afternoon without a pair of shoes on my feet, and if you think I am you've got another think coming!'

In the event, it was Victor's late Uncle George who rode to the rescue with a pair of outsize brown brogues Victor had remembered seeing on one of his recent odysseys through the attic. And, grumbling that he would have preferred something in more of a dark taupe but he supposed this would have to do, the Electricity Man slid them on and stomped away, leaving his customer in peace.

'Don't suppose we'll ever see those again,' Victor muttered to himself as he wound up the alarm clock that night after another day of unfettered gloom.

'Will you give over moan-moan-moan,' said Margaret, sliding beneath the quilt. 'Just think of poor old Jean tonight – lying there in hospital having to have her stomach pumped! Can you imagine? Just when they thought she'd got over it, to suddenly go under again like that. Keeling over and spewing up everywhere and God knows what else. Doctor on duty said there were all *manner* of toxins sloshing about her insides. Said it was a complete mystery where they'd all suddenly come from.'

'Mmm. 'Tis a bit odd, that,' said Victor, snugly joining her and switching out the light.

Margaret waited until there was a steady rise and fall in the duvet beside her, and then revealed that she had booked a two-week holiday for them both in Greece departing on Thursday which she was sure would cheer him up and allow him to forget his troubles and come back to face his life of retirement thoroughly refreshed and flushed with a new sense of optimism.

At all of which Victor snored his whole-hearted approval.

Of course there was the small problem of broaching the subject again when he was awake, but Margaret decided to tackle that one when she came to it.

Victor hated flying. That was the top and bottom of it and the reason that Margaret had to tread warily where holidays abroad were concerned. He hated the mental strain of it all, he hated the physical discomfort of it all, he hated the food, he hated the smell, he hated the vibration and he hated the turbulence. He hated the way the plane always took off two hours and forty-seven minutes late, he hated the stewardesses who grinned like simpletons as they showed you what to do when the plane crashed into an ocean and he hated the little complimentary sachets they gave you containing three peanuts. And above all he hated the fact that when you slipped away unobtrusively to use the lavatory a sign lit up telling every other passenger on the plane.

Nevertheless, over the next few days, using dextrous feminine guile, Margaret somehow managed to win him round and by Monday night, as she watched him thumbing contentedly through a mound of tourist blurbs and Greek phrase books, she was almost prepared to swear he was looking forward to it.

And indeed there was some truth in this, although Victor would never have admitted it, even to himself. If the holiday served no other purpose it would at least allow him to get away from that idiot down the road who was forever yapping on about the price of lawn-mowers.

On Wednesday morning, after laboriously extricating an abandoned Nesquick carton from the privet hedge, he served notice that he was off down the market to hunt for some new summer shirts to take away with him. And that afterwards he might well call in at the garden centre to look for that concrete gnome he had been promising himself.

'Oooh!' said Margaret, suddenly remembering the slightly sneaky favour she had agreed to grant a week earlier in the florist's. 'You couldn't give Mrs Berenger's husband a lift down there while you're at it? Only I promised her I'd ask. Seems he can't get about so easily these days, not since they had their car repossessed.'

'Who's Mrs Berenger?'

'You don't know her, she comes in the shop. It's Cardigan Crescent so it's on your way.'

'Yes, I suppose,' grunted Victor. 'So long as he's not trouble.'

Forty-seven minutes later Victor was in the thick of it. The market square on market day being inevitably thronged with market-goers, his progress from stall to stall was more in the nature of a projectile making its way round a pin-ball machine.

No freshwater salmon at the best of times Victor was quite unable to resist the flow of surging bodies to swim upstream, and after a good ten minutes of being buffeted backwards and forwards found himself being spat out into a small jungle of crumpled separates presided over by a man in a cap who said:

'How we doing me old cock sparrow, you *need* any help at all?'

'If I need any help I'll call in Air Sea Rescue,' said Victor ungraciously, rotating a series of hideous blazers on a spindle.

'Right you are, I'll get out of your hair and leave you in peace,' said the man in the cap without going anywhere at all. 'If you want anything just give me a shout, oh yes, that's a lovely choice, sir. Look lovely on you, that one.'

Victor had just lifted down a particularly bilious-looking jacket in lustrous mauve and was staring at it in a state of total disbelief.

'You think so, do you.'

'Made to measure, sir,' said the man in the cap, and with the swift legerdemain of a stage illusionist he had tricked Victor out of his coat and inserted him into the offending article.

Victor stared at his image in the mirror.

'I look a right pratt.'

'Only from certain angles, sir,' said the man in the cap. 'And I mean look, it's got the nice little zip here. Keep your wallet nice and safe? Or how about this one, sir, in the blue?'

Victor felt a slight flutter about his chest, looked down, and found to his astonishment that he was now wearing a stomach-churning number in blue corduroy.

'This one hasn't got a zip.'

'Yes, well, only keep sticking, don't they – bloody zips, I don't know. Looks a treat on you, that one, it really does.'

'*Does* it,' said Victor. 'And what about this pair of trousers to go with it? What do you think?'

The man in the cap eyed the green twill slacks Victor had just plucked from a rack and even he hesitated for a moment, searching his conscience, before replying:

'Ye-es .... Yes, I see your reasoning, sir. Very good choice, sir. Very good colour combination.'

'I was also thinking about sticking this paper bag over my head,' said Victor, suiting the action to the word. 'What do you reckon?'

'Ha ha ha,' lied the man in the cap, 'You're a comical charac-ter, you should be on at the Palladium. Shall I wrap these up for you now then?'

'You can dump them in the Thames with five hundred tons of industrial effluent,' said Victor, tossing the lot to the floor and striding over to another rail. '*I'm* not buying them. I could actually do with something more in a brown tweed, I lost one the other week. Ah yes, this is more the sort of thing....'

He paused, suddenly, in the act of fingering the hangers and stared, dumbstruck, at the garment in his hands.

'W— J— Where did you get this jacket?!'

'Er – that one, sir?' said the man in the cap, stalling somewhat, 'I'm not sure I can remember where that one came from...'

'Can't you! What a terrible shame!' stormed Victor, throwing it over his arm with a sulphurous growl. 'Because I know *exactly* where it's going!!'

'Here! What the Hell d'you think you're doing! Give that back here!'

The man in the cap leapt at Victor, who with a defiant lunge sent him toppling backwards into a carousel of corsets, snatched up his coat and shopping bag and prepared to storm off.

'Oh no you d—' began the man without a cap, stumbling to his feet. And then he froze. For as Victor's bag fell open he caught, suddenly, a glimpse of something inside.

It was a brief glimpse, but it was enough.

'Take your hands off me, you scabby little octopus, if you value your life!'

Oddly, the scabby little octopus did not persist.

The muzzle of that firearm glinting seriously beneath a packet of frozen peas was quite enough to demonstrate that this particu-lar mugger meant business. And Victor, who was so engrossed in the retrieval of his rightful property that he had quite forgotten the starting pistol was still there in his bag at all, was soon away down the lane and lost to view in the crowd.

The senior consultant at the hospital said that if puking into a basin were an Olympic sport he'd be proud to have Mrs Warboys in his team. And quipped one of the junior housemen who yet again found himself threading something rather slippery and nasty down her oesophagus: 'Sod much more of this, next time I'm calling in Dyno-Rod.'

But fortunately that was all behind her now.

For now she was back in the reassuring womb of her own bed; and, considering all that she'd been through, Margaret thought, looking surprisingly buoyant.

'It was just the shock of it suddenly coming on again like that,' she squeaked feebly while sifting through the books, magazines and videos her friend had deposited on the bedside table. 'They said the only thing they could surmise was that the original bug – that we all thought had been killed off – was still there. You know, lurking about inside my stomach, waiting to strike again at any moment. *Alien?* What's this about, something nice?'

'Victor got those out of the shop, I'm not really sure,' said Margaret eyeing the sterile-white rental box dubiously. 'Well, you like *Mork and Mindy*, don't you.'

'Oh yes. *Star Trek*, that sort of thing. Yes, I'll watch that tonight, cheer me up a bit at any rate.'

Margaret said she'd better scoot now as she'd still got a lot of packing to do for tomorrow, but she'd call round for the video in the morning. Skeltering back to her own house along the connecting crescent of crazy pavement she very nearly collided with the large young man who was standing outside her front door.

Victor had already had a right gutful of Mr Berenger. He wished, now, he had never agreed to give the bloke a lift in the first place.

Still smarting from the incident in the market, he had called round at the house in Cardigan Crescent in good faith and had been kept waiting twenty minutes in the back garden while Berenger just sat there in his wheelchair finishing off a crossword if you please. With absolutely no hint of embarrassment he had then decided he needed to go to the toilet, so Victor had been obliged to heave him into the stair-lift, then give him a piggy-back along the landing to the bathroom where he plonked him, with exhausted relief, onto the lavatory seat. He was still leaning on the bannister outside, wheezily trying to get his breath back, when Berenger shouted chirpily through the door that if Victor wanted to go as well there was a loo he could use downstairs.

By the time he had lugged his passenger all the way down

again, hoisted him back into the chair, wheeled him outside to the car, manoeuvred him onto the front seat, driven him to the multi-storey, parked, and then struggled up from the lower basement to street level with the cheery old soul clinging precariously to his back and amusingly whacking Victor's bottom with a rolled-up newspaper in the style of Willie Carson, Victor had just about well and truly had a complete basinful.

But no.

Yet another joyless hour had ensued. An hour of pushing the jocular bugger round the highways and by-ways of the garden centre with a large wire trolley in front of the wheelchair like a pair of coupled railway trucks.

'Beep! Beep! Mind your backs please, ladies! The Rhododendron Express is just coming through! This trolley will be calling at Hyacinths, Lupins, Liquid Fertilisers and Dwarf Beans! All aboard! Beep! Beep! Onward please Commander! Coming through now, mind your backs!'

Leaving a trail of brainless housewives guffawing foolishly at his hilarious antics, Mr Berenger sailed onwards into the Pets Department where he continued to reduce customers and staff alike to helpless mirth. And by the time they pulled up outside among the pots and trellises Victor was beginning to feel as if his hands had been welded to the back rail of that wheelchair for all eternity.

'Nnno . . . .' said Berenger, scowling disparagingly at the items on offer. 'I don't fancy any of these.'

'Well what *are* you looking for,' growled Victor, his patience now wafer-thin. 'Anything?'

Clonk!!

Went the paving slab.

'Shiiiiiiiittttt!!!'

Went the little old lady who had just dropped it on her toe with a nerve-jangling crunch.

'Hells bells and buckets!' cried Mr Berenger, flying out of the chair to her immediate assistance. 'Are you all right, love, what've you done to yourself? Come and sit down here, for God's sake . . . .'

Victor just stood and goggled.

'W— Y—'

Coherent speech had momentarily deserted him.

'What the bloody Hell are you doing!!!' he bellowed.

'This lady, didn't you see? Just plonked that slab on her foot, the poor darling....'

'*You!!!!*' shrieked Victor, his face simmering like a pan-boiled lobster. 'You can *walk!!!*'

Mr Berenger considered this obvious statement for a second and then said:

'Yes?'

'How long have you been able to walk!!'

'Since I was about two years old I suppose, I can't actually remember.'

'Bjjj- Yhhh- I've been wheeling you around in this bloody thing all morning!'

'Ye-es ..... To be honest with you I thought that was a bit strange,' said Mr Berenger, rather reasonably. 'But as I don't really know you. I thought I won't say anything. He probably thinks he's doing me a good turn.'

'Doing you a good turn???' It was all that Victor could do to refrain from disembowelling the man with a potato-dibber. 'What were you doing sitting in this in the first place when I called round for you!'

'I was waiting for you,' replied Mr Berenger with irrefutable logic. 'It's my wife's chair. She's disabled, and I was just sitting in it, waiting till you turned up.'

'Y— I carried you up three sodding flights of stairs from the car park!'

'Yes, I wondered why you did that. But as I say, you don't like to interfere, do you. I didn't want to go hurting your feelings.'

'Hurting my feelings, what about hurting my bloody back, it bloody nearly killed me!!'

But Victor was done with arguing.

'You can take your sodding echinopsis and make your own bloody way home!' he bawled. And thrusting the small prickly succulent into Mr Berenger's chest, he performed a sharp wheely with the garden centre trolley and careered off in the direction of the check-out.

After all he had endured that morning Victor could have done without the cheering news that a nice young detective constable had called round while he was out and returned his stolen brown tweed jacket.

'It's even still got your best fountain pen inside,' chirruped Margaret, laying it before him. 'Apparently they were carrying out a routine drugs raid on one of those tower-blocks and that's where they found it. Lining a dog basket. Sure the hairs'll come out with a good scrub.... What's the matter, I thought you'd be pleased.'

Victor, who had wilted backwards into an armchair with his face the colour of self-raising flour, peeked timorously into his shopping bag and said: 'I think I've just committed an armed robbery in broad daylight.'

'Fair enough,' said Margaret, and went back upstairs to finish sorting out her blouses.

Was there, Victor pondered, with his senses mashed to a pulp by the soddishness of circumstance, anything else that could possibly go wrong for him today? Or was Destiny, sated in its lust for cruel, vindictive sport, finished for the time being and ready to leave him in peace?

Sad to report, Destiny had not yet even started.

'Impossible! No, no, it's just bloody impossible!' screeched the manager to the spindly youth who, until three minutes ago, had worked for him at the garden centre. 'You can't just mislay a bloody seven-foot-long Indian python! What have I drummed into you time and time again about sticking the lid straight back on this tank the minute you've fed the slippery bastards!'

He pounded his knee violently against the reinforced glass and instantly regretted it. The two other snakes in the box twitched in their sleep and one of them made a rude sign with its forked tongue. It wasn't their fault their youngest daughter had suddenly decided to run away from home: she was at that difficult age. What were they supposed to do, tie a knot in her? And they didn't care for that reptilist use of the word slippery either. What happened to all things bright and beautiful?

'Ohhhh, God our help in ages past!' they heard him shout, as visions of horribly crushed babies and pensioners garotted in their sleep danced alarmingly before his eyes. 'If that snake's got out of this building God only knows where it might end up! It could be anywhere by now – absolutely *anywhere*!'

Fortunately for everyone else in the world except Victor Meldrew the snake wasn't anywhere, but somewhere.

Like many rebellious offspring before it, it was already pausing to reconsider its rather hasty action earlier in the day, and wondering if it shouldn't, after all, have stayed where it was.

Initially it had all been a bit of a lark, slithering through the azaleas sucking a sparrow, and frightening that old lady into dropping a concrete slab on her foot. But then everything had started to go wrong. Spurned with cruel indifference by a fickle hosepipe, it had slithered away in a snit and fallen asleep inside a large wicker pot-holder on someone's trolley. Half an hour later it had awoken to find itself on the back seat of a car listening to some miserable bastard moaning on about wheelchairs. Since then it had bided its time. It had waited until the basket had been carried indoors and the big bag of mulch lifted off the top. And then, undetected, it had made its escape over the side and sought refuge under a pile of washing just inside the kitchen door. There, coiled cosily amongst Victor's underpants, it dared to hope for a bit of peace and quiet.

'People ... people who need people ....'

Oh God no, it was him back, that weird bugger. By the looks of him a Giant Tortoise that had escaped from its shell, and had somehow learnt to strut about on its hind legs. Obviously some evolutionary dead-end: even the fittest of reptiles couldn't survive a face like that.

'Are the luckiest people ... in the *worlllld* ...'

At least he seemed to have perked up a bit now, but he was still making far more noise than was strictly necessary just to re-pot a spider plant. Perhaps with a bit of luck he would go home in a minute, wherever that was.

Yes! At last. He was heading for the front door, presumably on his way back to the Galapagos Islands. Pity about that irritating ringing noise that had just started up though ....

Victor, having opened the door and said 'Yes?' to the dustman, spent the next five minutes wishing he hadn't.

The man wore a small woollen hat, presumably to conceal his lobotomy scars, since to all intents and purposes when he spoke it made no sense of any kind. His accent bore strong traces either of Geordie or a pelican being put through a kitchen mangle, and at times had more in common with the sound of a men's glee club tumbling down a spiral staircase. Whatever its regional origin, it was of such a thickly strangled cadence and diction that Victor could make neither head nor tail of it.

Until, that is, after a tirade of apparent drivel during which Victor had caught only the word 'hat', the dustman suddenly produced from behind his back, with consummate glee, a thing of extremely boring grey felt, shaped all too ominously like Mrs Warboys' trilby.

Victor wilted with a dismal groan...

... while the dustman continued to prattle away jauntily before him.

To the naked ear he appeared to be describing in detail how he'd lost his virginity to Stanley Baldwin's dentist in a drawer of spoons. But Victor knew that couldn't be right.

Clearly the sputtering fool was explaining how he had spotted Victor's hat going into the crusher on the dust-cart, and had only just managed to rescue it in the nick of time. Erroneously assuming he had done Victor a good turn, the man was now hanging around for a tip. And Victor, who decided it would be a quid well spent to evacuate the lackwit from his front doorstep, said: 'Right thank you very much, just wait there a second,' and disappeared into the sitting room.

When he returned he found the dustman making even less sense than before: to all intents and purposes burbling on about a snake on the stair carpet. But in reality, one presumed, asking if he'd put all his newspapers out.

'Yes, I have,' said Victor, trying to close the door but finding his caller was not yet done. Somewhere in the middle of it all he thought he discerned the words 'pet snakes myself', and then for a second it sounded just as if he was cataloguing a collection of strange reptiles that he kept in the potting shed: two boomslangs, a rearfang, a rhombic night adder....

But by now, fortunately, Victor was getting the hang of the translation.

'Right, so in other words there'll be no collections on Easter Monday. Thanks then, bye!'

This time he got within an inch of shutting the dustman out before the toe of a grubby boot interceded, wedging open the door. It seemed he wanted to be sure that in future Victor left his wheely-bin on the boundary of his property or they couldn't guarantee it would be emptied. (Because of his impenetrable accent you could easily have mistaken it for a question about pet alligators, but quite patently that would have been absurd.) So Victor just cheerfully replied 'Yes! Absolutely! Very good then!' before finally putting one and a half inches of mahogany between the pair of them and flicking the catch.

He paused.

From the telephone table the boring grey shape stared up at him with infuriating smugness.

'Ohhhhh God! I don't know what's happening to me any more. People are going through my *dustbin* now and selling me back my own rubbish! Can't I ever get rid of this bloody thing!!!'

Saying which he snatched it up hysterically, mangled it between his hands, hurled it to the floor, jumped up and down on it six times, thoroughly ground his heel in it and then stalked back into the kitchen, without ever once noticing the creature that lay coiled around the stair-post, surveying him through glassy, membraned eyes from the landing above.

'Well, this time tomorrow we'll be up there,' scowled Victor, drawing the curtains on the dusk. 'Up in the *air*. As miserable a prospect as one could ever wish for. With nothing but a scientific principle to stop us all plunging to our certain death.'

'Are you ever going to give it a rest?' said Margaret from the ironing board. 'It'll only be a few hours in the air, it's not *that* long.'

'Long enough to plummet from the sky and be splattered on the ground in a million tiny fragments, I think you'll find,' said Victor, airily picking up his evening paper.

'At least it's hot and a long way from London.'

'So's the planet Mercury, I can't say I'd fancy a fourteen-day package holiday there.'

But truth to tell, he was feeling a lot more sanguine about the prospect now. His original declaration, that he'd sooner spend three weeks in a seaside guest house run by Pol Pot than go anywhere near an aeroplane, had really been so much bluster. The notion that they would both soon be jetting off to the Mediterranean sunshine together triggered, he found, a pleasingly warm surge of adrenalin in the well of his stomach.

That and the fact that, during his evening walk, he had dumped Mrs Warboys' blasted trilby underneath a hundredweight of rubble on a nearby building site had, in reality, cheered him up no end.

'What's for tea?'

'I don't know, I think there's a ghost in this house,' said Margaret, through a gush of steam. 'I left three kidneys on a saucer in the kitchen this afternoon. I don't suppose you've had them?'

'Why would I want to eat three raw kidneys, for goodness' sake?'

'Why do you do a lot of things? Then when I was drying my hair in the bathroom this afternoon, out the corner of my eye I could've sworn I saw that rubber pipe from the vacuum cleaner lying on the landing. Thought maybe you'd been doing some last-minute hoovering. But then when I came out it wasn't there any more.'

'Must've been your imagination,' murmured Victor.

But then again, was it?

Earlier in the afternoon he had gone up into the attic with the avowed intention of finally clearing out that mass of fusty old childhood artefacts, taking them all down to the garden incinerator and putting a match to them. But as he was stacking various boxes next to the hatch in readiness, he had hesitated. There was, on consideration, a Hell of a lot of stuff, and it would take an eternity to burn. He'd be far better off driving it up to the tip.

He had continued to pile it into a big heap – the books, the cigarette card albums, the chemistry set, the plastic Superman with catapult . . . and then he had reached his old dog-eared teddy bear, and hesitated again. It was already four o'clock, and the tip closed at six. What if there was heavy traffic, or a big queue up there?

No, best to leave it all till after his holiday, he reasoned, when he had more time. It was silly to try and tackle a thing like this now. But there would definitely be no backing out once he got back. This much he promised himself. There was no room for sentimentality. It was only junk, taking up valuable storage space, and it had to go. He would see to its removal the instant he returned.

Sitting there by the open hatch, deliberating on all this, he now realised that he too had seen, in the periphery of his vision, that vacuum cleaner pipe lying on the floor down below. In fact for some reason he fancied he had seen it twitch, as if being flicked about by someone at one end. But then afterwards when he had climbed down he had found the carpet empty, save for a thin wavy rut in its pile.

Oh well. It wasn't worth dwelling on, he told himself. There was always a natural explanation for everything.

In bed that night Victor dreamt that he was having a terrible nightmare, although he wasn't in fact, it was just a dream. In his dream he woke up in a cold sweat of immense relief and then realised to his horror that he was still asleep. In a panic he went downstairs and sawed his head off, hoping this would wake him up. When it didn't he became convinced that he was, after all, awake in real life and had just done something unbelievably stupid.

Next door Mrs Warboys was violently retching into an avocado wash basin with gold Victorian-style taps.

At 3.37 a.m. Victor woke up for real but found that his leg was still asleep. No matter how much he moved it or flexed it the leg appeared to remain totally numb.

Reaching down under the bedclothes he gave it a good hard rub but still could feel nothing, which was a peculiar and rather disturbing sensation. His skin felt unusually hard to the touch all of a sudden. Scaly almost.

Cramp, muttered Margaret through shuttered eyes. Lying in one position for too long. And would he please stop tickling her feet and sliding his hand up her nightdress, she wasn't in the mood for it at this hour of the morning. Victor nodded off again almost immediately and spent the rest of the night dreaming that he couldn't get to sleep. As a consequence he awoke at eight-fifteen the next morning feeling drained and thoroughly exhausted.

Margaret had already been up two hours when he finally padded into the kitchen, performing a sandpapering action down the back of his head and shaking his right leg about in the manner of a Morris Dancer.

'How is it this morning?'

'Yes, fine,' said Victor sitting down and briskly massaging his calf. 'Never had that happen in the night before. Completely lost all feeling in it. What's this?'

A cardboard box was what it was, about a foot square, lined with straw. Victor peered inside it curiously.

'Oh yes – you might have told me he was coming that early,' said Margaret, killing the blue flame under a bubbling saucepan.

'Who?'

'That dustman character. What did he say his name was – Rick? Said he'd brought the eggs for you as he promised yesterday. I said I didn't know anything about it. Strange, because he didn't seem to want any money or anything. Seemed in a bit of a rush, to be honest.'

'Perhaps he keeps chickens,' said Victor, plucking a large, irregular specimen from the clutch, and turning it over in his hands in a way that made the baby alligator inside feel extremely groggy.

'I don't suppose you'll be wanting a cooked breakfast today, not before the flight?'

'Just some toast will be fine for me,' said Victor, studiously replacing the object on its cushion of straw.

'Shame to let them go to waste though,' said Margaret, who had just spooned something resembling two steaming white rugby balls into a pair of egg-cups on a tray. 'I mean, we're not going to be here for the next two weeks, so ... I was thinking maybe Mrs Warboys would like a couple ....'

'Oh yes, how is she? She all right to start eating again now then?'

Margaret nodded. 'She's fine as long as it's something bland. So long as it's nothing that's likely to upset her. Do you want to pop this round while your toast's doing?'

'Yesss ... I suppose.'

Victor and the breakfast tray had scarcely left the house when the doorbell rang for the second time in half an hour.

It had started out harmlessly enough with a group of people going about their business on a spaceship. The dialogue was indulgently opaque, but that was to be expected in a Ridley Scott. The pictures were nice and colourful and it was the sort of film you could knit to without dropping a stitch.

In fact Mrs Warboys had been thoroughly enjoying *Alien* for the first twenty minutes or so, reflecting on whether the colour scheme of the Nostromo's flight deck would go with the curtains in her spare bedroom, when suddenly that horrific reptilian *thing* had come flailing out of its egg like a slingshot and lashed itself to that poor spaceman's face.

And that was Mrs Warboys back in the bathroom for a full fifteen minutes.

Steeling herself to spool onward in the hope that things might get better she quickly found that they didn't. As if that gentleman hadn't had enough grief in his life, being innocently hanged for murder in *Ten Rillington Place*, here he was again with his stomach violently exploding and his entrails splattering all over the ceiling as some monstrous lifeform erupted from his —

And that was Mrs Warboys back in the bathroom for another half an hour.

'Well I'm sorry about that, I really am,' said Victor when his neighbour had filled him in on her previous night's experiences. He set the tray down on the bed in front of her and began to plot his escape route. 'You know what it's like, the man in the video shop said it was all good, harmless entertainment. Anyway I can't stop, I'm afraid, we've got to be at the check-in desk for eleven, so . . . . '

'Well tell Margaret thanks very much for the breakfast, won't you,' said Mrs Warboys. 'And have a really smashing time. Both of you. And go easy on the ouzo.'

'Yes! We'll send you a postcard, bye!' said a voice from half way down the stairs.

Mrs Warboys, who had had little to smile about over the past few months, smiled. Nice to have such charitable neighbours. God knows there were few enough of them about these days. Picking up the knife Margaret had thoughtfully provided along with the freshly buttered toast Mrs Warboys tapped the top of the egg, peeled away the shell, sliced off the top and threw up for another two hours in the bathroom.

'How was she? All right?' said Margaret.

'Fine, yes,' said Victor closing the back door behind him and tossing a discarded Silk Cut packet in the pedal bin. 'Seemed to be more her old self again, I think.'

'Ohh good,' said Margaret. 'That parcel came for you while you were out.'

'Oh,' said Victor. 'Delivered by hand? Ahhhh! You know what this is, he's sent them back. Looks as if I misjudged him after all.'

'Sent what back?' said Margaret.

'The man from the Electricity,' said Victor. 'He's sent back Uncle George's shoes.'

Uncle George's shoes, certainly, would have fitted inside the brown paper package on the table an absolute treat. And indeed, having stripped away the outer wrapping, what did Victor discover inside but a large brown shoe box? No finer vessel in all the universe, surely, for housing a pair of large brown shoes.

'... I don't believe it!'

Victor unfolded the simple square of vellum notepaper that had been slid down between Mrs Warboys' trilby and the side of the box and read as follows:

Kindly refrain from dropping your cast-off trilbys in amongst the rubble on our building site. Rubble such as this is hard enough to dispose of as it is without all and sundry popping round every five minutes to discard items of unwanted headgear. May we respectfully suggest that on all future occasions you take your crabby old hat and bugger off out of it.

'What the Hell do I have to do to get rid of this thing?' seethed Victor, with much gnashing and wailing and whatever the expression was. 'I suppose if I strapped it to an inter-continental ballistic missile and fired the sodding thing into outer space someone would come up to me outside Tesco's the next day and say, "*Excuse me, is this your hat?*"!'

Why was nothing ever simple these days? What was it that made that last bloody teaspoon always cling on for dear life in the washing-up bowl every night? Even if you hadn't used a teaspoon one always seemed to appear from somewhere. In one of Victor's legion of recurring nightmares wild-haired zoologists had completely drained all the water out of Loch Ness to see if there were any monsters ... and there, lying on the bed of the lake, wedged defiantly in the mud, was a giant sixty-foot-long teaspoon.

'*God!!* What have you got in this thing, it weighs a ton!' gasped Margaret, struggling to negotiate a blue bulging mass with handles down the stairs. 'You talk to me about packing too much stuff whenever we go away ....'

But the story of the sad reptile that suffocated to death in

Victor's flight bag has been so ably documented – by, among others, such noted twentieth-century chroniclers as Mrs Biswell, Mrs Bracewell, Mrs Althorp, Mrs Grummitt, Mrs Gridley, Joyce who works in the dry cleaner's, Fat Agnes and the man at the bus stop – that it requires no further elaboration here. The moral, presumably, of the whole tale is that if you are ever a serpent of the genus *python molurus* you should never slither curiously inside any form of hand luggage that you can't unzip from the inside. Not a particularly useful moral, but a moral nevertheless.

And so Victor went on holiday.

He boarded the plane and he watched the stewardesses grin like simpletons as they explained what to do when the plane crashed into an ocean, and he ate his little complimentary sachet containing three peanuts, and he took off in the plane two hours and forty-seven minutes late.

And he unzipped his bag to reach in for a sucky sweet, and he pulled out a dead snake, and he wrestled dementedly with it in his seat for several seconds, and then he danced up and down the aisle with it and threw it into the lap of an elderly gentleman with a weak heart who, in turn, tossed it round the neck of the woman dozing off next to him, and so on like a game of pass the parcel all the way down the cabin until the poor animal came finally to rest in a champagne bucket in First Class where, taking it to be some exotic new *spécialité de la maison*, a lady in pearl earrings carved a delicate sliver off the tail, rolled it around her palate for a second to relish the flavour, and then spat it out all over a photo of Olga Maitland on page eighty-nine of the *Tatler*.

And Victor, having been placed under heavy sedation for the rest of the journey by a doctor on the plane who just didn't like him very much, had the best flight he could ever remember, and alighted at Athens Airport the other end on such a drug-induced high that absolutely nothing in the world would have fazed him.

And by an uncanny lack of coincidence this was exactly the very same state of mind that he wasn't in when he landed back at Luton Airport, England, a fortnight later.

CHAPTER FOUR

The Cruellest Month

Mrs Warboys ran over a squirrel on her way to the airport without even noticing it. The squirrel noticed it. But then, very shortly afterwards, stopped noticing it.

The Road to Luton was paved enough with pestilence and pain at the best of times, which these weren't.

The morning was, as previously reported, a grey and soulless one. Brooding clouds banked low on the horizon, weighting down the drab charcoal sky. Spring should have been here somewhere, but had probably gone back indoors to stay warm.

Twenty-one point four per cent of the population were at that moment going to the lavatory, which was well in line with the seasonal average.

Mrs Warboys, wisely anticipating the traditional snarl-ups on the motorway, had left home early that morning and managed to miss the traffic. She had not, of course, managed to miss the squirrel, but that was because she could no longer see straight. She was, in fact, out of her mind with worry. Every inch of her tastefully furnished frame sang with anguished predicament. Had her body been entirely sculpted from the carcass of a large dead jellyfish – which, as those who knew her well would readily testify, it was not – she could hardly have quivered about more in her driving seat.

This was the moment she had been dreading for the last ten days, and it was almost upon her. Her duty now was clear, and she would discharge it to the best of her modest ability.

For Mrs Warboys was that day the bearer of the most unutterably dreadful news.

To say that Victor's rectal examination was not a pleasant affair was like saying a rhinoceros was not a set of fitted wardrobes. Certain statements are, not to put it mildly, bleeding obvious, and this was one of them.

The moment that Victor, lying in a position usually reserved for childbirth, heard the crisp snap of that disposable plastic glove around the man's wrist was the moment that his last shred of dignity fizzled into the ether, like the flame of a guttering candle.

For two and a half hours he and Margaret had stood waiting forlornly in Baggage Reclaim before finally being forced to concede that their suitcases, like shy baby pandas at a zoo, were not in fact going to emerge through the big rubber flaps. Victor had then had seven arguments with people connected to computers who had all tapped things into their keyboards, shaken their heads sadly and apologised in such an unconvincing manner that Victor was convinced they were all reading it off the screen.

'Bloody Greek baggage handlers! *They're* all in the Mafia for a start,' he had moaned to Margaret as they parked their empty trolley back against the wall. 'Two hundred quid's worth of new clothes down the swannee! Never see any of that again.

'Still, looking on the bright side, I've still got my Greek fungal infection to treasure for always. A wonderful souvenir to remind me of the holiday every time I try and sit down without a cushion. Ointment hasn't done a bit of good, I might just as well have stuck a spoonful of taramasal—'

'Yes! Well I think you've made the point, haven't you!' snapped Margaret, as they trooped dismally along the carpeted corridor in search of light at the end of the tunnel.

'Fourteen days! Of utter misery, imprisoned in the most polluted city on earth during a bloody coach drivers' strike! Lace sellers wading out to you in the sea .... Had just about enough of it all, I have straight!'

Ahead of them, like the swirling waters of Scylla and Charybdis, loomed the red and green channels of the dreaded Customs Barrier. And like Odysseus before them Victor and Margaret dared to sail through ....

There was a perverse logic about two holiday-makers who had just lost all their baggage entering an area labelled 'Nothing to Declare'. And once again Victor, in trying to adopt an air of utter innocence – for the simple reason that he had nothing to hide – managed instead to assume the nonchalant posture of a member of the Baader-Meinhof Gang shopping for Semtex.

At which point he pounced.

A crisply-laundered piece of work with a blond moustache who, hitherto, appeared to be working as a back-up to the X-ray screening unit by mentally undressing anyone in a skirt. Sliding his buttock off the polished formica table he beckoned Victor over with a twinkle in his eye that said we're going to have some fun here, matey.

'Good morning, sir,' he began, with cloying civility. 'And how are we today?'

To which Victor, whose taste for jocular banter had long since deserted him, replied:

'Bloody awful! And so would you be if you'd just spent two hours squashed into a rock-hard seat with this crack in your bottom!'

For the next hour and a half Victor lay spreadeagled in the interview room while the drugs officers searched for it. Men with unpleasant instruments, men with clipboards, men with little torches shaped like pencils, men with horrific clamping devices in gleaming chrome.... Victor could even swear he'd seen a man with a pair of binoculars in there somewhere.

Protestations about misunderstandings were now superfluous. In an unguarded moment he had blurted out his guilty secret and must expect to suffer the consequences.

To say they were thorough was the understatement of all time. Bastards to a man, they were determined to prosecute their investigation with all the vigour at their disposal. It was a well known fact that some of these smugglers were devious buggers, stashing it all the way in as far as it would go. Well two could play at that game....

Try as he might, Victor could not make them understand. Several times he attempted to broach the subject of his embarrassing condition and was met with callous indifference. Indeed one of the officers, apparently under the impression that a skin fissure was a type of river bird with a long beak, said he never ceased to be disgusted by the sexual depravities of some people these days.

And Victor, who now regretted spurning an early offer of an old sock to bite on, could only lie back and reflect that at this rate if he ever filed a complaint about the incident they'd have to dust his prostate gland for fingerprints by way of evidence.

There was a cafeteria at the airport that sold, in accordance with Civil Aviation Authority policy, nothing you would ever want to eat.

There were, in the centre of the cafeteria, in accordance with strict Government quotas regulating restaurants throughout the country, thirteen tables that wobbled about the minute you sat down at them.

Seated at one of these tables were two what can only be described as women, although the casual observer might well have taken them for exhibits in some sort of taxidermy retrospective.

Their eyes were vitreous and vacant. Their faces waxed and wan. Had visitors from a far-off wobbly table at the furthest reaches of the Waitress Service Section landed here they would, for certain, have reported no evidence of Life As We Know It.

Mrs Warboys had told Margaret.

For days she had been composing her speech; desperately thumbing through her Thesaurus to find nice ways of describing it. But in the end it all added up to exactly the same thing, so finally she had just taken a deep, deep breath....

And told her.

If Margaret had been the sort of person who got hysterical and screamed and shouted she would not have got hysterical and screamed and shouted. The news was far too mind-numbing for that. It was the sort of appalling news that crystallised the blood and stiffened every muscle in the body. And it had left Margaret in a state of brittle petrification, like the frailest vase that a movement will shatter.

So Mrs Warboys, too, sat in fossilised silence, her eyes focused on infinity.

And for the first time in recorded history, with two people sitting at it, the cafeteria table did not wobble.

But of course the worst was still to come. Mrs Warboys knew it, and for the last fifteen minutes had thought of nothing else. Any minute now it would lurch into view through that archway, kicking over a tray someone had propped against the wall, shouting abuse at the world in general and Her Majesty's Customs and Excise in particular.

Krrllackkkk!!

Yes, that was the tray gone....

'Bloody officious bastards!! Ninety minutes of that! *Ninety minutes!* Can you believe that? That was with time added on when one of them found he'd lost his signet ring! Never been so humiliated in all my natural born days – morning Mrs Warboys how are you? – it was like bloody Billy Smart's Circus in that room! Cracking jokes and God knows what, while I'm just lying there! If that one with the peaked cap had shouted "Come on Dave pull your finger out" once more they'd have been carrying out a rectal search for his bloody Gauloise!'

'Victor....' Margaret's thin, reedy voice began nervously to re-emerge from hiding. 'Jean's got ... some bad news.'

'What?' said Victor, easing himself tenderly onto one of the plastic cushioned chairs with a flinching gasp. 'What is it? What's happened now?'

'Promise me you won't go berserk or start bashing your head up against the wall or doing anything silly....' said Margaret.

'I won't!' snapped Victor, realising now that all was very far from well. 'I won't go berserk, I won't bash my head against the wall, I won't do anything silly! Just tell me – what's happened?'

Mrs Warboys braced herself and then went for it.

'Your house has been demolished.'

After all the dust had settled and Victor had finished going berserk, bashing his head against the wall, and doing a multitude of things that were extremely silly, and after the other customers had all been pacified and some semblance of order restored to the airport terminal cafeteria, Mrs Warboys grimly proceeded to explain.

'It ... what happened was, first of all it caught fire. Somehow or other, two days after you left. As luck would have it most of us down the street were all out for the evening watching Kenny Rogers and the First Edition. It was Mrs Althorp across the road who first thought she could smell something burning....'

'W— y— well didn't she *do* anything?' stammered Victor.

'Well ... yes....' Mrs Warboys looked away awkwardly. 'She turned down the gas under her cauliflower. Later on, when the blaze was at its height she did finally latch on to the fact and tried to ring the fire brigade ... only with the arthritis in her fingers and everything I'm afraid she dialled the wrong number and got through to a singing telegram agency. Mind you, they were on the scene *very* quickly, you have to give them the credit for that.'

'Who were?'

'W— the three men in gorilla costumes....'

57

'*Three men in gorilla costumes!!!* Well that was the answer to all our bloody prayers then, wasn't it! What did they do, swing backwards and forwards between the lamp posts carrying buckets of water??'

'I know this is a terrible shock, Mr Meldrew, I've been dreading this moment. We did think about contacting you while you were away, but then, knowing what a good time you'd be having, enjoying yourselves and everything, we thought, well – at least let's not spoil their holiday.'

To this Victor, who had said more than enough for one day, said nothing.

'You see, they did manage to put the fire out, eventually,' continued Mrs Warboys. 'It was very badly gutted, but it *was* still standing.'

She paused, unable to look him directly in the eye, and fiddled sheepishly with the strap on her handbag....

'That was before the hurricane...'

Victor's face froze over like a lake.

'By then it was getting extremely hazardous, and collapsing onto people in the street and what-have-you, so to make it safe, they had no choice but to ... well, knock it down with a giant wrecking-ball.

'I ... I don't know what else to say, Mr Meldrew. There's nothing else I *can* say. I'm just so terribly, terribly sorry. Ummm.... So ... if you're both ready now, I suppose I'd better drive you home.'

Home. It had been that for more years than he liked to remember. It had been the Universe. It had clothed the two of them like a second skin, it had been their dearest friend. It had been the cocoon in which they had both developed, matured and ultimately begun to rot.

And no words can describe the sensation of dread with which Victor and Margaret stepped out of Mrs Warboys' car several hours later to gaze upon the debris and dust that once were 37 Wingate Crescent.

Daylight had long since ceased its vigil over the country, for it was way past its bedtime.

The streets sprawled still and silent now, dark-draped by the black-cowled spectre of night. One sun had set: a billion more had risen in its place. Amid their pin-pricks a silver sliver grinned its crescent grin. Mindful of those who took a giant leap across its virgin craters a generation before, it seemed to smile as far below a faltering figure dared to step upon the broken bricks that were the wreckage of his life.

The wind, which was clearly having a rather restless night, billowed sharply up the back of Victor's gaily-coloured Mediterranean tee-shirt, giving him fleetingly the appearance of some hump-backed body-snatcher, lurching about the mountain of rocks in wide-eyed disbelief.

And then, off in search of further sport, it howled up Margaret's thin cotton dress, hoisting and tossing it exuberantly in the manner of a flamenco dancer, and finally proceeded to curl about her legs in a vicious updraft that set every particle of her on edge, shivering and chattering.

'I'll go and get some coats for you both,' said Mrs Warboys, scurrying indoors. 'You'll both catch your deaths out here otherwise.'

Victor, meanwhile, was privately questioning whether death would not in fact be a merciful release from this mother of nightmares. From the distance, borne on the wind, came the midnight chime of the town hall clock, heralding a new day and a new month. But if this were some wacky April Fool's prank it was a singularly heartless one.

It was hard, now, to imagine that it had ever been a house at all, so efficient was the job of demolition. Like a defenceless creature that had put up no resistance against its predators it seemed simply to have keeled over and surrendered to the inevitable. Charred roof timbers mingled with mangled stair-rails, and a scree of fallen mortar lay scattered upon the beach of ash that once had been the sum of his possessions.

The front door had survived intact. Insolently it stood smoke-scarred in its frame, wreathed in a halo of ragged brickwork: the entrance to a world that had been extinguished along with the furnace that had raged inside.

A Gateway to Hell.

'I don't *believe* it!!'

Stumbling half-blindly in what used to be his hall, Victor came to a sudden halt. Surely his eyes were deceiving him . . . .

He bent down and picked it up.

'I do not *believe* it!!'

In the name of sanity, what was *happening* to the human race?

'Look at this!'

Furiously, he flapped it at the skies as if anxious that any aliens scanning earth for intelligent life would do well to take note.

'Ab-solutely un-believ—. Look at this!! The entire house has been razed to the ground and they're still delivering the bloody newspapers!! You see this? Those free ones they keep shoving through the letter-box every Thursday – how many times have I rung up and said I don't *want* the sodding things?? Look at it, it's tonight's edition! Some mental-case has actually come up to this front door and stuck this through *tonight!!* Can you believe that? ... Right! Where is it?'

Margaret, who in contrast to her husband had remained rooted to the spot in silent grief, watched with alarm as Victor began feverishly rifling through the pages in the light of the street lamp.

'What are you looking for?'

'Here we are! "Your Fortune in the Stars! Pisces! You will return home from the worst holiday of your entire life today to receive an extremely humiliating rectal examination carried out by several men in short-sleeved shirts! Your luggage will all go missing on the other side of the world never to be seen or heard of again, your house will be completely consumed in a hideous fireball, and you will end up tonight freezing to death on a God-forsaken demolition site that used to be your sitting-room!" Absolutely uncanny! He's certainly hit the nail right on the head this time and no mist— Ohhh I don't believe it ... look at this, there's more!'

Doubting the evidence of his senses, Victor reached down amid the rubble behind the disembodied doorway and fished out a small glossy sachet that was stapled to a card.

'A free sample of HP Spicy Sauces!!! The entire world has gone stark raving loopy!! I mean couldn't they *see*, for goodness sake, when they came up the bloody path in the first pl—'

'Oy you!!!'

From across the road a small bedroom light was now burning amid the blackness.

'For God's sake keep that bloody row down!!! Haven't you got any consideration??'

Victor spun round as if pirouetting on ice-skates and stared up at the window in disbelief.

'What the Hell's it got to do with you?'

60

'I'm trying to get some sleep up here, thank you very much! And I'm not having much success with you down there yakking nineteen to the dozen about rectal examinations and spicy sauces!! Do you know what time it is?'

'Time you bloody well shoved your face into an electric buzz-saw!!'

'Victor!!' Margaret hissed hysterically behind him. 'You'll waken the whole street!'

But Victor was just getting into his stride. If that gormless goon at Number 28 wanted a scrap in the dormitory after-hours he was most definitely going to get one . . . .

'I have just come home from holiday to find my entire house has been burnt to the ground!!'

'Don't I know it!' came the retort from somewhere inside a pair of net curtains. 'I didn't get any sleep that night either!! Fire engines and God knows what till the early hours!'

'Oh!! I'm so sorry if they disturbed you!' bawled Victor. 'Next time I'll ask them if they'd mind tippy-toeing up the ladders in their stockinged-feet, how's that for you! I'll get them to fit a silencer on their sirens!'

'Is that him back again! Old misery-guts?!'

From two doors along now, another white square of light flashed on, and a window was thrown open.

'I thought it was too good to last! Do you have to make such a bleeding racket all night long! I've got a six-month-old baby up here and my deceased uncle laid out on the dining room table! Much more of you jabbering away, they'll *both* be waking up!!'

'If I want to jabber away I will!!' jabbered Victor at the top of his voice. 'And if you don't like it you can both bloody well lump it! The pair of you!!'

'Awkward old arse-hole!!'

'Cantankerous old bleeder!'

And the two windows slammed shut.

And the silence returned.

This time it was a piercing silence that penetrated the marrow, like the cold, evil wind. A stark silence, heavy with horror, and laden with insidious implication. A silence that screamed.

Margaret watched as the shattered shell of their home began to disappear in the spattering rain that flowed not from the skies but from her own tear-ducts. In the space of seconds she saw it swim and then drown in the deluge of her utter desolation. Victor enfolded her with his arms to absorb the force of her emotion, but there was no human shield against the brutality of fact.

And then . . . .

It was at that moment that the pinch of salt with which, in the end, we must all take our life, blew suddenly back across his shoulder into the yawning maw of his wound. And in an instant all his anger and frustration gave way to a different agony: one which he would never have admitted to a living soul. For his eye – blurred, suddenly, by a curious moistness – had just caught sight of something poking through the scorched detritus . . . .

It was the last thing in the world that he wanted to see at that moment.

It was a face.

One, moreover, that was a part of his past. A part of his life. A part of his very existence. And he knew, now, that he had never had the slightest intention of consigning it to a bonfire, or of taking it up the corporation tip, or of ever relinquishing it in any way whatsoever.

For the value of that which is truly dear to us cannot be measured by its cost or by its capacity, or by its beauty or by its efficiency.

On all these grounds, for sure, the toasted remains of a sixty-year-old teddy bear with a plasticine ear would have scored very lowly indeed. Its true significance lay in something far more profound: something deeply rooted in our own transience; in the acknowledgement of Time and times now lost forever.

And now it was gone. All of it. Not only the Present, but the Past too. He had vowed to destroy it, and now, strangely, it had destroyed him. For it was ironic that his very hesitancy in the disposal of that trove of boyhood treasures should have been the cause of their ultimate demise.

Left unstacked and undisturbed, in their quiet resting-place among the tea-chests and suitcases of Victor's loft, it is entirely probable that certain combustible substances in his old chemistry set would never, as long as the house remained standing, have been disastrously introduced to certain items in his box of indoor fireworks.

But that is by the by and, being mere idle speculation, has no place in a factual account such as this one.

And since all that is certain is that in Victor's long and luckless life another gloomy chapter had once again closed we would be well advised to follow its example.

CHAPTER FIVE

The Wilderness Years

In the wake of Victor and Margaret's distressing loss, what was quite incredible was the number of friends and relatives who quickly rallied round to offer their support. Quite incredible because you'd think it would be more than two.

Mrs Warboys was a tower of strength, of course, and said that for the time being the pair of them were more than welcome to her spare bedroom, as long as they didn't mind sleeping on a snooker table.

This last remark was added by way of a joke, to try and jolly up a rather harrowing situation. But it was lost on Victor and Margaret who, unwilling to hurt their neighbour's feelings, endured seven nights of acute lumbar pain trying to get comfortable on a green baize slab that Mrs Warboys would happily have dismantled and propped up against the wall.

Indeed it was an arrangement that proved especially traumatic for Victor, who, having risen one night to go to the toilet in a state of semi-conscious delirium, was embarrassingly discovered chalking his member and about to aim for the centre pocket.

Margaret argued that it would be more sensible to go and stay at her mother's in Kettering.

Victor argued that it would be more sensible to plunge your head into a pan of boiling chip fat.

Margaret, as ever, prevailed.

Margaret's mother couldn't do enough for them. She bought them food, she cooked for them, she tidied up after them and she gave them her loving attention, all with perfect equanimity. If they had gone for a walk in the park together she would probably have thrown them a stick to bring back in their teeth. For she had not enjoyed the pleasure of such live-in company since her two Irish terriers died under suspicious circumstances following an interview with a police dog.

Above all, she was the perfect listener to their problems. For hours on end she would sit knitting in her great marshmallow of an armchair, nodding with patient understanding as Victor or Margaret poured out to her their catalogue of woes. And then, when they had finished, she would rise with a simple unrepining smile, cross to her beloved old gramophone, and play an album by The Grateful Dead she had found in W H Smith's under 'Easy Listening'.

'No wonder she's bloody deaf,' Victor had moaned one afternoon as he and Margaret came back to find her merrily slumbering beside a shrieking alarm clock. 'I prized open her hearing-aid last night, the battery looked as if a pigeon had crapped on it. If she could *see* anything it would be a start. Lost her contact lens down the back of a chair last week. What happened? Next day we found her blundering about the house with the remains of a half-sucked glacier mint stuck to her eye. Much more of this and that'll be it: I'm off to rest my neck on a railway line. I'm telling you straight, Margaret, I can not stick one more day of it.'

But Victor stuck seven more weeks of it. All courtesy of the friendly insurance company who were attending to their claim for compensation.

If he and Margaret had lived in a television commercial all would, of course, have been resolved in the twinkling of a star-filtered eye....

Standing there amid the intoxicating blues and silvers of his demolished home, rim-lit against a haunting swirl of frothy smoke and a battery of design awards, he would have turned in poignant close-up to behold the arrival of an angelic male model with a brief-case ... a latter-day Adonis who would, with a flourish of his gleaming gold pen, have signed the magic cheque there and then for whatever sum his claimant so desired. And to an orgasm of sweeping keyboards the man would have sailed away to re-join the host of heavenly charity-workers who populate all our banks and building societies and beneficent financial institutions, leaving Victor and Margaret – seen from a circling helicopter – to wave after him, dewy-eyed, in boundless gratitude.

But Victor and Margaret did not live in a television commercial. And they met with no angelic male models, and no gleaming gold pens, and no magic cheques.

They met with rigorous, rancorous bastards in drab suits who looked at them as if they were an unpleasant smell coming from beneath the floorboards. They met with endless sheafs of intimidating paperwork and weeks of pugnacious interrogation. They met with constantly engaged phones and un-returned calls and blatantly ignored letters. They met with unco-operation and accusation and indecision.

And finally, when the referee moved in and stopped the fight, they received exactly half of what they had asked for, and knew there was no point whatever in appealing for more because, after all, the insurance company itself was terribly strapped for cash, what with all the burgeoning costs of blue filters and smoke-guns and helicopter camera crews it had to contend with.

And as the budding days of Spring passed them by, and the crocuses and the daffodils and the tulips shook their petalled heads free from their wintry tomb to gaze for a few brief moments upon the world before departing it forever; as ambitions rose and aspirations fell, and the days grew longer and their lives grew shorter, Victor and Margaret saw through the season to its close.

Of their beleaguered quest to find a new home, and of countless hours spent inspecting vile *delightful semis* and squalid *well-maintained e.o.t's*, we will say nothing.

Let us lay, instead, their ten tortured weeks of hideous house-hunting humanely to rest. Summer was here now, to kick-start their fortunes and dapple their days with the sunshine of regeneration.

Better times were around the corner.

The world was their oyster.

And live scorpions on toast make a delightful bedtime snack.

CHAPTER SIX

Like Whirlpools

If there was one thing designed to drive Victor Meldrew totally up the wall – and on certain days ninety-eight per cent of the Universe appeared to fall into this category – it was the infuriating expression 'back to back'.

More accurately, it was the infuriating way that people persisted in using the expression 'back to back' when they really meant 'end to end' or, more commonly, 'next to one another'. He had often seen television programmes referred to in this way: 'the two shows will be transmitted on Sunday night back to back' ... presumably indicating that the second of the two would start with its closing credits and then proceed in reverse chronological order until it reached the opening titles.

Similarly, the estate agent who had sold him his new house had described the street as 'a delightful, well-maintained row of properties running back to back' when – so far as Victor could see – they did nothing of the kind. Could he gaze out of his rear bedroom window directly into that of his next door neighbour? Mercifully, he could not. Thus during an angry exchange in the estate agent's office one day he had suddenly produced a large, reputable dictionary and ordered the primped youth behind the desk to look the bloody thing up and learn how to speak English for a change. And blow me down if he didn't find that the ruddy thing gave 'consecutive' as one of the definitions! More horrific still, he found that it listed 'alright' as 'an alternative spelling of all right'!!

Which only serves to demonstrate, of course, that our language is in a state of constant evolution and merely adapts to fit current popular usage. However, since this naturally impressed Victor not one jot his reaction was to storm off through the double doors and ceremonially lob the dictionary down the nearest sewer, before recalling that he had borrowed it the day before from a mobile library.

And so, to begin without unnecessary digression and with due deference to the subject of our narrative....

Victor's new home was the third along in a spruce little modern terrace of six two-bedroomed houses that did not in any way at all, by any manner of means, or in any sense of the word whatsoever, run back to back. The garden of course was a lot smaller than his old one. And if the properties suffered from any design fault it was a certain box-like uniformity. The front aspect of the block comprised twin stripes of gleaming white brickwork surmounted by a brow of copper-red tiles. The bow windows had a faintly Georgian look with their thinly moulded architraves, and jutting out from each house was a dinky little lawn that could easily have been mistaken for a door mat.

On their third morning there Victor came suddenly scampering into the front room from upstairs all of a white-faced fluster.

'What is it! What's caught fire now!!'

But the sound he had heard was just Margaret crunching up a huge chrysalis of crackling polythene she had recently stripped from their new three-piece suite.

'I'm still wondering if we should have had the green,' she mused. 'Go over there and sit in the armchair.'

Victor went over there and, dutifully, sat in it.

Margaret stood for a moment considering.

'Slouch down more. Like you do at nights.'

Victor slouched down more.

Margaret appeared reassured.

'No! That'll be fine!'

And she resumed her crunching and crackling.

Victor surveyed the room with a shudder. The carpet was invisible now beneath a rolling ocean of protective wrapping and bubbled sheeting and strange fibrous shrouds and brown paper swathes and packing and packaging of every description.

'Is there any necessity for all this clutter every time you buy anything these days?' he grumbled, crossing the floor with all the dexterity of someone capering through quicksand. 'What did this have in it, the Taj Mahal?'

'That was the food-mixer,' said Margaret, hooking aside the voluminous cardboard box that was blocking his way. 'I'll need that to send it back in when it goes wrong. And be careful with that!' she snapped, as she spied him picking up a small engraved glass from the mantelpiece. 'That's from Mrs Burkett, she sent it as a moving-in present. And after all that you did to her that time I reckon it was an extremely generous thought.'

'What is it?'

'What does it look like? It's a commemorative Jubilee tumbler, it's got the Royal crest on and everything.'

'Ohhh goody,' said Victor, glaring at it with barely disguised contempt. 'So I can strike that off our list of priority purchases then, can I? One genuine Queen Elizabeth Jubilee T— just a minute. Isn't this the glass that she always—'

'Yes,' said Margaret.

'Used to use to keep her t—'

'Yes,' said Margaret.

Victor poked his nose inside with a surly sniff.

'You can still smell the Steradent as well.'

'Just please put it *down*. We can at least keep it there till the house-warming's over. I don't want her coming round and thinking we didn't appreciate it.'

'Huh.' Victor jammed it back on the shelf and resumed picking his way through the obstacle course on the floor. 'Thought you'd have had enough of house-warmings after our last place burnt to the gr— Hohhhh Godd, this bloody polystyrene! It's everywhere! Look at it – the ultimate proof that we're descended from apes. The second you take it out of the box it's completely and utterly useless. What are we supposed to do with this thing now?'

He held aloft a boggling bone-shaped mass in a manner that really needed a burst of *Also Sprach Zarathustra* for full effect.

'Look at that! You can't fold it up, you can't squash it, you can't flatten it or anything!'

To prove which point he began snapping the object into pieces, creating, momentarily, the illusion of a hailstorm in the centre of the sitting room.

'Will you stop that!' Margaret bristled, snatching it from him and sinking huffily to her knees. 'Now there's little white globules everywhere, they go right into the carpet like dandruff, and you know the vacuum cleaner's not coming till Monday.'

Victor heaved an expressive sigh that said: 'I'm sorry, but it's all this upheaval: a new home, a new street, I'm not used to living in modern buildings, I don't fit into them properly, they all look the same to me as it is.'

While aloud he just said: 'Bloody new house!'

Privately, he was thinking that it took him back to the first year of their marriage, when, long before a mortgage was a gleam in their building society's eye, they had stayed with his mother and father in their poky little terraced house in Dibley Street. Four of them under the one roof, with his Dad's home-made nettle and apricot wine festering in the scullery below like primal soup. It was said the smell used to knock budgies off their perches up to six streets away, and their bedroom was right over the top of it.

He remembered the Sunday mornings, when his father would get up at four-thirty sharp and stride down to his shed at the bottom of the garden to strangle a chicken for dinner; until later in life, when he lost the feeling in his fingers, and then he would simply stake the bird out on a paving slab and jump up and down on a broom handle he had placed across its neck.

Happy days.

Then of course there were the Sunday lunchtimes when they had all clustered around the wireless to listen to the BBC Light Programme: *Meet the Huggets* with the chirpy Cockney humour of Jack Warner and Kathleen Harrison.

They had never laughed once.

And that special way his mother had, of making the brussels sprouts taste as if they had been char-broiled in carbolic soap. He never had found out exactly how she achieved the effect, but he could still taste them to this day. Just the very thought made him feel quite sick.

Then one day, all of a sudden, there they were, venturing out into a place of their own. Starting off, just as now, in a brand new home.

Yes, it was time to forget the past. The important thing was to look forward and, for the first time in his life, to think positive.

A doorbell was ringing.

Jerking free of his reverie he looked round to discover that Margaret had disappeared upstairs. And so capering back through the quicksand he located the front door and hastily donned, as if it were a hat from the clothes peg, an expression of affable self-assurance before throwing open the door.

'Morning! Mr Meldrew is it! Nick Swainey, I'm your next door neighbour. How you settling in now, all right and everything?'

Less a man and more a dawn chorus, he strode past into Victor's hall in a pair of tartan carpet slippers and a ribbed jersey the colour of nothing on earth. His face glowed with pockets of enthusiasm like a hot chestnut brazier and one could imagine that he had, in his bedroom, several large canisters of glee with which he rubbed his hands every morning. You could take your pick as far as age was concerned, for he had both the weathered stoop of advanced senility and the gurgling inanity of babyhood. The real clue lay in his teeth, which were clearly twenty-nine years old, putting him somewhere in his mid-thirties.

'Yes I've been meaning to pay you a visit, just to say hello and that, you know,' he twittered. 'I was in two minds whether to come out yesterday afternoon when I saw you kicking that kiddy's tricycle off the front lawn, but I didn't like to impose, well you don't do you? What with everything these days.'

'Yes. Right. I'm very pleased to meet you,' said Victor, sublimating his urge to say 'What the bloody Hell do you mean by barging into my house as if it's a public library?' and straining to think positive.

'Yes, I was saying to Mother this morning while I was sponging her bunion, I'll just stick my head round his door, let him know who we are, put his mind at rest, or he might be wondering who he's moved in next to otherwise.'

At this he broke into a crazed torrent of sibilant yawping noises that very nearly prompted Victor to ring for an ambulance until it gradually dawned on him the man was laughing.

'Ah. Right. Yes. Fine,' Victor said, deliberately using four words that were vague enough to mean absolutely nothing of any kind.

'Anyway, she sends her regards to you,' said Mr Swainey, dabbing the mirth from his eyes with a crumpled square of Andrex. 'She would have popped round herself but she can't get about very much these days. Last week, I don't know if you heard, we had a power cut here and she was stranded half way up the stairs for twelve hours in her chair-lift. She did manage to hook her walking-stick through the cat's collar for a bit of company, but it wasn't a lot of fun for her, I'm afraid. To be honest I can't remember the last time she had a good laugh, I think it was when Agent Cooper underwent demonic possession in the final episode of *Twin Peaks*.'

'Ah. Yes. Fine. Right,' said Victor wondering where, if indeed anywhere at all, this was all leading.

'Yes, to be honest with you it's nice to see this house occupied again after such a long time. Nice to see a pair of curtains back in the windows .... '

'Yes. I'm sure. Well ummm .... '

'I mean it's silly in any case, isn't it. People being put off, just because of what happened with old Mr Gittings up in that bathroom. I mean what difference does it make?'

'Well I mean exactly. It's absolutely ridicul— what do you mean?'

Victor broke off suddenly and stared at his neighbour, who was now gazing philosophically up at the ceiling.

'What do you mean because of what happened up there? Happened up where?? What about old Mr Gittings?'

'Oh,' said Mr Swainey, switching rather awkwardly to abort mode. 'Well, what does it matter now? What happened to him happened, I mean no one wants to dwell on the gory details, do they? I mean it's not a very nice subject for discussion is it, chasing people round the house with a meat axe and all that. And in any case those Marley tiles are *very* good, they reckon they got most, if not all, the blood off in the end, you might find the odd little dried-up speck here and there in the grouting, but that's about all. No, no, no. It's best to put the whole thing right out of your mind, I shouldn't really have brought it up in the first place.'

'Gory details? Chasing people round the house with a meat axe? Marley t—? Got all the blood off the— What are you talking about??' Victor could barely rise to a gibber.

'Oh! And talking of bathrooms, that reminds me,' said Mr Swainey spinning off down the nearest available tangent. 'I wonder if I could be so bold as to ask you not to use your lavatory after twelve-thirty at nights, only it sets off a noise a bit like an air-raid siren our side of the wall. Goes right through all the pipes in *our* loo for about five or ten minutes. And once Mother wakes up that's it for the rest of the night I'm afraid. What do you reckon, if it's not too much to ask?'

'Oh! Right!' said Victor, finally doffing his air of affable self-assurance, rolling it up and slinging it across the room into a waste paper bin. 'And what time would you like me to hold my bladder until, of a morning? Eight o'clock be all right for you? Or I can keep dancing round the room in a sailor's hornpipe till half past if you'd prefer it?'

'You *are* kind,' Mr Swainey said, from behind several inches of hippopotamus hide. 'You sure that's not putting either of you out at all?'

'Not at all,' glowered Victor. 'We'll keep a couple of buckets on the bedside table.'

'That's an amusing idea, isn't it!' Mr Swainey said, through another gush of hissing and yukking. Then, remembering why he had called round in the first place, he reached inside his pocket and drew out a spongy A5 manilla envelope which he placed into Victor's right hand.

'Oh, I nearly forgot – this came through our letter-box by mistake, I think it must be yours. Better pop along now then, if you need anything just give me a shout won't you. Bubb-bye to you Mr Meldrew!'

'Yes! Good bye!' snarled Victor, and slammed the door behind him.

Dried-up specks in the grouting? What the bloody Hell was going on?

Somewhere, a mist began to clear in the back yard of his memory.

It had struck him as rather odd at the time .... Upon first receiving the estate agent's printed blurb two months ago, his attention had been strangely drawn to a thick ribbon of Tipp-Ex at the foot of the last page. Most of the deleted text had been completely impenetrable. However, by holding it close to a table lamp, he had just been able to make out the phrases 'our duty to warn' and 'of a nervous disposition'. But then, dismissing this as some office prankster's idea of a joke, he had thought no more about it.

Until now.

Now certain curious features – glossed over at the time – were starting to take on a more ominous aspect.

Features like finding that cleaner's mop on the landing the first day he and Margaret had come round to view. When Victor had queried why it was standing beside what appeared to be a large bucket of red wine he had been given some cock and bull story about clarets needing to breathe, and the mop simply being there in case someone accidentally kicked it over. Not, he realised now, the most satisfactory of explanations.

And what if there were more than met the eye to that white outline of a man's body on the bathroom carpet? The one where he appeared to be holding a railway signal flag in his left hand?

Again, the estate agent's patter about mischievous children with a box of chalks was beginning to appear wafer thin.

'Was that our new neighbour?'

Margaret, having now clopped down the stairs, was back in the room with a screwdriver and a sharp knife to set about fitting a plug to their new television.

'You might have called me down to meet him, what was he like, all right?'

'I didn't like the look of him,' said Victor, firing a frosty glare into the wall. 'He had a very sinister dimple.

'There's something very odd been going on in this house, and he knows a lot more than he's saying. I knew we should never have bought it when we found that little piece of tape caught on the rose bush in the front garden. The one that said "Police – Do Not Cross". Knew there was something dodgy about the place then. A pound to a penny that's why they'd knocked five thousand quid off.'

'Who's that from?'

'Sorry?'

Victor, who had quite forgotten the A5 envelope in his hand, looked down gruffly at the smudged Greek postmark.

'Urhhhh. From Athens. Must be about our suitcases at last. And about bloody time . . . . '

Ripping through the gummed flap with his index finger Victor tugged out a brief scrap of paper and read aloud . . . .

'Dear Mr Beldrew. Thank you for your series of letters concerning your missing luggage, and list of contents. These have been widely circulated among our office staff, all of whom have much enjoyed your constant abrasive wit and use of flowery language. I am afraid that as yet we have been unsuccessful in our attempts to trace the items you describe, although we have reason to believe the enclosed may be of interest to you. Assuring you of our utmost attention at all times . . . . What the bloody Hell's this??'

He had now thrust his hand deep inside the manilla package and drawn it out clutching a single Argyll sock. One of his own Argyll socks, to be sure, for he instantly recognised the darning around the big toe. Having then upended the packet, shaken it several times, and shone a torch inside to ascertain that it concealed nothing further, he tossed the lot to the floor and began positively to froth at the mouth.

'Is that *it???* After two and a half months spent scouring the Aegean Peninsula for our belongings? One bloody sock???'

'Well I suppose it's better than nothing,' shrugged Margaret.

'*How??* How is it better than nothing? Hang on, I'll just slip it on, saw my other leg off and hop round to the Greek Embassy to express my undying gratitude! We may as well face the fact here and now! We're never going to get any of *those* clothes back again! Probably all been sold off to the local yokels in that bloody flea market they have on Sunday mornings! God alone knows where they'll have ended up by now!'

On which optimistic note he plodded out the back door to plant some lobelias and shout at a family of starlings.

Margaret wasted no more than a reflective 'Tch' on his departing back and finished tightening the screws on her plug. Then she popped it into the socket and clicked on their new television.

No problems there. Instant power. Lovely colour. Nice crisp picture of that handsome young man reading the lunchtime news.... Not that she'd got the time to stand around and ogle *him.*

And in any case they'd cut away now, to some filmed report about the Greek general election. Just a lot of fuzzy shots flashing up of men and women on the streets and in the countryside being asked how they were planning to vote....

Margaret leaned forward to jab the Off switch. And then paused, gazing curiously at the screen.

It wasn't the grizzled old peasant who stood jabbering toothlessly at the camera himself, as such.... Or the slightly manky looking goat, tethered loosely to a nearby cypress tree....

But wasn't there something eerily familiar about that beige check shirt and Marks and Spencer's pullover he was wearing over his grubby old farming trousers? And was there, or was there not, something suspiciously recognisable about the broad fawn cap that had been jammed onto the goat's head, with two slits cut in the top for its ears to poke through?

Another moment and the image was gone, to be replaced by a different bunch of old goats and peasants sitting on a nice green leather bench closer to home.

Margaret frowned. Then blinked her eyes hard two or three times. And then shook her head, switched off the television, and backed sharply away from the set, slightly cross with herself.

Absolutely ridiculous even to think it....

Clinkkk!
Oh God, no .... What had she knocked off the mantelpiece with her elbow *now?*

After he had unscrewed the lid on the small round jar the old man sniffed inside to make sure it wasn't Marmite before dabbing it onto his boots. He had only once polished his best black shoes with Marmite, and that was when he'd had a very bad head cold, and that stupid woman from the Social Services had tidied up his kitchen and put everything away in the wrong cupboards. A fussy, sterile piece of work, he could smell her now: all underarm deodorant and pine disinfectant.

Like most of the 'ladies' they sent round to 'see he was all right' (but in reality to disrupt his carefully ordered routine and generally turn his life upside down) she treated him not as a human being but as a small pot plant. Feeding him and watering him, occasionally squirting things at him, and asking how he was doing today OK was he getting on fine was he jolly good that was the ticket that was what she liked to hear.

So he looked forward with eager excitement to the days when no one came round to 'see he was all right'. Of which today was one. Which made it a special day on two counts.

Having picked up his boots in one hand and his polish and his cloths in the other he made his way into the front room and sat down in the armchair to begin work.

He had no difficulty tracing the armchair because it stood directly in front of the sideboard on which he had placed a small bowl filled with dried lavender. And of course the bouquet from this was quite distinct from the pot-pourri of eglantine on the coffee table, and the tiny saucers at each end of the mantelpiece filled with rosemary and sandalwood.

The door that opened into the hall was also easy to locate because twice a week he buffed up the handles with a pleasantly sharp-scented citrus beeswax. And the bathroom at the end of the corridor was so sweetly perfumed with its pomanders of musk and rose and his birchwood and his lemon balm soaps that he was able to find his way directly there, without the slightest hesitation, in the middle of the night.

And the middle of the night was where Albert Warris had lived for the last sixty-three years.

The worn corners on the arms of his threadbare chair kicked back the gleam of sunshine that had managed – against all odds – to thread its way over the rooftops opposite, through a gap in the flaking railings at pavement level, and down the pitted stone steps to his basement home.

He enjoyed bright, midsummer days like this one because it meant that from approximately nine o'clock in the morning until half past eleven he could sit just here by the window of his east-facing flat and feel nice and warm on the top of his head. As if Someone, with higher authority than the local district council's, was benevolently shining a giant torch down in his direction, just to 'see he was all right'.

Which of course most days he was.

His breathing was a lot easier now since the doctor had changed his drugs. And although he hardly ever went out he got most of the things he needed from a lady who called round every Monday morning smelling of Arid Extra Dry and bleach.

And though his curtains had long since faded and died, and his carpets been laid to rest, and his furniture wheezed and creaked and threatened at any minute to expire, and the clothes that he shuffled about in had lost all sense of self respect somewhere around the time of the Munich Crisis, Albert dwelt nonetheless in the immaterial paradise of his imagination, amid the fragrant spices of kings and the honeyed essences of Nature.

For forty-five minutes he sat with his temples aglow, and his hairless head blushing pink in the narrowing square of golden sunshine from the open window, and he dabbed and rubbed and shined at his shoes until he could see his face in them . . . .

It was a soft face, alive with hopes and expectations, with a quiet pudgy nose, sparkling hazel eyes, and a broad toothy grin that spanned his jaw like the edge of a saucer.

It was the face of a seven-year-old child.

Yet sadly it was the only face he had. A face he had last beheld in his father's shaving-mirror on November 5th 1929 just before cycling off to a friend's fireworks party. And never again since.

'Oh . . . . '

He smelt the woman outside a good five seconds before he heard her loudly rapping on his door.

On the wings of a flimsy summer breeze they wafted past into his room: carnations, chrysanthemums, lilies of the valley. And he wasn't certain, but there may have been some freesias in there somewhere too.

From one blackness he lurched into another. In the second blackness found a round milled knob at shoulder height which he turned, causing the front door to swing back on its rusting hinges with a scratchy groan.

'Good morning! Got a special delivery for you from the Floral Basket.'

A cheery voice, it came not from the lungs but the heart. Suggesting straight away she was no social worker. With not so much as a hint of pine disinfectant or bleach about her anywhere. Just that heady floral rush from somewhere amid a mass of crackling polythene.

So she hadn't forgotten after all!

Mentally he scolded himself for ever doubting, in the first place, that his niece Ruthy would remember his seventieth birthday upon this morning of all mornings.

'*Thank you*! That's *very* kind! And very sweet of you . . . . ' he said, reaching out as if desperate to cradle a new-born infant.

'Errrmmm . . . . '

Margaret suddenly paused. She was staring now at the large glittery lettering on the bouquet that read 'Congratulations – 21 Today' and realising she had committed the most ghastly error.

'Is this . . . 62 Toland Terrace, or 62a?'

'62a yes,' said Albert, relieving her of the bundle and passing it delicately beneath his nose like a fine wine.

'Ermmm, I'm . . . s – sorry, I'm afraid I seem to have come to the wr—'

'Yessss, I was right – there *are* freesias,' Albert said, looking up and smiling approvingly at a particularly gross obscenity that had been etched in his brickwork. 'She knows I've always had a weakness for freesias. No, I knew she wouldn't forget me when it came to it. Not on my seventieth. Not my Ruthy. I mean she doesn't get a lot of time to write or pop down these days . . . . After all she's got her own family to worry about now hasn't she, so . . . . It's just that, well . . . . Surprising how much a little thing like a few flowers can mean to you, isn't it? When you get to my age.'

'Y— Yes. I . . . ermmm – was trying to say th . . . . '

'Sorry, my love?'

But had she possessed a heart of stone, or even that of a social worker, Margaret could no more have wrenched back that spray of flowers from the sweet old gentleman now than she could have single-handedly clawed his liver out.

So she simply said: 'Umm, l-let me put them in some water for you . . . .'

And then followed him inside and closed the door.

V ictor put down the large magnifying-glass that had been advertised at half price in one of the Sunday supplements and grunted. It was not much of a magnifying glass because the lens was slightly flawed. Which was, of course, why it had been offered at half price. And although the advertisement had actually mentioned this fact it had done so in such tiny print that Victor would have needed a really good magnifying glass to read it.

'Bugger the whole bloody business!'

He had scoured all the grouting around the bathroom tiles now, both with his eyes and with a Brillo pad, and was still none the wiser. Admittedly he had found a few specks of something here and there, but whether they had originated in a human artery or a fly's bottom he could not say for sure.

The thought of moving into a house that had once been the domicile of some crazed axe murderer was, of course, not a comforting one.

Following his alarming conversation with Mr Swainey the day before he had dropped into the offices of the local newspaper to make one or two discreet inquiries. From which, as far as he could gather, it appeared that the previous occupant of Number 19 Riverbank – one Norman Frederick Gittings, aged seventy-four – had one day completely taken leave of his senses while emptying the pedal bin, and become convinced that his wife was a cucumber.

A few days later the horrific remains of what he presumably took to be a light green salad had been discovered in his bathroom, together with the body of Mr Gittings himself who, being of a rather timid and squeamish disposition, was deemed to have died of acute shock.

Or had he?

As he padded back down the stairs Victor's thoughts returned to that pair of tartan carpet slippers and that gruesome, piping laugh, like Shirley Temple on bad acid.

And that foolish, goggle-eyed grin that seemed to be saying 'I have currently got five human heads boiling in a saucepan on top of my cooker.'

There was no question about it, if the Chamber of Horrors were looking for new material Mr Nick Swainey was a gift. Who was he? And what was one to make of that 'Mother' he kept oddly referring to? The more Victor thought about it all, the more he didn't like the looks of it one little bit.

'You had your shower?'

Margaret, who had just come away from the mantelpiece in the front room, was peeling off a pair of yellow rubber gloves and scrunching up an old sheet of newspaper that had been spread across the table.

'No, I don't think I'll bother tonight,' Victor said, with an affected nonchalance that was a long way short of being successful.

'Oh I see. Still on that caper are we?'

'Caper?'

'You! Too frightened to set foot inside your own bathroom! I don't wonder people go slaughtering their partners in this house. It all happened over a year ago! It was tragic, I know, but it's just one of those things. Now let's please just forget all about it.'

'Just one of those things? When a woman's body's been diced up like a gherkin in your wash basin? We don't know *what's* still up there in those pipes, do we?? Could be an elbow or something still lodged in the overflow. God Almighty, Margaret! I mean, here we are, moving into the human equivalent of Smithfields and all you can say is let's just forget all about it???'

'I see. So it's going to be *The Shining* all over again is it?'

'What's that supposed to mean?'

'Sitting up in bed all night with the light on and a poker in your hand? Well if that's going to be the case I'm sleeping in the spare room.'

'And besides, we don't even know for sure it was him that did it!' Victor shouted after her as she disappeared into the kitchen. 'I mean you move into a new neighbourhood you don't know anything about anybody. We could be living next door to the Manson Family!'

But Margaret was past arguing. When he was in one of these

loopy moods there was no reasoning with him. He didn't know where he was well off, that was *his* trouble. He could learn a thing or two from that poor old blind chap she'd sat chatting to for half the morning. Now there was a real victim of misfortune. Yet somehow he managed to confront it all with a sense of humility and tolerance that positively defied description. It was really quite astonishing.

Peeling off her gloves she shook her head sadly at the iniquities of existence, tossed her scrunched up newspaper into the bin and disappeared upstairs to run a bath.

In the front room, Victor darted a shifty glance at the hall door to make sure he was unobserved . . . then shuffled across to the other side of the room and squarely applied his right ear to the wall. Through the width of a brick and various layers of plaster and anaglypta he could barely make out a muffled yattering on the other side. Two voices, possibly? One low, the other higher, conversing animatedly and chuckling to each other . . . ?

Or one voice doing both parts?

At this distance it was almost impossible to tell. But that was where Mrs Burkett's Jubilee tumbler suddenly came into its own . . . .

By placing the rim of the vessel against the wall and then squashing his ear hard into the other end Victor could now hear, much more distinctly, the macabre, throaty tones of a woman talking horrifically about a brutal son . . . about hundreds of people being burnt in grease . . . and about a high-pressure front bringing a heatwave from the Eastern Mediterranean . . . .

Come to think of it, she did sound a bit like that weather fore-caster Ian McCaskell . . . .

'Victor, what the *Hell* are you *doing*!!!'

Margaret, on her way back to the kitchen for a fresh flannel, erupted down the stairs in a molten volcanic fury as she spotted her husband crouching against the far wall of the sitting room.

'Victor take that away from your ear this second!!!'

'Sshhhhhh!!!' Victor thrust a hasty finger to his lips as she came bounding towards him. 'I can hear a loud whirring sound now! They're either hoovering the carpet or revving up a chain-saw . . . .'

'I have just put *Super Glue* on the bottom of that glass!!'

'What?'

There was a moment of frozen infinity during which the words

80

sailed into his free ear, went straight through his head without so much as a by-your-leave, and emerged the other side into Mrs Burkett's glass tumbler. Here they buzzed about for several seconds without getting a lot of joy and then, taking a deep breath, grudgingly all trooped back up to his brain where they finally managed to gain an audience.

'Super Glue???!'

'Just before you came downstairs! The bottom fell out yesterday when I knocked it on the floor, and I'd just that second stuck it back in and put it on the mantelp—. Ohhhh for Heaven's sake, Victor! Don't you ever notice *anything??* And you know how quickly this stuff sets!!'

'GGGnnnaarhhhhhh!!! Don't pull at it, woman, you'll rip the whole bloody thing off!' squealed Victor as she leaned over him, attempting to prise the object free.

'Just try holding still, I might be able to slide my finger-nail in between the skin and just—'

'YYYNNNIIIIIGHHH!!!'

But it was no good.

The industrial strength bonding agent had done its work. Unhampered by any sense of human logic it had assumed that its mission was to cement first a glass disc to the bottom of a glass cylinder, and then, in turn, to solder the cylinder to a gentleman's head. And both these tasks it had carried out with commendable speed and efficiency. Victor was now totally and utterly unable to take the glass away from his ear.

'Ohhhhhhhhhhhh .... *Brilliant!!!'*

Still supporting the receptacle in his hand for fear of it falling to the floor to the hideous sound of tearing flesh, he flopped into a nearby armchair and glared daggers at God.

'Abso-bloody-lutely *brilliant!!!!* How I've longed for this, all my life!! How I've prayed for this precious moment! When I could sit here with Mrs Burkett's Royal Jubilee Tumbler welded to the side of my head for ever and a day!! How absolutely and positively spiffing!!'

'Well what were you doing sticking it against the wall in the first place! Why don't you look before you pick things up!'

'Oh yes, I always carry out a spot check on all my tableware for lethal adhesive solvents before I use them! But for that, I don't like to think of the number of times I'd be walking around with my bottom lip glued to the edge of a teacup! Or a soup spoon flapping from the end of my tongue! I mean this is all I bloody needed isn't it!! What the Hell am I going to do now??'

Margaret flinched as she heard the toilet flush, causing the pencil in her hand to skid across the notepad upon which she was writing her shopping list. Another second, and then she heard the light-cord roughly tugged and the door to the bathroom slammed in anger. She shifted uneasily in the bed and braced herself.

Through the door there appeared a small thunderous black cloud, hovering approximately six feet above ground level. Managing exactly to keep pace with it underneath was her husband, dressed now in his pyjamas, but frozen still in the posture of someone intently listening to a large sea shell.

'Did you manage all right in the toilet?'

'I got by thank you.'

'With only one hand?'

'I got by thank you. Ghhhhhhh— these bloody mats!!! Look at this! Every time I walk into this room I have to move that rug back six inches! Every single time! How the Hell do they keep sliding about everywhere? I mean, what do you do, oil the carpet?'

'Just leave it and come to bed.'

'If I leave it it'll be half way to Abergavenny by the morning.'

'I suppose you can see the hospital's point of view,' said Margaret meekly, as Victor rattily threw back the covers with his free hand and awkwardly clambered into position beside her. 'It's not exactly an emergency as such. If I run you down the health centre first thing I'm sure they'll soon manage to get it off.'

Victor made a short sharp grunting sound, rather like the one a sausage might make if someone had just invited it to a barbecue, and heaved the covers onto his chest. Six minutes of deafening silence followed, during which he fumbled about single-handedly with his newspaper and Margaret resumed jotting down her groceries.

'Got an ear-ache now,' grumbled Victor, at length.

'Which ear,' said Margaret without thinking.

But before Victor could respond with the piquant barb he had just nicely lined up, the phone began squawking on Margaret's bedside table.

'4291?' she said. And then: 'Oh, yes, hallo Mr Swainey! W— sorry? Ermmm, yes we did flush it a few moments ago actually, but I d— Oh dear. Is it? No, funnily enough there's no noise of any kind on our side. Oh. Right.' Cupping her hand over the mouthpiece she whispered to Victor: 'He's going to hold the phone against their downstairs cistern to give us an idea of what it's like when we fl— Ohh right!! Ohh yes! Yes, I can hear *that* all right. It is a bit of a racket isn't it? Yes, well we'll try not to in future, yes. Sorry to have disturbed you then. Night night.'

Victor, who had not only had to listen to this but had had to listen to it magnified several times through a small crystal resonating chamber, confined himself to a loud fiery snort and pointedly turned to another page.

'I'll ring the Water Company tomorrow, see if they can sort it out,' said Margaret, scribbling a small reminder on top of the notepad before returning to her list. 'I suppose four loaves will be enough for the party? It's only twenty people, top whack . . . . Oh, by the way, your cousin Ivor called today, said he was going to try and get along. Perhaps he'll bring one of his musical instruments with him.'

'Oh goody,' grimaced Victor. 'Like he did at Aunty Vi's funeral, when he tried to play *Abide With Me* and got that miniature harmonica stuck in his throat? Ended up reciting the Twenty-third Psalm like *Sparky's Magic Piano*.'

'Cheer up,' said Margaret, cheerlessly. 'It'll be fun having a housewarming. You see. Be a real chance to enjoy ourselves for a change.'

And even as she said it she knew there was not the remotest chance in all the world that she would be proved right.

The steamy warmth of a hot June night hung over Victor's house like a wet flannel on a bathroom radiator. Outside, the air was charged with the sultry musk of jasmine and honeysuckle, and somewhere in a neighbouring garden a hedgehog was lapping at a saucer of milk that had been left out for the cat, prior to taking its evening stroll under the back wheel of a Volvo.

Victor and Margaret had gone to considerable lengths to make tonight's house-warming party a memorable one. Margaret had lavished considerable care on the vast spread of sandwiches and pastries and cakes and bowls of salads and assorted dips. And

Victor had suffered excruciating agony at the hospital having an engraved glass tumbler chipped off his ear specially for the occasion.

It can be said with some degree of accuracy that the party began at exactly seven o'clock, because that was the time Victor had written on all the invitations. But just what time it finished was more difficult to ascertain.

As a rule of thumb the end of any party can normally be defined as the moment when the last guest leaves to go home. A rule that broke down in the case of Victor's house-warming, as no one had actually bothered to turn up in the first place.

'Where the bloody Hell's everyone got to?' fumed Victor, nursing the back of his heel where his new shoes were carving off skin like a bacon-slicer. 'Quarter to ten!! Three hours I've been sitting here like King Canute with these bloody things on! Never going to buy a new pair of shoes ever again! In future I'll just shove a razor blade down each sock, it'll be a lot cheaper.'

'Where are you going?' said Margaret as Victor sprang suddenly to his feet and headed across the empty room.

'Well I thought I might just mingle, you know? Circulate among some of the pilchard sandwiches for a bit....'

Margaret looked thoughtful.

'It definitely said seven on the invitations because I checked them all before I posted them.'

'Eight tins of sodding pilchards. Well that was money well spent, wasn't it!'

'They can't *all* be this late. Surely.'

'The pilchards were here on time. They arrived in their droves, they couldn't get here quick enough.'

'There were at least a dozen people rang up to confirm: Jean ... Alice ... Mr and Mrs Prout....'

'I hereby sentence you to a diet of pilchard sandwiches each and every night for the next eighteen months, and may the Lord have mercy on your soul.'

'Perhaps there's been a traffic jam or something.'

'It's not even as if either of us *likes* pilchards....'

'*Ohhhh for God's sake!!! Will you give over about the bloody pilchards!!!*' shrieked Margaret, exploding like a powder keg in his face. 'I'll go out tomorrow and buy a cat! I mean it's not my fault if no one's here to – Ahh!!'

There was no mistaking it this time.

The doorbell had rung at last.

Shooting Victor a look that said pull your stomach in, Margaret hurriedly slalomed her way round the furniture and flew into the hall to open the door and usher in the first belated throng of party guests....

Five seconds later she was back.

'Where did we put that Christian Aid envelope?'

Victor relaxed his stomach with a choleric groan of anti-climax.

'Here it is,' he said, locating it beneath a nearby plant pot. 'Hold on! I'll just see if I can cram five French loaves and two pilchards into it....'

Margaret yanked it from his hand and slid a coin inside on her way back to the front door. When she reappeared in the room her brow was knotted in puzzlement.

'Your cousin Roger ... is he still driving that old bottle-green Anglia?'

'Driving it? He'll probably be buried in it. Why?'

'It ... appears to be parked outside a house at the end of the road....'

Victor stared at her, nonplussed for a second or two, then kicked off his shoes, eased his slippers on, and headed for the front door.

'Wait here.'

Outside in the street the night had gone all gooey. From being previously a mixture of nitrogen, oxygen, carbon dioxide and certain inert gases the air now appeared to have graduated to a mixture of nitrogen, oxygen, carbon dioxide, certain inert gases and melted tar.

Even the silence was sticky. As he walked to the end of the road Victor could feel the ambient hum of the hushed housing estate congealing around him like a thick curtain of glue....

Yes, it was Roger's car, all right. The half-faded swastika was still there, gummed to the back window. Right where Aunty Gertie had slapped it fifteen years ago when she presented him with life membership of the National Front, claiming it would grant him free admittance to any stately home in Britain. And wasn't that Mr Prout's rusty Ford Capri up by the bend, its bonnet nosed round the corner like the snout of a giant ant-eater? And didn't that look like Ivor's Escort camped on the grass verge ... and Uncle Robby's Mazda ... and old Mrs Grummitt's Harley Davidson?

Victor felt a small pearled light bulb start to flicker somewhere in the middle of his head as gradually the grisly truth began to dawn....

From a nearby window came a brainless thumping noise like sixteen bass guitarists jamming with Jack Bruce, together with the unmistakable sound of various women in girdles hooting riotously at a joke involving a bent chipolata.

Victor turned and stared. Cast against the curtain in the front window he could see what appeared to be the shadows of several people having a fit on a trampoline, while others, with heads thrown back dementedly as they quaffed from their glasses, affectionately recalled John Barrymore in the silent movie classic *Dr Jekyll and Mr Hyde*.

'What in the name of – '

With brows keenly knitted Victor followed the path up to the front door which he discovered was slightly ajar. He pushed it open and then stepped curiously into the hall. The din was louder now: the hoarse speakers of some mediaeval sound system croaking out a forgotten hit from the Sixties, and beneath it the rumbling prattle of a room full of revellers making whoopee on sherry and six-packs.

But not just any old revellers.

As he stepped forward into the sitting room doorway and gaped inside, Victor recognised at once the host of merry-makers within ... many of whom were already grinning in his direction and toasting him with their glasses in a hearty fashion. Preposterous as it might sound, there could be absolutely no doubt about it. For the evidence was here, before his very eyes....

Victor's house-warming guests were having his party in someone else's house.

'Victor! How's it going! Haven't seen you all evening, where've you been hiding?' said a fat bespectacled voice at his elbow.

And turning he found himself facing two refugees from his old neighbourhood, Mr Prout and his wife.

'I must say you've done a superb job, in such a short space of time. I was just saying to Pam, wasn't I, you've turned it into a real home. It's a real credit to you! Excuse me while I just nip and get a top-up will you....'

'W – w – w– w . . . ' said Victor, in remarkable imitation of an old Morris 1100 on a cold morning.

But the Prouts were now bound for the kitchen and another transfusion of red wine.

'W – w – what the bloody Hell's going on in here??'

'Mr Meldrew! There you are!'

From another direction through the crowd there appeared a half-eaten sausage roll, closely accompanied by the chomping jaws of Mrs Warboys.

'I must say, I love what Margaret's done with the curtains in here, it's a real change of style for you both isn't it, when you always used to go in for those awful drab greys and browns. It really freshens the place up. Where is she by the way, I haven't had a chance to talk to her yet – ohhh! Brenda!! Did you get a refund on those fish-cakes in the end . . . ? Excuse me just a tick won't you, Mr Meldrew.'

'What are you doing!! Come back h— What's everybody doing in this h— *This isn't my house*! You're all in the wrong bl— Will someone for God's sake listen to me instead of waltzing away whenever I'm talking to them!!'

But his voice was lost beneath the discordant warble of someone called Heinz singing *Diggin' My Potatoes*.

At this point a sudden gap appeared in a line of high-kicking old ladies, while one of them went over to retrieve her right shoe from a bowl of fruit. Through this gap Victor spotted a tiny weasel of a man in a rocking chair with his hand wrapped round a large glass of rum. Bobbing backwards and forwards to the music with his purple-veined cheeks puffed out in a jaunty smile he was clearly having the time of his life. He was the one person in the room Victor did not recognise.

'Excuse me!!'

With some difficulty Victor insinuated his way through the gauntlet of girdled paunches and artificial hips to confront the gentleman eye to eye.

'I said excuse me!'

'Yes?'

'Is this your house?'

'Yes?'

'B— this is my party! What are you doing with my party in your house! These people should be in *my* house! I've been sitting like a simpleton waiting for them to arrive for the last thr— how long have they been prancing about in here for goodness sake!'

As the little man's face sagged into a dismayed frown he appeared suddenly to age twenty years.

'Well . . . they all came round here with bottles and drinks. And little presents for me. I thought they were from the social services.'

'Social s— Right!! Hallo! Hallo everybody! Excuse me, thank-you!! Your attention please?!!'

Receiving – instantaneously, as if by magic – nobody's attention whatsoever, Victor hurled himself at the record player and unceremoniously disengaged the needle.

Scrrrryyyeeeecckkk!!!

And finally the room fell silent. Bodies fell suddenly still. And another shoe fell in the fruit bowl.

'Hallo everyb— Look! Yes, good evening Mrs Burkett, how are you? – look! I'm very sorry but there's obviously been a huge mistake made here, you've all got the wrong address! You shouldn't be here, any of you, it's all gone horribly wrong. So, look, if you'd just like to come with me please – this way if you would . . . .'

'What do you mean?' said Mrs Grummitt, going nowhere. 'What do you mean we've all got the wrong address?'

'I mean I don't live in this house!'

'Well what did you buy it for then?' said Mrs Warboys.

'Because I w— I *didn't* buy it! I bought a house just up the road! Five doors further along!'

Mr Prout wrinkled his nose in confusion.

'Well why are you having the party in this one then?'

'What??'

'Why are you having a house-warming party in someone else's house? Didn't want to mess up his own carpet maybe.'

'Look! It's perfectly obvious!' Victor breathed hard. 'You've all misread the invitations, somehow or other . . . .'

'Well this is Number 10 Riverbank, isn't it?' said Mrs Warboys, squinting at the little white card she had just produced from her handbag.

'Number 10 Riverb— that says *Nineteen!*' said Victor, snatching it from her indignantly. 'That's a nine, not a nought!'

'That's never a nine in a month of Sundays.'

'It's a nine!'

Which appeared to be a cue for everyone in the room to fumble and fish about in pockets and purses and launch into an impassioned debate on the subject of nines and noughts.

'No one does their nines like that,' said Cousin Roger. 'Would you say that was a nine, love?'

'*That's* a nine,' said Uncle Robby, clicking open his pen and demonstrating with grand authority to all around him. 'Like that, you see? And that's a nought. But that's definitely never a nine.'

'He's always had trouble with his nines,' said Mrs Warboys. 'They come out like whirlpools.'

'He's not too clever with his letter H either is he?' observed Mr Prout. 'Looks more like an M half the time. I thought it said mouse-warming party when I first got the card.'

'I did as well!' said Mrs Biswell. 'I was in two minds whether to bring some toasted cheese.'

'*Mouse*-warming????' Victor was close approaching the point where steam would begin issuing from his ears. 'Why in the name of sanity would I want to hold a mouse-warming p— I mean that's quite clearly a letter H, anyone with half a brain would know it's meant to say house-warming p— Look!! It doesn't *matter*, in any case, what it looks like now, so can we please just leave this gentleman's house and have the party in *my* house! Where it should have been in the first place!! *Please*! Before the Earth gets sucked into the Sun!'

Saying which he began herding the assembled tribe like Moses out of the front room, through the hall, and into the street, amid a confused babble of protestations and an on-going dialectic about the wisdom of inviting one's friends and relatives round to witness the combustion of a small rodent.

When the house was finally evacuated Mr Drewett – for that was his name – blinked pathetically round the room from his old rocking chair, and in sadly stricken tones muttered:

'I was enjoying that.'

... while out in the street Victor was not in the remotest sense of the word enjoying it as he struggled to steer twenty-eight men and women with hastily retrieved coats, glasses and handbags back down the road to his own house.

'Come on everybody, that's it, it's only just down here ... for God's sake what are you putting your motorcycle helmet on for,

Mrs Grummitt! . . . it's only a few more yards . . . yes, this is the one, look, just down here please . . . . '

Looking up now he could see the astonished face of Margaret, gazing down upon this spectacle from the bedroom window. As he gestured to her with an exasperated shrug of his shoulders she sharply snapped the curtains shut and disappeared from view. Victor sighed hopelessly and with the efficiency of an old English sheepdog managed to funnel his guests down the path to the front door, which was still slightly open, and into the semi-blackness of the sitting room beyond.

When the last party-goer had thus been packed inside, and the cheery chink of bottles and glasses and the chatter of people enjoying themselves had once again begun to fill the air Victor dared to heave an immense sigh of relief.

At that point, from the downstairs toilet, he heard a lavatory suddenly gurgle, and the door opened and Mr Swainey appeared, sporting a pair of paisley-patterned pyjamas and, yes, those bloody tartan carpet slippers. In his hands he was nervously brandishing a large monkey wrench and a clutch of adjustable spanners.

'What the bloody Hell are *you* doing, at this time of the night??' snarled Victor, in no mood now for any of this tomfoolery.

'Hallo Mr Meldrew, I was just seeing if I couldn't sort out that little problem with the cistern . . . . '

'Yes well you can bloody well sort it out some other time, thank you very much,' said Victor, brusquely chivvying him to the front door. 'We've rung the Water Company and they're supposed to be looking into it and that's as much as I can do for the moment. So can you please stop pestering us every five minutes and leave us in peace to get on with our party, we've had quite enough bloody set-backs tonight as it is, thank you very much. Good *night!*'

With a deft turn of his hand on top of Mr Swainey's head he spun him sharply round through 180 degrees and thrust him out of the front door, closing it soundly behind him with an express-ive slam.

'Victor??'

It was Margaret's voice, creeping strangely down the stairs above him.

'What have you just done?'

'I'm sorry, but I'm not having *him* round here, tinkering about to kingdom come while we've got guests! Never know *what* he might do! I'm surprised at you even letting him in, in the first place – coming round like that, armed to the teeth with blunt instruments!'

'Victor – '

'On top of everything else tonight ... do you know what was going on? They were only holding our house-warming party down at Number 10! Can you believe that?'

'Victor – '

'I mean can you believe the stupidity of people? Never even noticed we weren't there, if you please! And then, to come back and find *him* buggering about round the lavatory pan, I'm afraid that was the bloody limit....'

'Victor, *this is his house.*'

'What?'

'You have just thrown Mr Swainey out of his own house!'

A small underground nuclear explosion of the metaphorical kind rocked Victor's insides, causing him for a second to totter drunkenly and then steady himself against the foot of the bannister.

For several moments he looked at Margaret.

Then he looked at the wallpaper. Then he looked at the carpet on the stairs. Then he looked at the lampshade. Then he switched on the light. Then he looked at them all again.

And then he said:

'Wh – I y – jj – but....'

Which was amazingly articulate of him given the nature of the situation.

Then finally he managed to compose himself enough to add, blankly:

'What are *you* doing in here then?'

Margaret fixed him with a withering Medusa glare.

'He called me round to help put his mother to bed ... She'd just had one of her nasty turns, and he said he needed a hand t— OOuuurrghhhh!!! I just don't *believe* you half the time!! Didn't you even look at the *number???*'

Striding forward she flung open the door again to reveal a pathetic figure in crumpled winceyette cowering timidly on the front step. Smiling lamely at Victor he pattered past him sheepishly and bolted upstairs to safety.

Victor scoured the floor of the hall, searching in vain for a large hole that would swallow him up. It wasn't his fault all the houses in the row looked exactly the same. With their identical white bricks and their identical red tile-work and their identical front lawns like doormats. And their bloody 'back-to-back' configuration designed to confuse everyone under the sun.

From Mr Swainey's sitting-room came a noise like a Red Indian war dance as twenty-eight people joined in with the whooping noises on the chorus of the Rolling Stones' *Brown Sugar*.

Victor wished he was dead, found that he wasn't, girded his loins, and strode forth into the gyrating mêlée of bodies, looking for the record-player.

Scrrrryyyeeeecckkk!!!

Now came the difficult part.

CHAPTER SEVEN

The Horror of
the Creeping Man

It all began innocently enough one morning with Victor eating a cockroach for breakfast and a brontosaurus poking its head through the letter-box.

During the night there had been an improbably fierce storm which had left the ground unusually soggy. This was bad news if you were planning to mow the back lawn, but rather good news if you were planning to jam your beak into the soil and yank out a number of fat, wriggling worms that didn't want to come.

And wouldn't you just know which category Victor Meldrew fell into!

So Victor stared out of the bedroom window at the steaming, overgrown rain-forest below – with what appeared to be the signature of Henri 'Le Douanier' Rousseau in the bottom right hand corner, but was in fact the trail of a large slug on his garden path – and said 'Bugger it.'

It was 8.23 a.m.

Twenty-one point two per cent of the population were at that moment going to the lavatory, which was well in the line with the seasonal average.

As Victor trudged down the stairs that morning he was convinced they would take him all the way to Hell. The night before he had been hitting the whisky and Smarties and, as ever, they had proved to be a lethal combination. Why did he never learn? For three or four hours he'd sit there, horizontal in the armchair, guzzling and crunching, bidding the problems of Mankind goodbye as he sailed giddily away to a crapulous utopia. The next morning he'd wake up feeling as if he'd just been through an autopsy.

'Hohhhhhhhh *Godddd....*'

Whatever it was that still remained in his stomach was sloshing about like the Bay of Biscay. Plus he had a searing headache that would have made the sensation of two men pulling a long piece of barbed wire backwards and forwards through his ears perfect bliss by comparison.

When he got downstairs he realised there was something missing in the kitchen. He blinked around for a moment with a saturnine scowl, but couldn't quite put his finger on what it was, so he trudged back into the hall and began miserably to trawl the front doormat for unwanted items of litter . . . .

There were four this morning. One from a firm lying about how interesting a set of books were; one from a firm lying about how much your life would be enriched by a subscription to several extremely dull magazines; one from a firm lying about 500 'smash hit' videos that a famous rental chain had paid them to take away in the first place; and one from a firm of inveterate liars who had employed one of the country's top professional lying agencies to tell, with inestimable flair and proficiency, a catalogue of utter and complete lies.

'Crap, crap, crap, crap,' said Victor eloquently, and proceeded to drown them all deep within the suppurating sludge that lurked in the bowels of his dustbin. 'Everywhere you look it's the same. Sell, sell, sell! Drives you round the bloody bend!'

Saying which he switched on the radio where a former alternative comedian was doing very nicely thank you on the voice-over circuit, talking about several rather good private health-care plans and one or two really neat washing-up liquids. In the front room he briefly switched on the television where someone very famous was copping something close to the national debt of a Third World country by persuading people to run up bigger and bigger phone bills. So he switched it off and picked up a Sunday newspaper full of adverts for vast unsecured bridging loans, out of which fell a glossy supplement with little perfumed flaps that you pulled apart and sniffed, next to photos of girls with glossy thighs that were clearly designed to appear just as accommodating.

But it wasn't all bad news. When he lifted up his empty Smarties tube from last night he heard a lone chocolate bean still rattling about inside that he'd very nearly missed . . . .

Slam.

At the sound of the back door opening and closing Victor suddenly remembered that what was missing in the kitchen was his wife. Sloppily re-tracing his steps he was amazed to find Margaret breezily entering the house dressed in no more than a wispy nightdress and her quilted dressing-gown.

'Oh, are you up?' she said, tossing a book of crossword puzzles onto the kitchen table. 'You might have put the kettle on . . . .'

'Where the bloody Hell have you been?' said Victor, in the high screechy register that he reserved for moments of peak bewilderment.

'They found a huge unexploded bomb in Mrs Lacey's back garden,' said Margaret, setting down two teacups and spooning sugar into them. 'You know, from World War Two. So the whole street had to be evacuated, just to be on the safe side. Did you bring the milk in?'

'Unexploded b—. Whole street had to be evacua—. When was this?' spluttered Victor, following her to the front door and back again like a trusty spaniel.

'About half past three in the morning, I think it was, the policewoman called round. I asked you three times if you were going to get up or not – all I got was "Tell them to send for the A-Team", and then you shoved your face into the pillow and went back to sleep again.'

'B— Y— What if it had gone off, for God's sake!!'

'It couldn't have been any worse than your snoring. Like sleeping with a troop of howler monkeys, it was a relief to get away for a few hours. Now. What are you going to do with yourself today?'

'What?'

'You won't be able to cut the grass, it's too wet. If you want a job you can start pulling down that old worm-eaten shed in the garden. Thing's a complete eyesore, and it's *crawling* with maggots.'

'Yesssss! I *know*! It's all in hand, I'll get round to it when I'm ready,' said Victor, who didn't much like the way she had managed to change the subject, but was feeling generally too fuddled to do anything about it.

And in any case, there was the front doorbell.

While Victor plodded out to see who was there Margaret picked up the empty Smarties tube he had placed on the worktop and was puzzled to find the creepy-crawly thing she had used it to trap last night by the skirting board had now vanished . . . .

'Yes!' said Victor, flinching momentarily as somewhere inside him a small black bug passed through an assortment of digestive juices like a Volkswagen entering a car-wash.

'Good morning to you, sir!' said the sinuous being on his doorstep, who could himself have been mistaken for a cockroach had it not been for the gift of speech. 'Another scorcher by the looks of it, makes you wonder what's happening to the old climate these days – I kid you not, I had snowdrops coming up in my garden in October last year, you can't tell me there isn't something wrong somewhere.'

'What are you, a door-to-door meteorologist?' snapped Victor. 'I've got a splitting headache and whatever it is you're selling I'm not remotely inter—'

'No, no, I'm not selling anything!' exclaimed the salesman, segue-ing into his sales patter. 'What we're offering is more in the way of a free advisory service on infant psychology and its role in the bonding process between you and your grand-children.'

'How do you know I've got grandchildren?' said Victor. 'I might be completely sterile.' But he was talking now to a bald patch on the crown of the man's head as the latter bent forward to reach inside a small suitcase.

'It's so all-important, isn't it, to foster that rapport while they're still young and impressionable, for all too often our personality flaws can be predetermined in the formative years of our childhood and with Christmas just round the corner what better gift than a bendy dinosaur? They come in three sizes, ten pounds, twenty pounds and fifty pounds, this is the smallest model, it's made of a new extra-tough pliable resin so you can twist it into any shape without the slightest fear of it breaking. I've got two kids myself and they never put them down.'

Whereupon he held up a series of small prehistoric reptiles, swivelling their bodies and legs about in various configurations to produce, by turns, the preposterous image of a triceratops doing aerobics; a pterodactyl dancing the Charleston; and a stegosaurus walking about like Max Wall.

'You give it a try yourself,' he said, thrusting one of the monsters into Victor's chest. 'You can bend that neck every which way, it won't snap, I promise you.'

'Thank you very much but once I start snapping necks I find it very hard to stop!' said Victor, who had now had more than enough of this asinine mummery.

'Let me at least leave our brochure with you, sir, it's chock full of exciting gift ideas for the festive – '

The rest of which was lost behind the large wooden door that Victor slammed in his face.

'Bloody rubbish they try and palm you off with,' he moaned as he tramped back to the kitchen, oblivious to the long-necked brontosaurus now making a phallic gesture behind him through the letter-box.

Bendy dinosaurs indeed!

It was clearly going to be one of those days.

M argaret closed her eyes, and through the power of positive thought refused to be tickled by the fingers that were slowly caressing her neck. Sensitively they followed the line of her chin, tracing the finely downed camber of her high cheek arches, exploring like a curious butterfly the curve of her eyelids and then curling downward in a gentle stroking action to the upturned tip of her puppy-dog nose.

'You've a very pretty face,' said Albert. 'And you look after your skin. With, I would say, something containing coconut milk and . . . .'

A long, deep sniff.

'. . . cucumber and . . . not avocado, or is it?'

'Gosh, you talk about Sherlock Holmes. You'd give a bloodhound a good run for its money, wouldn't you?'

Albert chuckled and relaxed back in his chair with his steaming mug of tea. It was nice to have made a new friend at last.

In the three weeks since she first called round he had grown very fond of the lady from the florist's. He always looked forward to her latest news, and the hilarious tales that she made up to amuse him about a barmy old man who accidentally brought home snakes from the garden centre and glued glass tumblers to his ears. Indeed, on one occasion when she had regaled him with a yarn concerning airport drugs officers with cold fingers he had very nearly choked to death on his digestive biscuit.

'I'm glad you came today,' he said, after he had mopped the tears of laughter from his cheeks following a priceless story about the man being duffed up by soccer hooligans. 'There's something you can do for me, if you wouldn't mind. Read this letter out from my son Mike, in Australia. It's one of his big fat ones so I know it must be full of news.'

'Oh I'm sure it is,' said Margaret, draining her cup and accepting the bulging envelope the old man had scooped off the dresser.

'I've got three grandchildren out there now and two great grandchildren. Little Danny and Tracey. Soon have to start thinking about what to get them for Christmas. I always try and send a little something off if I can. Haven't had a proper letter for ages, you start to wonder if they've forgotten all about you after a while.'

'Oh rubbish, they'd never do that,' said Margaret. 'Now let's see what he's got to say for himself . . . .'

Saying which she broke into the letter and entered, to her unaccountable dismay, the dread domain of the Devil and all his works.

'Oh,' she said, her eager anticipation arrested, tried, convicted and put to death all in a single instant.

'I know – his writing,' said Albert, weighing her sudden hesitation. 'Like a spider crawled out of an ink-pot. But just do the best you can.'

And Margaret, who would not for all the world have snuffed out the flame of faith in his heart by telling him he had been personally selected to receive one of six major prizes at a time-share-selling ceremony in Leicester Square, did the best she could and read to him a letter that had never been written. During which Albert sat perfectly still before her, listening eagerly as she told him how wonderful the weather was out there, how much they were all missing him, and how fast little Danny and Tracey were growing up now . . . . And he smiled to himself and ran the elbow of his matted cardigan across his glistening eyes. Because this time he knew she was not making any of it up.

'Would either of you like another custard tart?' asked Victor, stretching forward in his chair.

'No thank you,' said Patrick.

'No thank you,' said Pippa.

'Another chocolate finger?'

'No thank you,' said Patrick.

'No thank you,' said Pippa.

'Can I get either of you another cup of tea at all then?'

'No thank you,' said Patrick.

'No thank you,' said Pippa.

Victor nodded, and continued to smile inanely from ear to ear.

He had not had a good day. After that bastard with the bendy lizards had called first thing he had begun the business of emptying the garden shed, prior to pulling the whole thing down and erecting a new one. Hardly had he been in there ten minutes than he suddenly became aware of a disturbing humming noise in both his ears. Imagining that he must have accidentally set off an old power-tool of some description, he began foraging frantically through all the drawers and cupboards, kicking and whacking them violently with a large garden spade, before discovering to his horror that the entire shed was surrounded by a swarm of runaway bees.

The next half hour had been spent desperately plugging up knot-holes with bits of decomposed parsnip and shouting at the bloody things to bugger off back where they came from, as they had no business being there in someone else's garden in the first place. Whereupon the bees, who were not used to being spoken to in such a cavalier fashion, did not bugger off anywhere at all, but stayed where they were and made a point of deliberately buzzing about even louder.

Eventually Mrs Lacey, who had been standing on a ladder three gardens away clipping her cockerel, spotted what appeared to be a giant vibrating tea-cosy next to Victor's fence, and immediately rang the police. The owner of the bees, Mr Robin Parslow of Robespierre Close, was alerted and whisked along in a squad car to retrieve his property, and after seven hours of captivity Victor Meldrew had finally been released.

An hour or two later he had been returning from the late-duty chemist's with a glowing ear and assorted tubes of antihistamine cream when he had spied a young gormless-looking couple in waterproof blousons emerging from a dark blue Vauxhall Nova outside his house.

Turning as he approached, they had hailed him with great gusto saying how nice it was to see him again, and what a relief it was to get here at last because they were both dying for a cup of tea. And then to his astonishment they had begun heaving three huge suitcases down from the car roof.

Victor, who couldn't quite place the pair of them for the moment, said he was thrilled to bits they had arrived like this out of the blue. And pausing only to retrieve a twisted Tango can from the petunias he promptly ushered them into the front room and put the kettle on. But if he had nursed any hope that their identity would become clear as the evening wore on he was horribly mistaken. Fourteen tea-bags, four custard tarts and twenty-nine chocolate fingers had now waxed and waned, and the more he stared at them with his oriental stockinged-face grin the more he realised he didn't know either of them from a bar of soap.

Beyond ascertaining, via various tangled skeins of conversation, that their first names were Patrick and Pippa, he was still puzzling over who the bloody Hell they were and how they seemed to know *him*, when the scraping of a key at the door finally announced his wife's return from work.

'Sorry I'm a bit late,' she called from the hall. 'I popped by to see that old blind chap again, and he'd had this letter that he th—oh! Hello!'

Clopping wearily into the sitting room she stopped suddenly in her tracks at the sight of their two guests, who had risen cordially to greet her.

'How are you, Margaret!' said Patrick.

'Keeping well?' said Pippa.

'Y-yes ... yes, how are you both?' said Margaret, flashing them a broad, sociable smile.

'Oh fine thanks,' said Patrick. 'We were telling Victor – it took us five hours to get here from Bath. Bloody M4 was choked solid.'

'Oh dear, I know,' said Margaret. 'And it's getting worse isn't it? Ummm ... would you ... excuse us both just a second – won't be a tick ....'

Inserting her fingernails casually through Victor's pullover and deep into the flesh of his midriff she escorted her husband into the kitchen, delicately closing the door behind them.

'Well?' she demanded in a scalding stage whisper.

'Well what?' returned Victor blankly.

'Well who the Hell *are* they!'

Victor stared at her.

'I haven't the faintest idea! I thought *you'd* know who they were when you got home! They just turned up on our doorstep as I was coming back from the chemist, with three bloody suitcases!

Names apparently are Patrick and Pippa – I've never clapped eyes on them before in my life!'

'Patrick and Pippa....'

Margaret's eyes creased into a frown.

'Doesn't mean a thing. They must be relations.'

Victor shook his head adamantly.

'I sneaked upstairs an hour ago on the pretext of a kidney disorder and went through all the address books and the photograph albums. The closest I managed to find were Patsy and Peter, and they're both dead. And in any case they were your sister's goldfish. Oh it's too ridiculous for words, I'm going to come right out with it and ask them!'

'You'll do nothing of the kind!' spat Margaret, grabbing a handful of skin around his neck and propelling him back against the cooker. 'Make us both look like a couple of half-wits. It'll come to us eventually, it has to.'

Patrick and Pippa's legs were apparently rigged to the kitchen door by some elaborate hidden mechanism, for having sat down the second it closed they jerked at once to their feet the moment it re-opened.

'Actually, I was just saying – we're both a bit bushed,' declared Patrick, making a move towards the door. 'If it's OK with you we'd quite like to get to bed.'

'If you don't mind us both having an early night,' chuckled Pippa.

Victor, whose face was starting to ache from the forced muscular contortion he hoped was being taken for an expression of warmth, could hardly believe it. Two complete and utter strangers had trooped unceremoniously into his house and bored him rigid for three hours with tales of cones and contraflows, and were now announcing their intention of kipping down there for the night! And unbelievably – constrained as he was by English etiquette – all he could hear himself saying was:

'Yes! Right then, I'll take your things upstairs for you, just follow me....'

While Margaret, who behind two twinkling pupils was ransacking her memory like a thing possessed, said:

'And I'll just go sort out some fresh soap for you, I'm sure you could both do with a bath.'

Patrick and Pippa, having managed to wade knee-deep in pleasantries as far as the foot of the stairs, now suddenly paused.

'Take our things upstairs?' said Patrick.

'Sort out some soap?' said Pippa.

'Yes you can sleep in our bed,' Victor said, cupping his fingers under the handles of two massive cases, and with a swift yank managing to anchor his arms to the carpet like guy-ropes.

'Sleep in *your* bed?' said Pippa, in something approaching scandalised tones. 'Why on earth would we want to do that?'

'Why, what's wrong with it?' said Victor, who was beginning to find this lofty attitude a little offensive, to say the least of it. 'It's a perfectly good bed and we haven't got round to buying a spare one yet.'

'Ummm! Well, no, we wouldn't want to put you to all that trouble, would we, darling?' said Patrick, snatching the suitcases from Victor's hands. 'All things considered, it's probably time we were getting home, so . . . .' With which he proceeded to make a brave lunge for the front door.

But Victor was having none of it. Who did they think they were, traipsing in like this and turning their noses up at his Slumberland mattress? If it was good enough for him it was good enough for them.

'Don't be so completely ridiculous!' he snapped, retrieving the cases and staggering off with them in an apparent desire to fold his spine in half. 'We wouldn't dream of turfing you back out at this hour – what sort of people do you take us for?'

'Thank you very much but I think we'd prefer to go home!' said Patrick. And clambering after Victor he began to wrest the luggage from his hands while Victor, for his part, clung on for dear life, sparking an unseemly brawl for supremacy half way up the staircase.

In the kitchen Margaret's blood suddenly chilled, and she felt her veins crack like a frozen water-pipe. For she had just experienced epiphany under the S-bend. Withdrawing her head from the cupboard by the sink she flew back into the hall where something approaching all-out gladiatorial combat was now threatening to wrench the bannisters from their sockets.

'For goodness *sake*, man! Give that here, I won't have it!'

'Can we please have our cases back!'

'It's a pretty poor do if we can't put you up for the night! Now just let go, for Heaven's sake – please!'

'*Victor*! If they want to go perhaps we should just *let* them!'

Victor gazed down at his wife and melted into jelly. So crisply assertive was her manner that he knew better than to offer resistance.

'Thank you! Very much indeed,' said Patrick, the balls of his eyes swivelling minaciously round the room like a gun turret as he picked up his belongings. Together, he and his wife then backed carefully out of the front door with the technique of two lion-tamers leaving a cage, and a second later were gone.

'Ohhhhhhhh God, nohhhhhhh...' whimpered Margaret as her face fell limp against the door. 'We *have* met them before! I suddenly remembered ... I've remembered now where it is they've come from.'

Victor padded dumbly down the steps behind her.

'Where?'

Slowly she turned her corrugated brow to face him and said, with pathetic inevitability:

'Next door.'

'W— Y— but they j— *Next door??*'

'Don't you remember? The day we were moving in they were getting into their car, going off on a month's holiday to the West Country. We shouted hallos at each other across the front garden and that was about it. It was pouring with rain, we never really saw their faces that clearly.'

'B— You mean when they pulled up outside in their car tonight they were actually g— Ohhhhhh my Godddd ... what have I *done??*'

And as if in answer, he almost fancied he could feel it tumbling down his trouser leg and rolling obscenely across the floor into the corner of the hall.

Natalie, twenty-two, stood before the big gold mirror in the sitting room, intently re-defining mascara as a form of radical self-expression. The brushwork on her lashes, though clearly derivative of certain works by Rolf Harris, was bold and uncompromising, and there was much in the modelling of her eye-shadow that Francis Bacon would have admired. Coquettishly, she fluttered her lashes up and down, giving her pouting reflection the stroboscopic motion of a silent movie starring Fatty Arbuckle. Beneath her in every sense of the word her flat-mate Angie, nineteen, clothed in what appeared to be the wreckage of the Hindenberg Disaster, lay sprawled upon the carpet with the sinuous grace of a ketchup stain, flicking through the pages of a glossy bridal magazine. And in the big armchair in the corner Wilfred, seventy-two, sat with a tray of beans on toast lodged across his lap, dribbling Quick-Brew as he gazed avidly at them both and eavesdropped on their tasty chit-chat.

So far as he could make out, the two girls were engaged in a fiery debate about the relative lengths of their hair-styling wands ... except that for some reason the names Dave and Trevor kept straying into the conversation, so perhaps it wasn't hair-styling wands at all. Whatever it was Wilfred didn't care. He just enjoyed watching them because of the funny faces they pulled, and the way they kept plonking themselves down onto sofas with their arms crossed, and the hilarious way their eyes popped and their voices rose several octaves whenever the lady across the road popped by to talk about something called a multiple orgasm. Yes, even now he could hardly believe that this time tomorrow he would be watching the pair of them in the flesh, live in the television studio where the programme was recorded. Harder still to believe that his own reedy chuckle would be added to the sound-track of his favourite comedy show, to be beamed across the nation and eventually all over the world.

In the kitchen a tweeting phone brought Mrs Warboys scuttling in from the utility room where she had been pressing a pair of her brother-in-law's trousers.

'Phone, Wilf! Can you turn it down a bit please!'

'Oh right, Jean – sorry!' said Wilfred as with a jab of the remote control he reduced Natalie and Angie to a merciful silence.

Tomorrow would of course be his first night out since the dreaded triple by-pass operation three months ago, the trauma of which had left him rather confused and wobbly on his feet. Whether it had all been a success was hard to say, now that the surgeon had been taken away for questioning. For although he had provided Wilfred's local GP with a full written report it was in such a shaky hand that neither of them had been able to make out much beyond the words 'wouldn't go booking up any holidays next year if I were him'.

Since he came out of hospital his powers of concentration had waned considerably. And try as he might he could not remember a time when his memory had been as bad as it was now. Despite this, there was a part of him prepared to swear blind he had possessed two nipples when they wheeled him down to pre-op that Monday morning. Why, otherwise, during the delirious sleep that followed, would he recall a muffled voice shouting 'that's buggered it!' followed by the sound of two young women running about screaming? In fact the more he came to consider it the more he couldn't be at all sure he had emerged from the wretched experience alive. Suppose the doctors had not been levelling with him and he had, in fact, died on the operating table? Suppose everything that had occurred since had been some ghostly, out-of-body experience?

It would certainly explain the taste of this tea he was drinking.

'Wilf, I'm afraid I've got to go out,' said Mrs Warboys, appearing suddenly in the doorway and gravely jangling a set of car keys. 'It's ummm . . . something of an emergency.'

'Whatever for?' said Wilfred, fearfully. 'What is it – what's happened?'

When Dr Stokely had finished examining Victor Meldrew and put away his stethoscope he said the two words Victor was dreading most in all the world.

'You'll live.'

And where was the pleasure in *that*?

It was three hours since the garden shed collapsed on him in his back garden. Three hours since he had unwittingly lifted down a small seed tray from the top shelf, little guessing that it was holding the entire roof together. And that the roof, in its turn, was all that was keeping the four walls and all the shelves and cupboards on those walls and all the contents of those shelves and cupboards from caving in to the centre like a house of cards, and interring him at the bottom of the heap like the victim of some horrific mining disaster.

How long he had remained there in a state of exquisite suffering with paint and splinters in every orifice known to Man is not recorded. By the time the ambulancemen arrived the bright red emulsion had seeped far enough into his trousers to convince them, along with the razor-edged jag of glass jutting from his flies, that here was a text-book emergency needing immediate micro-surgery if the severed organ was to be saved.

And so it came to pass that a small lump of mouldy carrot was rushed to hospital in a special refrigerated canister normally reserved for ears and fingers, and might well have ended up being sewn to the end of Victor's foreskin but for the vigilance of the junior doctor on duty who knew a rotting root vegetable when he saw one.

'We've notified your wife at the florist's, Mr Meldrew, I gather she's getting a friend to run her up here straight away,' he said, reappearing from a small back room with a mug of steam and a Jaffa Cake. 'So in the meantime I think we'll just get a couple of the girls in and have them swab this little fellow down with turps. If you'd like to just sit back in the waiting room, we won't keep you more than five minutes.'

Interestingly, of all the words and phrases commonly in use at hospitals and health centres around the country, the expression 'we won't keep you more than five minutes' is the one guaranteed to bear least resemblance to its actual meaning. Just as the phrase 'I'm *sure* I remembered to switch on Mrs Catchpole's dialysis machine' implies, on the contrary, a sneaky uncertainty about the fact, and 'These eye-drops may sting a little' is normally a euphemism for 'Have you ever pondered what it's like to be the victim of an acid attack?' so 'We won't keep you more than five minutes' usually denotes a period of delay marked by various changes in the stratification of the earth's crust.

Thus, some two hours later, Victor Meldrew was still squatting on a burst plastic bench in Casualty waiting for his name to be called. Irritatingly, for the last twenty minutes or so, he had been obliged to listen to a grisly conversation behind him in which two nicotined hags loudly compared notes about their husbands' cystoscopies. In fact, so appallingly graphic were the details of this discussion that when, at one point, Victor turned round to see a young child sliding a straw into a bottle of Coca-Cola it caused him to emit an involuntary howl of pain like a wounded coyote.

Outside, the dog day dusk had already curtained the window in a vivid cobalt blue, and the first star of the night had begun to twinkle cursor-like in the top left-hand corner of a wordless sky.

Inside, the heinous vision of human congestion and the wailing woe of the waiting wounded brought inevitably to mind certain nightmare sequences directed by Ken Russell. For it is fair to say that comfort and confidence in this particular flagship of NHS reform were noticeable by their absence. On a cracked television screen above their heads a government minister was glibly demonstrating how creative use of treasury statistics could cure cancer and coronary heart disease, while over in the corner a man with his hand nailed to a roof timber was attempting to manoeuvre his way into the Gents where, doubtless, further logistical problems would present themselves in due course.

'I ummm ... how much longer do you think they're going to be,' murmured Mrs Warboys, nervously wondering if it was right that blood should be dripping through a nearby crack in the ceiling. 'It's been an eternity now, you sure they haven't missed him out?'

'I'm afraid that's hospitals,' said Margaret. 'Why don't you run along, we'll ring for a cab later.'

'Yes, you go on home, Mrs Warboys,' said Victor, cheering up for the first time that day. 'We'll most likely be here hours yet.'

'No, no, I'm quite happy to hang on till you're ready,' said Mrs Warboys, slipping on her gloves and fishing for her car keys. 'It's just that ... I don't like to leave Wilf there on his own for too long, not the way he is at the moment after his big operation and everything.'

'Is he still coming with us to the BBC tomorrow?'

'Oh yes, he's really looking forward to that. I think it'll do him good, to be honest, to get out for a change .... Oh! What with everything I forgot to say to you, there've been one or two more cancellations, so it doesn't look as if there'll be the full fifty-five of us going on the trip now after all, I'm afraid....'

'Oh dear,' said Margaret. 'How many is it now then?'

'Four.'

Victor swivelled his gaze to Heaven like an exasperated satellite dish.

'Chris can't get back in time you see, and Mr and Mrs Burkett have got a crossword to finish, and you know how people are. Anyway, it'll be their loss, we'll have a super time between us.'

'Oh yes? Like the last side-splitter you got us tickets for?' grunted Victor. 'Supposed to have been a glittering evening at Television Centre, the most exciting moment was urinating next to Peter Sissons.'

Situation comedies, it hardly needs emphasising, were not far from the top of Victor's all-time hate list, just below Nazi war criminals and people who parked mini-Metros right back against the wall in car parks to make you think there was a space there when there wasn't. It was bad enough having to watch all that tripe when it was on the box, let alone sit amongst cackling coach parties from Huddersfield in the studio where it was being made. Privately he had been hoping his injuries this afternoon would prove sufficiently horrible to excuse him attendance. But no such luck, it would seem.

'Bye then, Jean,' said Margaret. 'And thanks for the lift.'

'You're more than welcome,' said Mrs Warboys. 'Sorry the ride was a bit bumpy, I'm afraid I *still* haven't got used to driving Chris's car.'

With which she gave them both a convivial wave, and then hurried away to batter a sixty-year-old man senseless and lock him up for the night in her garage.

It is either ironic, or perfectly fitting, that accidents should happen in an Accident Wing, depending upon your viewpoint. And it goes without saying that this particular accident would never have occurred had the large sodium lamp located at the back of the Radiography Unit been in normal full working order. For one thing the far end of the hospital car park would have been sufficiently well-lit for Mrs Warboys to see which gear she was engaging when she set off in her husband's Montego estate. And for another, a short, raffia-haired electrician named Mr Saunders would not have been balanced ten feet off the ground changing a light-bulb when she suddenly reversed into the wall and sent him crashing face down onto the roof of her car.

Cursing her clumsiness Mrs Warboys threw open the nearside door and surveyed the damage. She had knocked a couple of dustbins flying, and an old workman's ladder had keeled over onto its side, but otherwise there was no real harm done.

So she closed the door with a shrug, re-selected First – quite pleased with herself this time that she had remembered the clutch pedal – and then, hunched uneasily against the wheel, jerkily steered the vehicle out of the gates and away down the road.

To be honest she was not sorry to leave the hospital behind tonight, what with the distressing sight of all those bodies, sitting battered and bleeding in that waiting room. Why, for most of the journey home she fancied she could still hear their ghostly groans continuing to haunt her, spookily from somewhere above her head.

When she finally purred to a halt beneath the automatic door in her garage and sealed out the world with a flick of the remote handset, she switched off the engine and unfurled a long cool whistle of relief.

The sooner she got her Peugeot back from the workshop the better, she decided, as she closed the internal door in the utility room and drove home the key in the mortice lock.

And Mr Saunders, had he not been draped unconsciously across her roof rack at the time, would almost certainly have drunk to that.

'Don't suppose that'll keep it out for one moment, but still,' grumbled Victor as he tramped back into the house that night after meticulously laying seven slats of shattered shed panel across the top of his big yellow rubbish skip.

'Keep what out?' said Margaret, knowing full well that the answer to her question was 'The busted mattress'.

'The busted mattress,' declared Victor, emphatically.

And although she knew exactly what he was talking about, because it was one of her husband's favourite observations about Social Behaviour in the Twentieth Century, she nevertheless gave him the satisfaction of trotting it out one more time by delivering the feed-line:

'What busted mattress?'

'The busted mattress someone always dumps in your rubbish skip whenever you leave one outside your house,' said Victor, bolting the back door before setting about mixing his nightly mug of Horlicks. 'It's a fundamental law of nature. Just as the cuckoo always lays its eggs in other birds' nests, so some bastard always comes along and slings a busted mattress in your rubbish skip. Always the same. You stick one of those things out in the road, it's like traipsing round the streets with a big hand-bell shouting "Bring out your crap!" Thought there'd at least be an old kitchen mangle in it by now ... or a dead walrus or something.'

'Are you coming to bed now, or staying down here all night talking to the saucepan?'

'Yessss ... I'll be up in a minute,' scowled Victor, crudely sundering the cardboard flaps on a fresh carton of milk and extinguishing a pilot light.

Bloody shed! He should never have tampered with it in the first place. Of all the injuries he had suffered today it was the blow to his dignity that had left the deepest scar: having to lie there while a pair of smirking student nurses snipped his underpants open with surgical scissors, and then proceeded to wipe down his manhood with all the discretion of someone grating a lump of cheese.

One of these days, he promised himself as he stumbled upstairs in the dark, he would learn to leave things as they were.

Margaret clicked the button on the cordless phone to the off position and replaced it in its cradle thoughtfully.

'What's happened,' said Victor, plodding half-dressed into the front room the next morning to hunt for a tube of Savlon. 'Has the BBC burnt down or is it bad news?'

The extensive bruising down his legs had now graduated from yellow to blue, and where the nurses had made a thorough job of scouring his bottom to remove all traces of paint it had left his skin rather dramatically inflamed, giving him, as he slid his pyjama trousers off that morning, the appearance of Clark Kent changing into Superman.

'Jean can't come to the show with us after all,' Margaret was saying. 'Says she's got to baby-sit for her god-daughter tonight at short notice, and do we mind taking Wilf with us? I said that was fine, we'd pick him up about six-thirty. Assuming you've no objections?'

Victor's objections, if he had any, would have been wholly indecipherable amid the sudden outbreak of rabid spluttering that now reached her ears from the other room.

'*I don't believe it! I just don't believe it!!*'

'What's happened!' cried Margaret, charging through in a paroxysm of terror.

'*I – do – not – believe – it!!!*'

Fleetingly, she was greeted by the image of her husband arched forward against the front window-pane with his lower jaw hanging open like an unlatched briefcase and his eyes ballooning forth from their sockets as if in some form of terminal seizure. And then, it must have been just as she blinked, he had vanished from the room and she heard the violent crash of the front door being thrown back on its hinges.

'*I – do – not – believe – it!!!*'

As she joined him on the doorstep to stare, goggling, down the line of the front garden path, she was bound to acknowledge that she, too, did not believe it, although of course there was no denying the evidence of their senses . . . .

Upended in Victor's rubbish skip at an angle of some forty degrees to the horizontal was the monstrous carcass of an old rusting, abandoned Citroen 2CV: its rear end in the air, its nose deeply immersed in the remains of a deceased garden shed, like some immense prehistoric armadillo foraging for food. An apparition of breath-taking nihilism, it seemed eloquently to evoke the disposable values of a consumer society. Inert and absolute, its tarnished hulk abased itself before them, a fallen idol from the graven statuary of the God of Transport.

'Who the bloody Hell's d— What do people think this is, a sodding drive-in scrap-yard!' bellowed Victor to no one in particular as he stomped murderously down the path. 'I paid for this skip, it's for my rubbish and no one else's!! What am I supposed to do with this now ... melt it down for Baco-Foil? I said this would happen! Didn't I say this would happen??'

'Where on earth's it c— has someone just come along in the night and *dumped* this here?' gasped Margaret in stupefied astonishment.

Victor stared at her with eyes like bradawls.

'Well! Unless a very large jackdaw was carrying it back to its nest and *dropped* it I should think that's a pretty safe assumption, wouldn't you? It never ceases to amaze me, the bloody-minded soddishness of some p—'

At which point his jaw fell open yet again as he spied, rolled up on the back seat of the forsaken Deux-Chevaux, what could only be described as The Worst Horror of All . . . .

How long it had been busted, and from whose scabby old bedstead it had originated, he did not care to speculate. For it was enough that his prediction had come to pass with alarming accuracy, and his abysmal estimation of the worth of Mankind once again vindicated.

'You heartless bastards!!' he bawled at the clouds, apparently in the hope that somehow, somewhere, his thunderous wrath would rain down upon its appointed target. 'You come round here slinging your crap on my doorstep another time, I'll murder the lot of you!!'

Having delivered which dire warning he turned round and tramped back indoors to put some trousers on.

The tragic death of Mrs Warboys' brother-in-law Wilf came as such a dreadful shock that he was not at all sure he would ever get over it. What had started out as a ridiculous fantasy the night before had, during the next twenty-four hours, ripened into a compelling hypothesis that sent a chill down his spine.

It was a hypothesis that went as follows....

The mental torpor he had been encouraged to regard as post-operative disorientation stemming from recent major surgery could, in fact, be described in terms far more prosaic.

He was dead.

He had died twelve weeks ago under the surgeon's knife, and no one had told him, which was typical of doctors. The blurred, milky haze through which he seemed to view the world these days was not due to cataracts at all, but some ectoplasmic perspective from beyond the grave. And that swirling, floaty feeling that had been diagnosed as labyrinthitis was, in reality, the natural locomotive sensation of a nebulous being from the spirit world.

There were of course still some questions he could not answer: such as why ghosts still needed to go to the lavatory; and why, when he had attempted to put his theory to the test that morning by walking through a wall, he had required two boxes of Kleenex to staunch the resulting haemorrhage in his nose.

Moreover, if he *was* dead, how was his sister-in-law Jean able not only to see and talk to him, but to knot a tie around his neck as the two of them were preparing to go out that evening?

The more he considered the implications, the more confusing and frightening it all became. And so he resolved, at length, to pull himself together and forget all about it.

'I'm so sorry I'm not coming with you,' said Mrs Warboys, patting down Wilfred's light grey collar and standing back to inspect the dark grey tie inside his mid-grey pullover. 'But I can't let Malc and Becky down, not with their anniversary dinner and everything. And I'm sure Victor and Margaret will look after you, so— you know, it's a bit sombre, Wilf, for a night out. Why don't you get one of Chris's from upstairs, they're hanging on the back of the wardrobe door.'

'You're probably right,' said Wilfred. And then added, although he immediately wished he hadn't: 'Don't want to look as if I'm going to a funeral, do I?'

Mrs Warboys snapped the clasp shut on her handbag and followed him out of the lounge with the words: 'Have a nice time, won't you, and I'll see you when I get back!'

'Yes, bye, Jean!'

Mrs Warboys marched briskly into the utility room and un-locked the door to the garage. She had just placed one foot inside the looming hollow beyond – without the slightest sensation of an itch in her ankle – when the front doorbell summoned her back to the hall to admit Victor and Margaret, and usher them both into the sitting room.

The itch in her ankle – or absence of it – is of course not significant in itself, and is mentioned only as a telling indictment of the casual way that our lives on this planet are governed by the merest random collisions of chance. For it is fair to say that had her ankle itched she would have bent down to scratch it. And had she bent down to scratch it she would have noticed the bloodied fingers of a crab-like hand, reaching out from the blackness of the garage and attempting to hook themselves into the back of her shoe. In which event she would have discovered, like Mr Trevor Bennett in the Sherlock Holmes story, the body of a creeping man crawling on all fours across the floor of her utility room. And she would have rung for an ambulance so that he could be taken to hospital and given whatever treatment is appropriate for people who have just spent the night totally unconscious on the roof of an Austin Montego.

But Mrs Warboys did not have an itch in her right ankle. And she did not see Mr Saunders drag himself, shakily, to his feet, mumble 'Excuse me?' and then lurch into the kitchen to be sick down the waste disposal unit, because she was too busy issuing Victor and Margaret with their tickets for the BBC, together with various sets of travel instructions.

'You run along, Jean, we'll be fine,' said Margaret as her friend continued to fuss around them.

'Yes, right – have a good time then – bye!' said Mrs Warboys over her shoulder as she fled back to the garage, and a minute later was grinding her way down the road inside a thick fog of belched exhaust smoke.

Victor held the three tickets in his hands at arm's length so as to make out the small print that said 'Children under the age of 12 will not be admitted to the studio.' Could there, he pondered ruefully, be anyone *over* the age of twelve who found the antics of this dippy duo remotely diverting? With their carefully contrived chalk-and-cheese personalities and their cornflake-packet class conflict? For the life of him he failed to understand why they were the country's number one comedy show when, as far as he could see, they were not remotely funny.

'An evening of fun and frolics to look forward to here by the looks of things,' he grumbled, wondering privately if he could feign a sudden fainting fit that would allow him to spend the recording doing brain-teasers in the toilet.

'If you're going to be grizzling away like this all night long while the rest of us are trying to enj— ohh!!! Hallo!!! How *are* you!!'

Victor turned round towards the door as his wife snapped open one of her deluxe fake smiles like an old-fashioned plastic rain hood and welcomed their companion for the evening. He was slightly surprised, not so much by Wilfred's scruffy appearance – for they were, after all, going to BBC Television Centre – as by the wild, startled look in his eyes as he tottered in from the kitchen blotting the corners of his mouth with a paper towel.

'So nice to meet you,' Margaret was saying with sing-song sincerity, while violently flapping his hand about. 'I'm Margaret, and this is Victor.'

'Oh.'

Mr Saunders blinked at them both without so much as a glimmer of understanding or any recollection at all of his previous existence.

'*Margaret* . . . and *Victor* . . .' he repeated slowly, in a display of mental agility normally associated with any Raymond Chandler character called Moose.

'Thaaaat's right!' sang Margaret, cordially.

'And who am I?'

'Sorry?' said Victor.

'I'm afraid I . . . can't seem to place wh—everything seems to have gone blank, I can't quite remember who I . . . .'

'You're *Wilfred!!*' Margaret chuckled merrily, picking up a dark-grey tie from the back of the armchair and looping it beneath his crumpled collar. 'You're Jean's brother-in-law Wilfred! You've been through a big operation and it's left you a bit forgetful . . . .'

'And where are we going now?' he said as Margaret steered him towards the door, brushing the sleeves of his jacket with a tissue. 'Somewhere nice?'

'I'm afraid not,' said Victor, without a hint of irony. 'We're going to the BBC.'

It was unfortunate that, of all the working-class state-educated employees currently on the BBC's payroll, neither of them was actually present when Victor and Margaret arrived at Television Centre for the show that evening. Instead, they were greeted by two willowy Sloanes named Teena and Heidi who purred plummily at them through their super-sheer ten-denier smiles and then led them on limbs of lycra into a large studio, where they all settled back beneath a constellation of overhanging lamps to watch the latest instalment in the nation's best-loved comedy series.

Victor had predicted the evening would be an unalloyed nightmare, and he was certainly not wide of the mark. Tonight's plot appeared to be a real barrel-scraper, revolving as it did around the rather hilarious counterpoint of a boyfriend's circumcision and the shrinking of the collar on Angie's pink polo-neck jumper. All of which was bad enough, without the added discomfort of your ex-neighbour's brother-in-law collapsing semi-consciously across your lap, dribbling spittle and groaning about a lump on his forehead the size of a Saxon burial mound.

Mrs Warboys had, of course, warned them that Wilfred might still be shaky on his feet, but this was ridiculous.

Since the moment they loaded him onto the back seat of their car like a sack of coke he had not so much as uttered an intelligible word all night. Worse, he seemed incapable of maintaining an upright position for more than five seconds at a time, and at various points they had been obliged to prop him up against a succession of walls and pillars, down which he would eventually slide like a rag doll, until either his body reached the floor or one of his nostrils became hooked over the door knob.

Most embarrassing of all had been the moment when the

Warm-Up Man invited questions from the audience and Wilfred, politely raising a forefinger, had asked why he had woken up on a roof rack that evening with the filament of a sodium light-bulb inside his left ear. When the Warm-up Man had confessed to finding this one a bit of a stumper Wilfred had become possessed of an acute desire to genuflect before the nearest lavatory pan, and mumbling a brief apology to his host and hostess, excused himself from the studio and stumbled away in search of the Gents.

Relieved, for the moment, of his charge for the evening, Victor relaxed to such an extent that he very nearly forgot himself and laughed when, for the umpteenth time that night, Natalie and Angie both failed triumphantly to say or do absolutely anything that could be considered, in any sense of the word at all, remotely amusing.

A t twenty-eight minutes past eight precisely Wilfred made a really quite fascinating discovery. What he discovered was that squinting through a pair of net curtains at a deserted street for two hours was a staggeringly pointless way of spending your life.

It is of course a popular fallacy that the act of squinting or peering through a set of curtains will accelerate the arrival of a visitor to your house. In reality no direct link between the two has ever been established, and it is accepted now among physicists that the time we devote to gazing out of windows looking for belated guests would be far more profitably employed having sex or strangling a Conservative MP.

Neither of these options being open to Wilfred, he remained gamely at the net curtains for another thirty-six and a half minutes, peering and squinting in the hope of seeing Victor's car draw up. And when Victor's car failed to do anything of the kind, Wilfred was obliged to concede that he was not, after all, going to be taken to London tonight to watch the hilarious antics of Natalie and Angie, and the funny woman from across the road who talked about multiple orgasms.

M r Saunders was not feeling at all well. After spending twenty-five minutes hunched over a lavatory making noises like a sea-lion that's failed to win the Booker Prize, he had, while coming up for air, met the toilet seat on its way down. The resulting thwack of durable plastic upon his conjunctiva had triggered a sudden temporary blindness, during which he had attempted to exit the cubicle without ascertaining that the door was open first. By the time he had disengaged the chrome coat-hook from the roof of his mouth and skated across several of his teeth into the BBC corridor a whole new sense of imbalance and utter confusion had set in.

He had no idea who he was, or where he was. He had already forgotten why he had come there and had never known who had brought him there. If his brain had been surgically removed from his skull and then mushed in a Kenwood Blender it was a safe bet it would be in better shape than it was now. The world spun dizzily all around him, appearing before his eyes the way it might to a pair of socks in a tumble dryer. People, faces, objects blurred in a foaming smudge of shapes and silhouettes, and a host of shrill sounds pulped his ear-drums. His head had been hammered like a nail, and he had little now in the way of personal ambition but to crawl away somewhere quietly and die.

He was conscious, vaguely, of staggering into a small room with mirrors all around the walls that was, for its size, extremely well-spoken. The moment he entered it said: 'Ground Floor. Going Up.' And then, a short while later after both its doors had purred shut and then purred open again it said, with the confidence that only comes with true breeding: 'Sixth Floor. Going Down.'

But Mr Saunders was not in the mood for conversing with small rooms, however well-connected they might be. And it was unfortunate that when the doors purred open the next time he happened to be leaning against them, because it meant that two seconds later he was lying face down on the floor with his nose in the shape of a jumping-cracker and a sound like five hundred canaries twittering inside his head.

Two girls named Uma and Cassie who were both clutching white cardboard cups containing white cardboard coffee asked if he was all right, then stepped over his head and pressed the button for the First Floor. The doors purred shut again, the well-spoken voice made a slightly suggestive remark, and the girls both laughed like elephants as they disappeared down the lift-shaft.

Mr Saunders, now in the posture of a giant grovelling newt, proceeded to haul himself across the opulent pile of the sixth floor executive carpet, through three sets of double doors, down a long tiled ramp, along a corridor lined with perspiring pot plants, through another huge swing door, up a different ramp past a woman with a drinks trolley who deliberately looked the other way, and finally through another set of doors beneath a flashing red light and a big sign on the wall that screamed 'Do Not Enter!'

Yes, it really was that easy to enter the BBC Newsroom during a live transmission.

It was not, of course, a particularly smart move for Mr Saunders to make, and as it turned out it was something he would regret for the rest of his life. Put another way, he would regret it for another three and a half minutes.

Plagued for most of the day with thoughts of death, Wilfred had sat down in front of the television to take his mind off it, and found himself watching an American TV movie about Californians with terminal illnesses who were so sick they only looked like half a million dollars. When he turned over to BBC2 he found it was screening a repeat of a programme in which Jonathan Miller sawed up a corpse, so he switched again to Channel Four where a young man wearing big red glasses was talking to a young Irishman with a curly beard about nothing of any interest to anybody in the entire world.

Finally he tuned in to BBC1 where the reassuring baritone of Moira Stuart describing atrocities on the West Bank enabled him to snuggle down and put the worries and the cares of the world behind him.

But what was this?'

Something was going on in the back of the BBC newsroom. While Miss Stuart continued to speak impassively in the foreground, in the middle-distance, behind her right shoulder, a blurred man with raffia-like hair appeared to be clambering drunkenly onto one of the desks, knocking down an in-tray and kicking over several cups of steaming coffee. A second later, two fuzzy figures in white shirts could be seen rushing in from camera left, apparently trying to restrain the first man by making a grab for his legs. And although the man on the desk, who was now staggering this way and that without any apparent purpose, managed to dodge them for several seconds, he succumbed, eventually, to a nifty rugby tackle that sent him crashing face-first into a computer keyboard, while his right foot ended up twitching convulsively inside an over-turned monitor screen nearby.

With cool professionalism Miss Stuart introduced a short film report about oil slicks and when, forty-five seconds later, the camera returned to her the shot had been hastily recomposed so as to exclude, almost entirely, the woman in a nurse's uniform who was now thumping the man's chest and frantically feeling the pulse in his neck.

By now Wilfred, who had had quite enough of this unscheduled mayhem, decided he would make himself a sandwich and get ready for bed. Switching off the television he entered the kitchen and put on some light music on the radio while he pottered about, preparing his supper. An hour later he had just finished drying a plate with a tea towel and was standing on a stool returning it to the top cupboard when he suddenly heard his own name being read out by a Radio 2 newsreader.

What the newsreader was saying was that he, Wilfred John Warboys, seventy-two, of Stevenage in Hertfordshire, had – tragically – died of a brain haemorrhage earlier that evening.

What the newsreader said next he was never destined to hear, for by that time he had keeled over backwards onto the table in a mortified swoon, the checkered tea towel had fluttered down across his face, and the plate lay in fragments on the floor.

He had told himself it was all nonsense, and for a while he had almost been convinced of it. But when no less an authority than the mighty BBC broadcast the fact on its airwaves, could there any longer be a vestige of doubt?

Wilfred *was* dead after all.

It was, at last, official.

Victor mis-dialled three times before he got through to Mrs Warboys at her god-daughter's house that night. His finger was quivering in that exact way that your finger always quivers when you're about to tell someone that the ageing brother-in-law they entrusted to your care for the evening has just wandered into the BBC Newsroom and dropped spectacularly dead in front of twelve million viewers.

When Wilfred had first disappeared from the studio half way through the recording to go to the toilet Victor's principal reaction had been one of relief. An hour later, when he had still not returned, Victor's relief had gradually turned to envy: if *he* was being forced to sit through this ham-fisted display of hamming-up he didn't see why anyone else should escape the torture. But then, just as he and Margaret were filing out at the end of the show, a man in a blue uniform discreetly took his arm with the words 'that old geezer you brought in's just croaked it', and slowly he began to experience a foreboding that all was not well.

Half an hour had passed since then, during which the full facts about the deceased had been laid before them – as indeed had the deceased, on a rather rusty old First Aid trolley. And they had both sunk stiff brandies to try and still their jangling nerves.

'Brilliant!' Victor had groaned. '*Absolutely brilliant!* You let someone out of your sight for five seconds and what happens? They bugger off upstairs and snuff it on the *Nine O'Clock News*! I told you he was in no fit state to come out tonight! Ten minutes of that sodding sitcom and he quite obviously lost the will to live ... tch! Wrong number again! Suppose we'll just have to hope she wasn't watching when it happened, that's all.'

'Or heard the news since,' said Margaret. 'They've no right to put his name out before the next of kin have been told. It makes you wonder how they get hold of information like that so quickly.'

'Yes, funny that,' said Victor, prodding the phone buttons again. 'Considering it all happened in the nerve-centre of the country's major national news network.'

'What are you going to say to her?' said Margaret, observing him with growing unease. 'She might get hysterical, or anything. They were a very close-knit family.'

'What do you *think* I'm going to say to her?' said Victor, listening testily to the ringing tone. 'That we got fed up carting him around and dumped him on John Cole's typewriter? I mean I'll just have to break it to her g— ohh! Hello?? Umm, yes, hello, Mrs Warboys, it's Mr Meldrew here, ringing from the BBC medical room. I'm afraid I've got some rather terrible n— sorry? Err, yes, *quite* funny I suppose, in parts – though to be honest it's not really my cup of tea in the first place ... but the thing is, I'm afraid, the reason I'm ringing is Wilfred. I'm afraid he's had a rather n— what? Yyyyy ... hang on, I'll ask Margaret ... did the woman across the road come in and talk about multiple orgasms? I think I must have nodded off at that point....'

'For God's *sake*, Victor!!!' Margaret began to steam like a spouting geyser. 'Will you give that *here*!!'

And relieving him sharply of the receiver with a glare that would shatter crystal she took the phone into a corner and quietly said whatever it was she had to say.

The windscreen wipers scratched and screeched in front of Mrs Warboys' eyes, sounding the tattoo of a tattered heartbeat as she trundled homeward down grief-lined avenues of sodden despair. Rain-swept street lamps scored a tangerine swathe through the blackness of her bereavement. And at no point whatever did she hum a merry tune, or pull over at the side of the road to skip up and down the pavement with glee.

For the news of Wilfred's death had devastated her beyond measure. And to think that it had taken place in such an apocalyptic fashion under the glare of the television cameras: in full view of half the population of Great Britain.

The whole scenario was just too appalling to contemplate. In addition to which she could not help feeling personally responsible for the tragedy, as the one who had considered him fit enough to be allowed out of the house in the first place. How horribly wrong she had been! And now she would have his awful, awful death hanging on her conscience for the rest of her days.

In the shock of the moment she realised she had forgotten to ask Margaret what would actually happen to her brother-in-law's remains. Presumably he would be transferred to a local hospital, pending the appropriate funeral arrangements. Certainly a dead body wouldn't be allowed to remain very long on BBC premises. There were all the health risks to be considered, for a start. And indeed, as Victor had observed to Margaret, the danger that he might accidentally be given his own chat show on BBC1.

As she steered her car into her drive she was a little surprised to see the soft glow of the kitchen light playing upon the birch tree in her back garden. Perhaps Margaret had decided to leave it burning as a deterrent to intruders. It was, after all, typical of her thoughtful nature.

Shakily, Mrs Warboys parked the car in the garage and locked it. Then she traversed the darkened utility room and opened the door to the kitchen.

At which point her heart leapt, figuratively, into her mouth, flapped about for several seconds in the manner of a freshly caught herring, and was forced back down by a large gulping action into her ribcage, where it proceeded to cannon back and forth against her chest like a lunatic in a padded cell.

And instantly all lingering reflections about her friends' thoughtful nature were eradicated by the barbarous vision that rose to greet her.

Having first had the decency to telephone and forewarn her of Wilfred's demise it was inconceivable that Victor and Margaret would be so heartless as to ferry the poor man's body home and dump it on the kitchen table with a tea towel across his face ... surely to goodness?

It was inconceivable, and yet it was a fact.

For there he was, duly delivered: plonked among the plates and pepperpots as if he were nothing more precious than a deep-pan pizza.

'Oh my dear God spare us ....'

Bravely, Mrs Warboys dared to lift up the flimsy checked cloth and expose the face of sweetly mottled putty beneath, its eyes hooded in silent death, its grey-lipped mouth thrown open wide as if attending the arrival of some spectral dentist.

'Poor, poor, Wilfred ....'

This could only be Mr Meldrew's doing, she reflected, as she backed biliously away from the bleak tableau before her. Any man who would wilfully feed his next-door neighbour boiled eggs with live lizards in them would hardly shrink from parking a fresh corpse on her breakfast bar. Was there no seam of sensitivity in the man of any kind? How much more trouble would it have been to carry the poor fellow upstairs and lay him out decently on a bed?

Mrs Warboys' head flopped forward as she surrendered her sorrows to a tempest of tears. In all her life she could not recall a set of events more deeply distressing.

Of course, had she known then that she would be spending most of that night in a drawer at the local mortuary it is not likely that her constitution would have much improved.

122

Exactly how it came about may never be known, for it is a story that has already become the stuff of legend. What is recorded fact is that shortly after returning home to find Wilfred slumped across her kitchen table Mrs Warboys picked up the phone and dialled for an ambulance. Minutes later, while steadying her nerves with a large whisky, something – call it the sudden appearance of her dead brother-in-law staggering in, dazed, from the kitchen – caused her to choke and splutter uncontrollably as if she'd seen a ghost.

We can only speculate as to what caused the considerable bruising found later on the back of her neck and the crown of her head. But it would certainly be consistent with a well-meaning relative having whacked her violently between the shoulder blades with a saucepan to try and free her air passages, and, having got a bit carried away with himself, accidentally knocked her unconscious.

It can confidently be supposed – although it has never been confirmed – that Wilfred then rushed next door to get help, at which point a pair of pimply young ambulancemen arrived, charged with the collection of a deceased body. Being the sort of paramedics who rushed mouldy carrots to hospital first and unzipped your flies later, they wasted no time trussing Mrs Warboys up in a large red blanket and whisking her straight back to base where the night-duty houseman drowsily signed her through to the cold meats department.

According to the hospital log it was 6.29 a.m. when a sudden outbreak of maniacal shrieking from Drawer 27D caused grown men in the hospital morgue to stampede hysterically into the corridor screaming for their mothers.

By 7.05, happily, someone had plucked up the courage to creep back in and release the reluctant corpse from her tray, and very soon the whole nasty mix-up had been sorted out, and you will be pleased to hear that Mrs Warboys was not inadvertently cremated or buried alive or anything unpleasant of that nature, but instead was allowed to return home where she and Wilfred both toasted their return from the dead with a plate of Sainsbury's bran-flakes doused in semi-skimmed milk.

CHAPTER EIGHT

Muscle Tensions

Doreen Mauleverer, having taken off all her clothes, lay down on the small, velvet-draped couch and prayed that she wouldn't get hiccups. On the floor, some eighteen inches away, was a dead match upon which she carefully fixed her gaze, and at which she continued to stare for the next ninety minutes while mentally plotting an exciting dinner party she was planning for Wednesday week. Although utterly undressed she soon began to feel quite hot, but that was due to the large Fresnel lamp behind her shoulder, angled so as to glance softly off the ceiling onto the robust curves of her ripened circumference.

Victor tried rubbing his finger across her nipples to see if he could make them stand out more. It was a trick he had seen performed by Mr Creamer, who sat next to him, and it had the effect of finely diffusing the shading on your drawing so as to give it a true feeling of three dimensions.

However, after several minutes of meticulous smoothing and smudging Victor found he had merely produced the horrific image of a woman with two enormous bullet-holes in her chest, so he flicked to the next page of his Rowney pad and started all over again.

He was on his eighteenth attempt at this particular life study when the caustic breath of the art teacher Mr Dewey-Dobson arrived like a hair-dryer on the back of his neck and he found himself being dragged out before the whole class so that his work could be publicly pulled to pieces.

'Tch tch tch! What on Earth's happened here, Mr Meldrew? Is this supposed to be a sketch of a nude lady? It's like the results of some hideous medical experiment.'

'I'm afraid I was never very good at drawing figures,' said Victor, casting a sheepish look at his subject, who remained throughout the discussion perfectly and immovably placid. 'I can't seem to get the proportions right.'

'That much is evident,' said Mr Dewey-Dobson. 'You'll find if you look at the model that her arms are of roughly equal length and that neither would be particularly suited for swinging through the trees in a jungle. Also, if you study the actual distance between the bottom of her chin and the top of her pubic hair you'll see that in real life there's no way the latter could be mistaken for a beard. Do you see? Look at where I'm pointing, Mr Meldrew.'

'Ye-es ... I see,' said Victor, looking carefully first at Mrs Mauleverer's chin, and then at a poster for a flower-arranging course on the community centre wall.

'And then of course we come to the head ... I mean y—'

At this point Mr Dewey-Dobson broke off, momentarily, to swivel Victor's sketch round through ninety degrees, and peered mordantly at it over his half-moon spectacles before resuming, in a voice encrusted with disbelief:

'What in the name of all that's holy *is* this, Mr Meldrew? I mean, it certainly isn't any known terrestrial life-form, we can be sure of that ... what was that film *The Thing*, by John Carpenter ...? I mean, what are these, up here next to her nose, for goodness sake?'

Victor's forehead creased into a frown as he squinted dubiously at his artwork.

'I'm ummm ... I'm not quite sure what those are, to be honest with you....'

'They look like tusks.'

'I'm afraid they do, a bit.'

'You see, if I'd wanted a pencil study of some heraldic beast suffering from various congenital deformities I would have brought one in – do you see what I'm saying? And got it to pose on the couch. And what are you using for this sketch anyway, some form of advanced diamond-cutting implement?'

'I've been using the 2H,' said Victor. 'I seemed to get on quite well with that for the cup and saucer last week, so I thought that erm....'

'Yes well this isn't a cup and saucer, is it, Mr Meldrew,' said Mr Dewey-Dobson, pointedly.

'Not really it's not, no,' said Victor.

'For goodness sake use something softer but keep it well sharpened,' said Mr Dewey-Dobson. 'And try to give a bit more thought to your perspective in future.'

'Yes. Right,' said Victor who, having retrieved his pad, sat down again to resume his professional examination of Mrs Mauleverer's thighs.

An hour or so later he was emerging from the hall into the narrow side-corridor when he very nearly walked right into a small woman with black, burnished hair speaking animatedly on a public phone. Because she was wearing clothes it was all of ten seconds before he recognised her.

'No! No you will not do anything of the kind! Leave it in the garage, there's quite enough death on the roads as it is – I'll get a taxi!'

With which she slapped down the receiver and flashed a benign smile at Victor, who was still standing alongside her, waiting to squeeze past.

'Lost his contact lenses again,' said Mrs Mauleverer, proceeding to burrow back into her purse for another coin. 'My father. He's a menace at the wheel at the best of times. Last time he gave me a lift I swore never again: claiming he'd electrocuted himself by accidentally ripping out the choke button. I told him, our car doesn't *have* a choke button, what you've got there is a cigarette lighter, that's why your fingers are burning, but of course he wouldn't have it. Old people are such a worry aren't they?'

She had a quiet voice, sweetly rusted by age. Her face was seasoned and warm, and her wise eyes nestled snugly beneath her glossy raven fringe.

Victor cleared his throat and asked her if she needed a lift home at all. And she replaced her purse in her handbag and asked him if he knew Sutton Crescent at all.

You could tell if you looked closely that the dawn was gradually approaching. What it was gradually approaching was the dusk. For the smoky twilight of late September was already beginning to fog the days, which were fast becoming shorter. And the white-hot lustre of summer had begun a slow cross-fade into the amber glow of autumn.

The sunshine months had brought mixed blessings to Victor and Margaret. True, they had, once again, a roof over their heads, but they had not exactly got off to a good start with the neighbours.

Hurling Mr Swainey bodily out of his own home in the middle of the night had, in the end, been the least of their worries. When the facts were explained to him the latter had immediately seen the funny side and for a full twelve minutes had rocked back and forth on his pouffe like a laughing sailor at a fairground, his face turning such a vivid shade of red that Victor had to be physically restrained from throwing a bucket of water over him.

Pacifying Patrick and Pippa had not been so easy.

While Patrick's initial alarm had now eased to some extent he was still not prepared to write off his neighbour's mad behaviour over that double bed just yet. Additionally, there was a rather nasty rumour circulating – though he had not been able to get to the bottom of it one way or the other – that Meldrew had been personally involved in the kidnapping and subsequent death of that hospital electrician on the *Nine O'Clock News* the other week. Put all this together with an eye-witness report by a local window-cleaner that he had been observed earlier that summer lying in the bath with a glass tumbler on his ear and it was clear that Victor Meldrew, if not exactly on another planet, was certainly in orbit somewhere outside this one.

Pippa, because she was the sort of person who saw things differently, saw things differently. While her husband prided himself on a special brand of dogged vindictiveness she was herself not physically equipped to carry a grudge for more than a few yards. Life was infinitely too complex and unpredictable to start forming opinions about the way people around you behaved. It was her experience that the human race rarely acted in anything other than a totally absurd and illogical fashion. So to try and work anyone out was a complete waste of time, and the best you could ever strive for was a kind of on-going peaceful co-existence. Unhappily this rather philosophical attitude only served to antagonise her husband, for although he could tolerate most things in life tolerance was not one of them.

That evening, when Victor had been safely packed off to his art class and Margaret was returning from the chemist's with a little something for his rather stubborn 'Greek problem', she noticed the light on in Pippa's kitchen and decided to drop by for a neighbourly chat.

'I'm sorry things have been a bit tense these last few weeks,' she said, plonking her shopping bag down by the kitchen table upon which Pippa was currently carrying out a stock-take of her vast hoard of vitamin pills. 'I'm afraid my husband can be a bit of an acquired taste ....'

Pippa chuckled and stood up to flick the kettle on.

'You don't have to apologise,' she said. 'Mine's as bad. I never told you this, but after that first night Patrick sat down and wrote an abusive letter to Victor, and the next day went straight out and put it in the post. No name or address on the envelope, just the words "To That Cretin In The Cap". I'm afraid that's the sort of mad thing he does to let off steam.'

'Yes,' said Margaret. 'The irony is we received it. About the quickest a letter's ever got to us I think.'

And then, surveying the vast metropolis of bottles and boxes spread across Pippa's table she added: 'Gosh, you're well stocked up on all your health-foods! Must cost you an absolute fortune....'

'That's Patrick's ginseng' said Pippa, eyeing the long foil strip Margaret was idly scrutinising. 'He takes it to reverse the ageing process.'

'Does it work?'

'Well, in that he's started acting like a five-year-old. Of course he's always *had* a childish side to his nature. Except when he was a child, oddly enough.'

'I wonder if Victor could do with anything like this to supplement *his* diet.'

'What sort of things does he eat?' said Pippa.

'*Anything*,' declared Margaret. 'Of any sort or description, in the most disgusting and hideous combinations known to Man. Foods you wouldn't even put in the same cupboard he'll quite happily slice up together on his shredded wheat. I think he lost all sense of taste years ago.'

'Here we are, get this down your neck,' Pippa said, placing before her an earthenware mug steaming with exotic fragrances. 'Soothe away all your problems. It's a special herbal tea made from camomile, jasmine, tilia and lemon-grass. They make it up down the health shop, it gives you a terrific night's sleep.'

Margaret dipped her nose into the squat, silvered tin from which Pippa had been spooning into the teapot and issued an approving sniff.

'Mmmmm. I shall have to get some of this for Victor next time I'm down there,' she said. 'Never know, it might help to calm him down a wee bit.'

Ironically, as things turned out, it would not so much help to calm him down a wee bit as reduce him, in the space of seconds, to a complete absolute nervous gibbering wreck.

The time on the video recorder was 19.36 when the back door slammed and Victor strode into the front room clutching a handful of something so unspeakably vile that it defies description. Which meant that it was exactly 22.15, for to this day they had not yet figured out how to re-set the clock.

'Mmm! I'm really glad I arrived home to find the half-eaten remains of this Double Whopper With Cheese in my rose bed!' bawled Victor at no one at all, for Margaret was still upstairs. 'Some people put manure on theirs but I'll have none of it! A half-eaten Double Whopper With Cheese is the thing, Harry Wheatcroft always swore by them.'

'You're late back,' said Margaret, materialising from the hall. 'How was it this week? What did they ask you to draw?'

'Bloody litter!' cursed Victor as he tramped back in from the pedal bin and began stripping off his coat. 'I'm thinking of compiling a special book, *The Observer's Book of Crap in Your Back Garden*. Give me something to do, to while away my twilight years.'

'I said what did you have to draw tonight?'

'There's a Bassets Liquorice All-Sorts packet flapping about in the guttering, we'll need a bloody turn-table ladder to get that down....'

'Am I talking to myself?' said Margaret, reaching for the giant sketch-pad Victor had leaned against the sideboard on his arrival.

'Sorry? Draw? Er, yes, a nude if I remember correctly.'

Margaret froze briefly in the act of flipping through various sheets of semi-vandalised cartridge paper to stare at him aghast.

'W— a *nude??* What ... a nude *woman?*'

Victor sat down airily to begin the business of unlacing his shoes and said:

'As far as one could tell, yes.'

'What – in front of everybody ... with no clothes on?'

Victor looked up at her.

'Yes?'

Frenziedly, Margaret found the offending page, goggled at it

129

for several seconds, then swivelled it round through ninety degrees and said:

'Why has she got tusks?'

'Oh, that was just an early attempt, don't look at that one,' said Victor.

Margaret stopped looking at that one and proceeded to look at the next one.

'Ohhhhh, *very* nice,' she said, focusing on Victor's handiwork through eyes of flaming petrol.

'Thank you very much.'

'I suppose it was necessary to draw her breasts in this much detail was it?'

'What?'

'You had to put *breasts* on her.'

'Had to put br— What was I supposed to do, ask her if she'd mind slipping them off for a few minutes while I did the sketch? Hang them up on the clothes peg next to her hand-bag? I mean for goodness sake!'

But Margaret was having none of it.

'You might have had the decency to rub them out afterwards!'

'Rub them out afterwards?? Well what's the point of her being nude then??'

'You tell *me*!' stormed Margaret. 'No wonder you're late home, having to tear yourself away from this orgy of flesh.'

'That had nothing to do with it,' said Victor. 'It's just that after I'd given her a lift home I got a bit lost in the one-way system, and it took me a—'

The loud *flllwacckk*! was the sound of an open sketch pad plunging suddenly from Margaret's hands to the floor.

'Gave *who* a lift home??' she spluttered. 'The naked woman??'

'Well, I didn't g—'

'The naked woman???'

'Well she wasn't naked when I gave her a lift!!'

'You've had a naked woman in our car??'

'Not in the car she wasn't naked!'

'She didn't sit in the *passenger* seat?'

'Ohh for goodn— No, I strapped her to the bloody roof-rack! Attracted one or two stares at the traffic lights ... I mean, she's not naked all the time, for God's sake, she does occasionally put some clothes on!'

Margaret was not to be deflected.

'She's naked by *profession!*'

'Naked by profession? What the bloody Hell's that supposed to mean? She's a model, that's all there is to it. She happens to be an artist herself, and she models for one or two of her friends, including this art teacher chap, and she was trying to ring for a taxi, so . . . .'

'Oh, you know all about her now, do you?' said Margaret, prosecuting him further with one of her sickly smiles. 'Where does she live, got a nice little place somewhere has she?'

'She lives in Sutton Crescent, near the hospital.'

'Oh yes, just on the corner, by the Sexually Transmitted Diseases Clinic?'

'What the hell's that supposed t— anyway, as a matter of fact she's offered me a little part-time job. If you must know.'

'Oh yes?'

'Cleaning round her house once a week. She's divorced now and she's got her father staying with her, who's apparently a bit of a handful, so. . . . Few extra bob in the pocket, it seemed like quite a good idea. I mean you've no objections, surely to goodness?'

'Objections? Why on Earth would I have any objections?' said Margaret, while – as she stared flintily at Victor's drawing of Mrs Mauleverer with two bullet-holes through her chest – a really quite barbaric idea suddenly entered her head.

The next morning Margaret stepped out of the shower, got dressed, put some lipstick on and slipped several pieces of bacon rind into her tights. Which was odd, because Margaret never wore lipstick. And no one was more surprised than the ageing tube of *Coral Blush* when it found itself being exhumed from an old vanity case at the foot of her wardrobe and studiously applied in front of the bathroom mirror.

What made this odd behaviour exponentially odd was that Margaret had no intention of leaving the house that morning. It was her day off from the florist's, which meant that she had a million (or more accurately, eleven) chores to perform around the home, none of which demanded immaculate facial grooming.

But then Margaret was not herself that morning. She was wrestling with a whole cluster of emotions that she would rather not put a name to. Irrational, adolescent emotions that she never thought she would feel again. And although she could perfectly disprove, by logic, that they were remotely productive, she remained hopelessly in their grip. And the visceral torture unleashed by her own insecurities forced her, like a helpless puppet, to say and do much that she knew full well she would later regret.

She was, for example, regretting already the remark about the Sexually Transmitted Diseases Clinic the previous evening, as well as her injunction that morning, when Victor was leaving for Mrs Mauleverer's, to make sure he had a rubber on the end of his pencil. Cheap shots, both of them, which she knew full well he did not deserve.

When she had finished binding the small nylon pouch filled with scraps to the branch of the cherry tree, and had twisted it into a position where the tits could happily peck their way through, her attention was suddenly arrested by a voice like a set of door chimes in the next garden which said:

'Morning, Mrs Meldrew! Is it me or is it moist?'

Simultaneously, to her surprise, one of the fence panels swung back through sixty degrees, to reveal Nick Swainey holding a large garden fork as if it were a dry Martini, and grinning like a village idiot who has just been given a turnip for his birthday.

'Ermmm ... yes, it does seem a bit on the humid side today,' stammered Margaret, slightly taken aback by the ingenuity of his entrance.

'Makes it a bit easier, doesn't it?' said Mr Swainey, indicating a set of brass hinges down the inside of his fence post. 'Saves all that trooping round to the front door every time either of us wants to say hallo. It used to come in very handy for keeping an eye on old Mr and Mrs Gittings, to make sure they were both all right and what-have-you. Up until their unspeakably horrific deaths, that is, at least.'

'Yes. I see,' said Margaret. And hastily changing the subject, she said: 'I see your rhubarb's going berserk down there . . . .'

'Yes, terrible business,' said Mr Swainey. 'Hacked to pieces in the bathroom, blood and guts everywhere. And do you know I'm not sure as they ever did find that other ear, it's amazing what'll go down a plug-hole sometimes isn't it. Anyway I expect it'll pop up eventually. Whole business hardly bears thinking about really. When you stop to think about it.'

'Ye-es,' said Margaret, and then, deciding to give it another try, she added: 'So! Did you have a good weekend then, Mr Swainey?'

'Oh yes, lovely, thank you very much.'

'You go anywhere nice at all?'

'To hospital. I'm afraid Granny took a sudden turn for the worse so I had to run Mother up there on a bit of a mercy dash. Which was a little fraught, we'd no sooner got her up there than her wheelchair accidentally locked into high-speed reverse and she ended up going on a mystery tour of the Clement Atlee Wing. And of course by the time we managed to find her she'd already gate-crashed three hysterectomies, so it was a bit of a day all in all.'

'Oh dear,' said Margaret dutifully. 'So how is your grandmother now. Not giving any cause for concern or anything?'

'Ohhh no, no, no,' said Mr Swainey with a sunny smile. 'Not now she's dead. Well she was ninety-three, I'm afraid, so.... They reckon it was a broken bone that finally did it.'

'Oh? I didn't realise you could die of a broken bone?'

'You can when it's stuck in your windpipe apparently. And of course she was always a great one for gnawing on chicken carcasses. The funeral's tomorrow, I don't think Mother's looking forward to it very much but I expect we'll manage to muddle through. Anyway it's nice having a nitter-natter, Mrs Meldrew, but I've just noticed it's time for Mother's poultice so I'm going to have to leave you and put another flannel in the sandwich-toaster. Be seeing you shortly I expect. Bubb-eye to you for now.'

And to Margaret's immeasurable relief, the fence panel had snapped back into position and he was gone.

B lue was predominantly what Mrs Mauleverer's house was. The wallpaper, which was a very profound blue, did not look at all right on the walls and was clearly homesick for its Sanderson's catalogue. The rugs, which were of hand-tufted Chinese washed wool, had more blue in them than you could shake a stick at, and sprawled languidly around the glazed pine floorboards like patches of sea bobbing about on a very large raft. The two Heals settees were blue and so were all the cushions scattered upon them. The light fittings were also mostly blue. The curtains in the lounge were not blue, but only because there weren't any.

The Venetian blinds were blue.

To begin with, the sitting room was empty. But then a curious thing happened. Through the door on the right a broad plastic brush appeared, emitting a strident hum as voraciously it gulped back any particles of grime and grit that were foolish enough to be standing in its way. At the same moment, through the door on the left, a broad plastic brush appeared, emitting a strident hum as voraciously it gulped back any particles of grime and grit that were foolish enough to be standing in its way.

Through the door on the right Victor hauled his vacuum cleaner into the room by its floppy hose-pipe and then stopped and stared at the man opposite him who was doing exactly the same thing.

He was a cadaverous gentleman, lean-looking and hunted, with lolloping arms and legs that appeared to have been inspired by the early animations of Max Fleischer. With his head and shoulders bunched forward in an obdurate stoop he appeared oblivious to Victor's presence as he continued to guide his slurping funnel across the floor.

'Excuse me!' shouted Victor, above the drone of both motors. 'I'm doing this room – there's no need for you to do it, thank you!'

Wherein the man, who did not for an instant pause or look up from his work, snapped back:

'I'm doing this room! Out of my way if you please!'

'There's no need for you to do it, I'm being paid to do it!'

'What?'

'Your daughter's paying *me* – you don't need to do it!'

'You're standing in my way, if you don't mind. Are you going to move or do you want this nozzle up your nose?'

Victor moved.

And Leonard Mauleverer surged forward with the subtle delicacy of a swarm of army ants devouring a dead horse.

'What on *earth's* he up to now!' cried a distraught voice from the hallway.

Mrs Mauleverer, her fingers crusted with wet clay, dived through the door and trod on his Off button, causing the appliance at once to wind down and expire. 'Father, I told you I was getting somebody in to do that, to make things easier for you! Why don't you *listen*.'

'I'm not entirely crippled,' rasped her father. 'I am still capable of doing a few simple jobs around the house, thank you very much.'

'Oh really, I suppose that hedgehog just leapt into the lawnmower for a haircut last week did it? I've told you, *I'm* not scraping it off the blades.'

Leonard eyed Victor with a look of undisguised scorn.

'Who the bloody Hell's this anyway?'

'This is Mr Meldrew, Father. I've arranged for him to pop round once a week.'

'You can arrange for him to sod off,' said Leonard.

'For goodness sake, will you stop being so truculent!'

'I don't like the look of him,' said Leonard.

'Yes well he can't help his looks, Father, can he. Any more than you can. Now will you please go back to your room and let him get on with his work.

'I'm sorry about this, Mr Meldrew,' she said as the old man finally relented and tramped upstairs in a snit. 'I did say he was a bit difficult.'

Victor smiled weakly and made a rather faint hissing sound that he hoped she would read as an expression of understanding and a demonstration of his own easy-going forebearance, but which she just read as a rather faint hissing sound.

Life clearly could not be easy with an ill-tempered old sod like him around the house day and night. Anyone could see that. And she surely deserved better, a woman in her position, at her time of life ....

'I'm sorry, Mr Meldrew. Is something wrong?'

'Hmm?'

Victor blinked, and suddenly his blood froze as he realised. He was staring at her breasts.

The way the tap kept dripping it was a wonder there weren't any stalagmites in Albert's bath.

Thought Margaret, as carefully she examined her hand.

But in truth the rhythmical per-plip on the lime-scaled enamel had become something of a landmark in the old man's sensory perspective: its reassuring pulse a sign that things were still all going wrong and that the world about him was functioning as normal. In fact today was actually better than normal because the lady from the florist's had popped round, quite unexpectedly, for a mug of tea and a ginger biscuit.

At first he had thought it was the man come back from the locksmith's to pick up the pencil he had left behind. He had quoted a price of £250 to fit a new dead-lock cylinder to the front door with security-locking mortice bolts, top and bottom, a solid steel security chain, and securing bolts to all the window sashes. It was a lot of money – in fact it was everything he had in the post office – but he had decided it would be worth it. His locks at present were both rusty and loose, and would offer little resistance to a determined intruder. So he had said to go ahead, and the man had promised to come back in two days' time and get everything sorted out.

It wasn't until she had actually spoken that Albert had recognised Margaret this time because she seemed to be wearing an unusually strong perfume. And when she had kissed him on the cheek he had detected a slight stickiness which had never been there before. The feeling he got (and of course he could have been totally mistaken) was that she had suddenly become anxious about her femininity. Her manner appeared less confident, and she had even made reference to his description of her face the other week as 'pretty', asking how he could possibly think such a thing when she was clearly so old and wrinkled.

After twenty seconds Margaret stopped examining her hand, stared into space for a moment, and then examined it again. It was, she felt, a good hand – although after she had triumphantly laid her double-six and Albert had trumped this with a six-three to score eight points she realised it was not so much which pieces you picked up in dominoes as the way you played them. And Albert, who in his time had been something of a grand master at the game, had little difficulty clobbering his companion four times on the trot as they faced each other that afternoon for a session of Fives and Threes.

'One more, or do you need to be getting back?' he said, as he shuffled the flat wooden bricks with their specially raised spots across the table top.

'I'd love to, but I dare say my husband will be wanting some tea when he comes home,' said Margaret, reaching for her scarf. 'All that skivvying for Lady Godiva, I imagine he'll have quite an appetite.'

'Lady Godiva?'

'Oh, just a naked woman he spends large portions of the day with. I've not actually met her myself but I've seen an artist's impression, and without going into details I don't imagine she gets to see much of her feet. Still, I'm sure she's a very nice person when you get to know her. Like Myra Hindley.'

'Oh.'

Since Albert (i) wasn't totally sure what she was talking about and (ii) wasn't totally sure he wanted to be totally sure what she was talking about he simply accompanied her to the front door and said:

'Keep your chin up, Mrs Meldrew. And whatever it is you're worrying about, just remember you're alive and got your health. When all's said and done you can't ask for more than that.'

And whereas, had these words been uttered by some fat oily tart on breakfast television, Margaret would instantly have disgorged her lunch into the coal scuttle, upon Albert's lips they had a curiously sagacious and settling ring. So she smiled warmly and said how much she had enjoyed his company this afternoon, and that she would look forward to seeing him again very soon indeed.

When he came home that evening Victor was whistling. Margaret couldn't make out exactly *what* he was whistling, but it sounded dangerously like 'I've been having a really terrific time today hanging out with my great new friend the nude model.'

Victor, had she asked him, would have categorically denied this.

So she didn't ask him.

In case he categorically denied it.

Thereby removing all just cause for the evening of brooding martyrdom she inflicted upon him from the moment he came in till the moment they went to bed.

Margaret desperately wanted to say something. What she wanted to say was 'Please tell me to stop behaving in such a totally illogical and immature fashion.' But she said nothing. And if Victor had told her to stop behaving in such a totally illogical and immature fashion she would have emptied a saucepan of scrambled egg into his cap.

Because as a matter of fact she liked behaving in such a totally illogical and immature fashion.

Victor, as it happened, also desperately wanted to say something. What Victor wanted to say was 'Can we please stop this ridiculous business, as it is clearly absurd to think I could harbour any romantic interest in a younger woman like Doreen who, for her part, would never be remotely interested in a tedious, balding old twerp like me.'

Doreen?

Where in Heaven's name did *that* come from?

He must have seen it this morning on one of those envelopes he was tidying up in her kitchen. . . . And somehow it had got lodged in his brain.

Well? There was nothing in that.

As far as he was concerned she was just plain old Mrs Mauleverer. And that was all there was to it.

Nice though the name Doreen was.

That wasn't the point.

And the sooner Margaret realised it the better.

It was Margaret's turn to lie awake for several hours that night. So she did.

As she lay awake she thought of then and now. Of poetry and prose. Of promise and denial. And she watched as the cast of past dreams skipped along shifting sands and splashed, as children, in a timeless sea. For the night was far off then, and the darkness of Eternal Dust forever shrouded in sunshine. Two spirits, devoted to each other's cause, whose simple sin was to trust in Truth.

Where were they now?

Well, one of them was lying with his elbow up the other one's nostril, generating the sort of ambient sound to which a pillion passenger on a Yamaha motor-bike would be more accustomed than an adjacent bed-fellow.

Margaret, since she rarely awoke to find herself at the controls of a bulldozer, was not easily able to move Victor on these occasions. She considered for a delicious moment the option of jabbing a safety-pin into his buttock but decided it would be unfair to wake the neighbours. Besides which she was now cultivating a magnificent headache that caused her positively to drool at the thought of an Anadin. So she tore herself free from the rumbling behemoth beside her, padded out to the bathroom in her bare feet, clicked on the light, and opened the door to the medicine cabinet.

The first thing she saw was something that was not a packet of Anadin. It was something that did not belong, nor ever had belonged, in the cabinet, or in their bathroom, or anywhere at all in their house. And as she gazed at it, with a skirling groan of despair, the words leapt from her lips to their certain death:

'Ohhhhhhh Godddd, Victor ... you *haven't* been ....'

M argaret could only apologise to Patrick in a tone of helpless ingratiation that she hoped would appeal to his better nature.

It didn't.

'*Right* then, Mrs Meldrew!' he said, after she had knocked on his back door the next morning and placed the item from the medicine cabinet into his hand. 'Thank you *very much* then. Thank you very much *indeed*.'

As ever, Patrick's manner was molten at room temperature, and the look he gave her laser-guided. But it was his deadly accuracy with italics that proved his most effective weapon in forcing Margaret judiciously to retreat.

'I'm umm ... as I say, it's all been a bit of a ...' she stammered, backing off towards the side gate.

'*Yes*, Mrs Meldrew?'

'Ihhh ... expect I'll see you around then, Patrick,' she signed off, lamely.

'*Indeed*, Mrs Meldrew!' said Patrick. 'I expect you probably *will*.'

Pippa was returning from the shops through the front door as Patrick slammed the back one and turned to face her with a glare that would have fused two hydrogen protons.

'Well! That's *that* little mystery cleared up then,' he smouldered. 'Cleared up and tied up neatly with a nice pink ribbon. It's nice to know there's never a dull moment living next door to *those* two.'

'What are you rabbiting about this time,' said Pippa, who really didn't much want to know.

'The mystery of my vanishing ginseng capsules,' said Patrick, flinging a long foil strip onto the table. 'You remember? I was hunting high and low for them all last night?'

'Oh right. Where were they then?'

Patrick left a beat of precisely two seconds for dramatic effect and then said:

'Mr Meldrew had been sticking them up his bottom.'

'I *beg* your pardon?'

'Yes, apparently,' Patrick said, flicking open a filter cone and tossing in two scoops of breakfast blend. 'I looked in most places, I think it's fair to say I never dreamed of looking *there*.'

'What on Earth are you talking about?'

'I don't know why I'm surprised really – the man seems to be capable of just about *anything* . . . .'

'How did he get hold of them, then?'

Patrick turned to face her with a look of unconcealed disgust.

'How he got hold of them is something I'd rather not con-template, thank you very much. Between the index finger and the thumb presumably. Beyond that, the whole image is too horrific to even think about.'

Pippa flopped into the chair with awful realisation.

'Tchohhhh . . . God. That's right, Margaret was fiddling about with them on this table the other night . . . they must have fallen into her bag . . . she *said* she'd just been to pick up his prescription . . . what happened? He must have found them in there and thought they w— Ohhhhh *dear* . . . .'

'I mean what have we got to do, put a statutory notice on the side of every bottle of vitamin pills now? *Caution – this product should not be shoved up Victor Meldrew's rectum??*'

'You're not throwing the rest away?' said Pippa, watching Patrick lob the remaining strips into the pedal bin.

'Somehow they've lost their appeal,' said Patrick. 'I can't imagine why.'

Pippa gathered up a small brown paper package from her shopping bag and headed for the back door.

'I'll have a word with her, I was just going to drop round in any case.'

'Unbelievable!' said Patrick after his wife had departed. 'Abso-lutely *unbelievable* . . . .'

Margaret wriggled both her arms down the sleeves of her coat and tried to collect her thoughts. The job of explaining to your neighbour that his miracle rejuvenation capsules have, for the last twenty-four hours, been used as suppositories to treat a rare fungal infection was never destined to be a painless experience. Still, it was done with now, and she could only hope the incident would be allowed to wither and die, and that in time full diplomatic relations would quietly be resumed.

She glanced at her watch and groaned.

The conversation with Patrick had delayed her departure for work, and she was in danger of being horribly late. Despite this, she paused while hurrying through the front room for her handbag to pick up Victor's sketch-pad and remind herself of its sordid contents . . . .

Pornography, she concluded. By anyone's standards. Decent ladies did not waltz into the local community centre and dangle their bare breasts over the edge of a couch before a group of gawping strangers.

Especially breasts like *those*.

To judge from Victor's generous rendering it would take only a slight draught from the door to set them slowly swinging to and fro, and within minutes the entire class would be in a state of deep, induced hypnosis. Come to think of it, where he had been at work with the rubber some of his sketches *did* look a bit on the blurred side. What, for example, was she doing in *this* one – rotating them both at high speed like a pair of Catherine wheels?

And then there was that phone call she was supposed to have made to her father later in the evening . . . .

To her horror Margaret now beheld, in her mind's eye, the boggling image of a woman twirling a telephone dial with an erect nipple in the holes . . . .

To say that Victor had an intimate knowledge of Mrs Mauleverer's body was grossly to understate the facts. After three hours scrutinising every square inch of her surface area there could not be a single goose pimple whose position he hadn't charted. Yet strangely it was not this that troubled her most. What troubled her most – and this surprised her – was the fact that Victor was now meeting the woman with her clothes *on*. In Margaret's eyes there was something perversely exhibitionist about a nude woman covering up her body in front of other people. For by putting on clothes was she not merely drawing attention to how naked she had been without them? In short, by getting dressed she was presenting Victor with a rather titillating memory test. And one, she didn't doubt, that he would pass with flying colours.

'Hallo! Anyone at home?'

Margaret's reflections were interrupted at that moment by a modest knuckle on the back door, followed by the pixie grin of her neighbour peeking into the kitchen.

'Pippa! How are you – I'm afraid I'm just off out actually .... I'm sorry about the ginseng, I'm afraid it hasn't improved matters much has it?'

'Ohhh, don't worry about it,' said Pippa. And then, carefully placing her brown paper package on the table, she added: 'I just wanted to give you this. I was down the health shop first thing, and ... well, remembering how much you liked it....'

'Ohhhh Pippa! That's *very* thoughtful of you,' said Margaret, lifting out a brand new pot of the herbal tea they had been discussing two days ago. 'How much do I owe you?'

Pippa waved her hand dismissively.

'Think of it as a peace offering. Remember, it's very good last thing at night. Very good if you suffer with a lot of tossing and turning in your sleep.'

Margaret chuckled.

'Victor does the tossing and turning. *I* suffer. Anyway, we'll definitely give it a try. And thanks again.'

A second later Pippa had departed and Margaret was about to do the same through the front door when she found her way blocked by a man dressed from head to foot in black, with a demeanour to match.

'Morning Mrs Meldrew.'

'Mr Swainey! You're looking a bit peaky – I suppose it's not to be wondered at. How did it go? Were there many there?'

'Not really,' said Mr Swainey. 'Six of us counting the corpse. I just wanted to thank you for the lilies. We were both of us deeply touched, Mother especially.'

'How did she take it?'

'Well she spent most of the service crying and blowing her nose: it was a bit like hearing *Abide With Me* being played on the tuba. And then of course she started getting her prickly heat coming on, so ... I've just parked her in the conservatory, give her a chance to cool down a bit, hopefully.'

'Ghhohhh, help!' said Margaret suddenly as the kitchen clock came into focus. 'I'm going to miss my bus....'

'Oh,' said Mr Swainey. 'You going to the shop? I can drop you right there after I've popped Aunty Ciss down the drains department.'

'You sure? That'll save my life! I've just got to get my purse, I won't be a tick,' said Margaret, and straightaway shot upstairs in a small cloud of dust.

Nick Swainey loosened his black tie slightly in order to breathe; took three deep breaths and then tightened it again out of respect for the deceased. As he waited for Margaret to return his eye travelled to the caddy of herbal tea Pippa had left on the kitchen table. He had just idly picked it up to look inside when Victor appeared with a bulging shopping bag and a soggy Rolos wrapper he had recently liberated from the wisteria.

'Oh! Morning, Mr Meldrew!' said Mr Swainey, suddenly looking up.

'Morning,' said Mr Meldrew, suddenly looking extremely down. There was, presumably, a good reason why this buffoon was standing in his kitchen dressed as one of the Blues Brothers, and he imagined it would become clear in due course. His cheeks, oddly, seemed to have lost their customary colour and had paled to a bright vermilion. And even Victor could detect a certain despondency in the air, so in a voice carefully gilded with concern he said: 'How are you. You all right?'

'Oh ... yes, I suppose,' said his neighbour gloomily. 'Just the worry of Mother I expect. Always knocks you for six, doesn't it. A death in the family.'

Victor paused in the act of setting down a six-pack of toilet rolls on the worktop and looked genuinely surprised. Margaret, as usual, had said nothing to him about this. But then for the last couple of days she had said nothing to him about anything.

'I'm very sorry to hear that,' he said, dutifully uncovering his head. 'When exactly did it happen?'

'Sorry?'

'When did she die?'

'Oh. On Sunday. Half past six, I'm afraid. Up the hospital.'

'I didn't know she'd been taken up there,' said Victor.

'Who?'

'Your mother.'

'Oh! Mother, yes. Yes, took her up there in the afternoon. No sooner got her up there than we lost her,' said Mr Swainey, his face dimpling into a bizarre ghoulish grin. 'Didn't Mrs Meldrew tell you?'

'She didn't tell me anything,' said Victor.

'Yes, it's all been a pretty gruelling experience. I've just got back with her from the crematorium actually. Just wanted to say thank you for the flowers.'

It was at this point that Victor was forced to clutch the draining board for support. Previously, he had paid no attention to the small silver vase Mr Swainey was holding reverentially in front of his flies. But at the word crematorium its hideous significance became transparently clear. And Victor, who for one complacent moment had allowed his guard to drop in the presence of this dangerously goofy person, was now obliged to acknowledge the awesome and terrifying truth . . . .

Mr Swainey's departed mother was here in this room.

'Yes . . . I was just telling Mrs Meldrew – she's still a bit on the hot side, unfortunately . . . .' he was saying, whilst – Victor could scarce believe his eyes – lifting the lid and sniffing inside. 'Take a little while to cool down, I expect.'

Victor now experienced a severe gastric rebellion. He had an awful feeling he was about to become re-acquainted with the two poached eggs he'd had for breakfast. The man surely could not be human.

Good God, was there no end to it? He was even taking a small pinch of her out now, between his fingers, and *tasting* her with his tongue!

'Oh by the by! I said I'd give your wife a lift in to work,' Mr Swainey said, finally setting the deceased down next to a jar of marmalade. 'You couldn't do me a teeny favour and keep an eye on Mother for me? Only it's just the thought of leaving her on her own – do you know what I mean? If it's not too much trouble . . . .'

To which Victor, his eyes magnetised by the offending urn, could merely stammer: 'Ye-es . . . no . . . errm – r-right.'

'Ready when you are!' called Margaret over a sound of galloping feet on the stairs.

'Coming Mrs Meldrew!' said Mr Swainey.

And amid a swirl of hasty goodbyes he and Margaret were gone, and Victor was left regarding the item on the table in much the way a frog might regard a book of French recipes.

'Ohhhhh ... my *Goddddd* ....'

It couldn't remain where it was.

That was the first thing.

Squeamishly, summoning every last ounce of courage, he lifted up the urn and began tenderly to carry it at arm's length into the dining room as if it were a severed head. Which, presumably, about ten per cent of it was.

That it was never fated to complete its journey only became clear when a sudden shriek from the telephone caused Victor sharply to trampoline several inches into the air, tossing the pot to the ground and spewing its deathly contents in a horrific swathe across the carpet.

'Ohhhhh ... my *Goddddd* ....'

Said Victor, for the second time in a minute. What he shouted into the phone at the young girl called Debbie who wondered if he was aware of an exciting breakthrough in cavity wall in-sulation can not, sadly, be reprinted in a BBC Publication before nine o'clock in the evening.

More crucial was the fact that the ashes of his next door neighbour's mother – not yet cool following her spell in the oven at Regulo 2000 – were lying scattered all over his floor like Gandhi on the Ganges.

'Ohhhhh ... my *Goddddd* ....'

He said for the third time, because under this kind of pressure his vocabulary inevitably shrivelled to just three words.

He considered, for a full one and a half seconds, the option of scooping the poor woman up and redepositing her, grain by grain, into the urn. But she had burrowed, by now, far too deeply into the pile to make this practical. Clearly, unless he approached it in the right way, there would be bits of old Mrs Swainey lying round the house for ever more. And the worst of it was you wouldn't even know which bits they were.

There was, plainly, but one course of action.

When Victor had finished the task of hoovering Nick's mother up and had emptied her, in a mass of fluff and dust and tangled hairs and dead woodlice, into the dustbin he washed his hands very, very thoroughly with Dettol and then paused, considering his next move. Probably best not to tell Mr Swainey his loved one was on her way to the corporation crusher. Far better to keep him in the dark by replenishing the vessel, then he'd never notice the difference.

Well, that shouldn't be too difficult to do. It was just a matter of finding something to burn.

'**M**ad as a bloody March hare,' said Patrick, peering through the Venetian blinds in the spare bedroom.

And Pippa was not so guileless as to ask him who he was talking about. Bearing in mind the angle of his vision and the venom in his voice, it was safe to assume the object of his curiosity was a gentleman who, twelve hours earlier, had been ignoring the instructions on his ginseng capsules by storing them in a place that was far from cool and far from dry.

'I'm off out now then. See if I can change this skirt,' said Pippa. 'You'll remember to video *Neighbours* won't you.'

'Ab-solutely mad as a hatter,' said Patrick, his attention riveted by something that was going on down below. 'He's just come out of the house and unravelled six toilet rolls into a cast-iron skillet. Then he scrunched them all up and set fire to them, if you please.'

Pippa sighed dismally.

'Yes! I daresay he did, now you won't forget will you.'

Patrick turned from the window to stare at her incredulously.

'What do you mean *Yes, I daresay he did?* What sort of remark is that? My God, you talk about being anally-fixated. The man must be shot away to buggery if you ask me. And you say he's normal?'

'*I* never said he was normal,' said Pippa, closing the flap on her bag. 'Now are you listening to me or what? *Neighbours*, at 5.30.'

'Yesss ....' said Patrick. 'Good God almighty! It gets worse, look. He's sprinkling Mazola cooking oil over them now, to make them burn ... and – I don't believe this – he's mashing up all the ashes with a rolling pin, like a mortar and pestle.'

Pippa paused in the bedroom doorway with her hand on the knob and said: 'While I'm out I may pop into the House of Commons restaurant and commit an unnatural act with Dr Rhodes Boyson on a bed of lettuce.'

'Yesss ...' said Patrick.

'Is that OK?'

'Yesss ...' said Patrick.

'*Right*,' said Pippa. 'I'll see you later.'

Two minutes after she had gone Patrick said:

'I wonder if we could get him certified on BUPA ....'

146

And then ten minutes after she had gone he said:
'A bed of lettuce ... ?'

When Margaret got back from work she thought she detected a faint smell of burning in the kitchen. And sure enough when she glanced into the sink she found a semi-charred frying pan and a blackened rolling pin that had been left there to soak. How extremely unusual, she thought, as she picked up Pippa's silver tea caddy from the work-top and stowed it away in a top cupboard. It was rare enough for Victor to cobble together a sandwich at lunchtime, let alone tackle anything so adventurous as a pastry dish.

What on earth had been going on?

Come to think of it there was a rather strong scent of cheap perfume about the place as well which, together with the first smell, suggested a slice of toast wearing a roll-on deodorant.

As Margaret threw open the door and flapped it to clear the air the unsavoury hypothesis that Victor had, in her absence, been playing host to a secret female guest sent a ripple of revulsion down her spine. Tawdry visions of her husband suggestively tossing crepe suzettes while Mrs Mauleverer rolled naked across the work-top flickered before her eyes. It was a nightmare scenario that could surely exist nowhere outside her own imagination.

Or could it?

If there was anything destined to confirm, beyond all doubt, that her fears were justified you would not expect it to be the wrapper from a strip of Orbit sugar-free chewing gum.

Yet unexpectedly it was so. For as it fluttered in from the back garden on the wings of an early evening breeze, it was about to tell Margaret the very last thing in the world that she wanted to know.

Three days had passed, during which the following had happened: Margaret had moved all her things into the spare bedroom, including her body at nights. Since Victor was unable to extract a single word from her he was unable to discern any motive for this eccentric behaviour. For a while he was convinced she had found out about Mrs Swainey's ashes and sentenced him to the dog house. But that couldn't be so. When he had returned that evening after paying the video rental the urn had been gone. Which could only mean that no one, including their neighbour, had rumbled the substitution. Plus he had been careful to mask any lingering smell of burning toilet tissue by liberally spraying the kitchen with floral air-freshener. So he was pretty confident that he had managed to cover his tracks.

Margaret had said nothing to Victor because there really was nothing to say. After she had picked up that Orbit wrapper and gone to throw it in the pedal bin she had stood with her foot on the little rubber block, staring among the potato peelings in a state of goggle-eyed disbelief. And even when she had fished it out to assure herself she was not dreaming it was still hard to credit the evidence of her senses. For this time it was no mere strip of misplaced ginseng capsules. Oh, no – this time it was something infinitely worse.

On the Saturday evening the phone rang and when Margaret answered it a husky voice on the other end said 'Hallo, is Victor there at all? It's Doreen.'

Margaret, resisting the temptation to ask what she had used to dial their number, quietly passed the call to her husband by dumping the phone in his spaghetti and stormed upstairs. Mrs Mauleverer sweetly asked Victor if he was free to come round the next morning as she desperately needed a man's body. When Victor, with an excited shiver, asked what she meant by this she said the doorbell was ringing which meant her dinner guests had arrived, so could he be a positive darling and pop round about ten? And Victor, who was beginning to tire of Margaret's campaigns of psychological warfare, decided it would be a relief to escape for a few hours, so he swiftly said yes and his role as a positive darling was assured.

For much of the night he lay worrying that he was about to embark on an act of devastating infidelity. Strangely, this was both alarming and yet somehow stimulating. After all, if he *did* enjoy another woman's company for a few hours, what of it? Hadn't Margaret brought this on herself in the first place, with her jealous carping and constant expressions of mistrust?

At 8.30 the next morning Victor climbed out of the bath and spent twenty-seven minutes trying to decide which shirt to put on.

At 9.30 he left the house and drove to Mrs Mauleverer's with his hands trembling so much they could hardly grip the steering wheel.

At 9.55 he arrived at Mrs Mauleverer's and was shown into the lounge.

By 9.57 Mrs Mauleverer had got his shirt off.

When Leonard switched on the radio he heard Derek Jameson talking, which was something he had absolutely no desire to do. But instead of switching the radio off again he took it into the bathroom, jammed it down the lavatory and pulled the handle. This did not stop Derek Jameson talking, it just made him sound as if he was talking at the bottom of a lavatory. So Leonard then flushed the lavatory again, and Derek Jameson then went on talking again. Next, Leonard used the lavatory, and Derek Jameson handed over to Sacha Distel who sang *Raindrops Are Falling On My Head*. Finally, Leonard flushed the lavatory one more time before stomping downstairs and striding, upside down, into the sitting room.

Victor thought how strange he looked upside down, as anyone would, but said nothing.

'Is *he* back again?' growled Leonard. 'What's he doing this time, picking cobwebs off the ceiling with his toe-nails?'

Victor was not picking cobwebs off the ceiling with his toe-nails, although Leonard could, perhaps, have been forgiven for thinking so. He was actually posing in a loin-cloth for a pencil study of a painting Mrs Mauleverer was working on, called *The Crucifixion of St Peter*. For reasons of historical accuracy he was obliged to balance precariously on his head with both arms outstretched and his feet against the wall, looking for all the world as if he was preparing to bore into the sofa like a human drill. Hence his distinctly upside-down perspective on the world.

'*I* could have done this!' growled Leonard like a wounded bear. 'I could have done this standing on my head. I'm not entirely incapable, you only had to ask me.'

'Yes well I don't think we'll risk it, shall we, Father,' said a voice behind a large drawing pad. 'Not with your corpuscles. They've got precious little sense of direction as it is.'

'And you needn't start on that again,' said Leonard, wagging a bony forefinger in her direction. 'There's nothing wrong with *my* circulation, and I resent the implication that there is.'

149

'No, and the M25 really speeds up around the Dartford Tunnel,' said the voice.

'Oh! *I* see! Right, well, I think I'll go back upstairs now, shall I, and get my gas mask,' said Leonard.

'Whatever for?'

'Well I presume it won't be long before you get someone in to exterminate me, will it? It's perfectly clear I'm nothing more than a household pest round here these days. I'm quite obviously too old and decrepit to do anything useful in this house!'

With which he slammed the door on himself and marched back upstairs with enough feeling to splinter the floorboards.

Victor, in addition to feeling extremely stiff, suddenly felt extremely awkward. But since he felt more extremely stiff than he did extremely awkward he ventured, at length, to ask the artist if it would not be a cunning idea for him to pose the right way up so she could simply turn the picture upside down afterwards.

'I'm afraid it doesn't work *quite* like that,' chuckled Mrs Mauleverer. 'The muscle tensions would be entirely different. Now do try not to move if possible, and keep your fingers well spread – remember to imagine those nails through the centre of your palms.'

'Yes,' said Victor. 'Right. Nails through the centre of my palms.'

On the other side of the room the clock appeared to say twenty to five, but in reality said ten past eleven.

Mrs Mauleverer took out a Stanley knife and tapered the end of her pencil, assuring him the sketch would not take more than another couple of hours and then he could relax. By which time it is fair to say Victor had concluded her intentions that morning were, after all, nothing if not entirely honourable.

As the credits for *Fatal Attraction* rolled across the television screen Margaret dabbed her eyes with a tissue and told herself she must stop watching videos with an unhappy ending.

Then she watched it again.

Then she sat for another half an hour in Victor's armchair biting the heads off jelly babies and filling in wrong answers to certain key clues on his Saturday Prize Crossword.

At 3.17 p.m. she looked at her watch.

It said 3.17 p.m.

Victor had been at Mrs Mauleverer's now for over four hours, during which time Margaret had hoovered and polished the house, cooked and eaten a Sunday lunch and carefully plotted eleven perfect murders. She was just in the process of ironing out some loopholes in number twelve when a scuffle in the hall told her the victim had returned home and was noisily kicking off his shoes in the downstairs toilet.

From the other side of the sitting room door Victor uttered a word that, as far as she could make out, was spelt:

'Ggghheeurrhhhh-jjjjj ....'

A second later the door was flung open and something that appeared to owe its choreography to a resurrected mummy lumbered into the room, grunting and gasping as if every step were a marathon, and continuing to utter the word that was spelt:

'Ggghheeurrhhhh-jjjjj ....'

Margaret, who for the last three hours had been rehearsing exactly what she was going to say to Victor when he came home – which was nothing – spontaneously abandoned her script and demanded:

'What's the matter with your back?'

'Ggghheeurrhhhh-jjjjj ....'

Tensing every muscle in his body, and with the expression of a trainee astronaut whose face has just been sucked inside out by a centrifuge, Victor attempted to lower himself onto the sofa in an agony of anticipation that he normally reserved for particularly cold lavatory seats.

'*A-a-a-a-a-hahhhhhh!!!*'

It was not to be. Scarce had his bottom dallied with the pattern on the cushion cover than it was immediately obliged to jerk upwards again. And Victor let out an involuntary bellow that loosened several fillings. Tenderly clutching the region above his coccyx he tottered grotesquely back and forth as if auditioning for *The Benny Hill Show*, did a lap of honour round the coffee table, and finally came to rest against the sideboard, groaning and wheezing in a positive paroxysm of pain.

'Hohhhh Goddd,' he spluttered. 'I remember having a mid-life crisis when I was thirty, no wonder I feel I'm about to die at any minute.'

'What's happened to your *back*!'

In reply, it was all Victor could do to squeak, feebly:

151

'I've put it out.'

Which told Margaret nothing that wasn't already screamingly obvious, for it was the cause of the injury that interested her more. And as she fixed him with a dangerous sneer, her right eyelid half-descending like a knight's visor in readiness for battle, she simply said to him:

'Oh yes?'

'At Doreen's,' wheezed Victor, attempting to re-angle his spine so as to minimise the agony. 'I should have known I wasn't up to it. I should never have let her talk me into it. In that position for *three hours*! God, I'm lucky I can still walk....'

'Position...?'

'Upside down with my feet against the wall while she just got on with it, to her heart's content. Wouldn't let me lie back or get comfortable or anything – said I had to be like that for her muscle contractions.'

'Mummuscle contractions...?'

Margaret fairly stuttered.

'Said it was very critical where I put my thumbs. And she said to be sure and flex my fingers wide apart or it wouldn't be anything like as good for her.'

'Fuffingers wide apart....'

'If it was that bad today imagine her getting me back to do it all over again in oil. I think I may have knackered my neck for good as it is....'

'Duddoo it in oil....'

That Victor should have perpetrated this squalid misdeed in the first place was vile enough. That he should stand before her now, boasting of his exploits in all their sickening gynaecological detail, beggared belief.

'You ... have ... absolutely no shame, have you?' said Margaret, finding her voice at last.

'Sorry?'

'No shame ... of any kind whatsoever....'

'What are you talking about?'

'I *found* it in the pedal bin, Victor! The other afternoon when you were out paying the video.'

Victor looked blank.

'Found what?'

The words smouldered on her lips, white-hot like barbecue coals:

'*The empty packet!*'

And still Victor could barely manage a frown of incomprehension.

'Empty packet of *what*?'

'Empty packet of *nothing*! Because it was *empty*!'

'Y— Well what was in it *before* it was empty!' said Victor, who for the life of him couldn't follow this one at all.

'*Some-thing!*' snapped Margaret, her voice pitching somewhere over a top C. '*You* know what was in it!'

'No I *don't* bloody know what was in it!' Victor shrieked back. 'What is this, *Twenty Questions*? Is it animal, vegetable or mineral? Would I be able to use this in the garden at all . . . ?'

'I wouldn't put *that* past you!'

'Well for goodness sake, *tell* me what the bloody Hell you're on ab—'

'*Con-tra-cep-tives!*'

Margaret finally spat the word at him in a fury of disgust.

'Do I have to spell it out for you?'

'Contracep—?'

'Where did you do it, upside down against the sink unit? With her naked breasts dangling over the double drainer? Whole place *stank* of cheap perfume. Smelt as if she'd been spraying toilet freshener under her arms. Next time you do this sort of thing you might at least make a better job of hiding the evidence. I mean, for God's sake, you must have known I'd *see* it in there! I don't think I've ever felt so sick in all my life. When I first read the words "banana flavour" I thought it was a carton of yogurt. I'm just . . . speechless, that's all. I don't know what to say or think any more.'

For a long moment the air hung heavy with the poison of her indictment. During which Victor's brow contracted first into a furrow of disbelief, and then gradually relaxed with dawning realisation.

'Is this what this has all been about? Sleeping in the spare bedroom, and nailing my spam sandwich to the bread-board the other evening?'

'What the Hell do *you* think!'

'B— I found that thing in the *garden* . . . underneath the rhubarb, next to a squashed Budweiser can. Could hardly say I was surprised, the stuff people sling over your fence these days. I mean you couldn't possibly have thought that *I'd*, b— God almighty, Margaret, what do you think I am? You've been in a sulk like this ever since I brought home those drawings of Mrs Mauleverer. And I can tell you this much, I know now what they have to go through, posing on those couches. And I think it's fair to say they deserve a bloody medal.'

'Posing on those couches, what do you mean?' said Margaret, whose fire had been all but extinguished by Victor's annoyingly credible explanation. 'You've been posing for her, today . . . ?'

'Ten quid she gave me, and a stale Garibaldi biscuit with my cup of coffee. Said that was the going rate. Well, never again! And I shan't stick that cleaning job either, I know that. Go through that every Monday morning with her old man – Goblin vacuum cleaners at twenty paces. Miserable old sod does nothing but moan and groan all the time. I don't know how she puts up with it . . . .'

Margaret opened her mouth to say something, but oddly this time he was saying it for her.

'. . . strange thing is, watching him there today, I suddenly realised it was like looking in a mirror.

'Hah-a-a-a-a-*hahhhh!!!*' he screamed suddenly as, bending to pick up a newspaper, he was rewarded with the sensation of two men applying a baseball bat to his kidneys.

'I think, if you don't mind, I'm going to go upstairs now . . . run myself a nice hot bath . . . step inside it . . . and then plug my fingers into the light socket.'

For the first time in over a week Margaret remembered what it was like to smile.

As she drove through the streets the next morning Margaret thought how incredibly beautiful death could be. And how the very presence of putrefaction and decay could bring the autumn branches alive with colour. All around her the glorious spectacle of rotting organisms filled the air. Joyous festoons of decomposing tissue that bucked and billowed in the breeze to form a kaleidoscope of browns and bronzes, of sorrels and cinnamons.

It was 8.47 a.m. and at that precise moment twenty-two point nine per cent of the population were going to the lavatory, which was well in line with the seasonal average.

The mellow haze of a new day was already wilting under the

pressure of the plucky little September sun, which rather conveniently mirrored the clouds that had lifted from Margaret's personal horizon. Following yesterday's rapprochement with her husband she was now experiencing the perverted pleasure of auto-castigation. With hindsight she had known all along that her suspicions were more to do with a crisis of confidence on her own part. And that she had, for the last seven days, treated her husband quite shamefully by subjecting him to a constant tirade of poisonous abuse.

Fun though it had been at the time.

Well, now she was happy to take the blame and admit she was wrong. And the spring in her step was matched by the gleam in her eye as she stepped onto the pavement outside Albert's basement flat with a cluster of freesias that she knew would bring a sparkle to his cheerless world of shadows.

The worn latch on the front door had for some time enjoyed no more than an on-off relationship with its housing, but this morning the two did not even appear to be on speaking terms. The door, indeed, was several inches ajar, and where Albert was obliged to slam it really hard so as to engage the Yale lock some of the woodwork round the frame had begun to fracture. Margaret noticed that the old man's daily pint of milk had been taken in, so she knew he must be up and about. At this time of the morning he would be out the back blacking his shoes for the day. But it was odd that he hadn't noticed the sharp down-draught curling in off the street and up through his hallway.

Margaret tut-tutted her way past the jagged woodwork that threatened to snag her coat and sounded a lively tap on the frosted glass panel.

'Mr Warris? Anyone at home? It's Mrs Meldrew!'

Immediately, in a cheerful reply from the kitchen, the familiar jaunty voice of her old friend, brushing away at his boots, could not be heard.

Inexplicably, the flat was dark and still.

In the sitting room the day had yet to dawn, for the windows were still thickly webbed by a pair of dense hessian curtains. As Margaret stepped forward into the unrelieved gloom of the interior she stepped as its tenant sightless into the vale of the night. For a moment she thought she could identify a familiar body, asleep in the wing-backed armchair. But as her eyes grew accustomed to the dimness she saw it was just three cushions he had propped on top of each other to ease his arthritis. Again she called his name, but the blackness seemed to swallow her words without compassion and offered nothing in return but the brooding silence of uncertainty.

At that moment she heard a sound coming from the bedroom.

A soft sound at first, but one which grew, chillingly, in significance.

Curiously she stumbled back into the hall and approached the open door.

It was a rapid, fluttering sort of sound with slightly squelchy undertones. Margaret knew that she recognised it but could not, for the moment, quite place it. It was, she felt sure, a sound she would normally have found quite reassuring. So why at this moment did it cause her flesh to crawl with a sense of unutterable dread?

She had reached the door now, and could hear it more distinctly.

A frisky, flapping noise ... a smacking noise ... a pattering noise like the wing-beat of a baby bat that stemmed from the far end of the room. Here too the curtains were undrawn and all was drenched in darkness. So Margaret hooked her hand round the door and flicked on the light.

It was then that she saw what was making the noise.

And it was then that the overpowering sickness surged to the surface, causing her hand to fly to her mouth and her knees to buckle beneath her. And at once a screaming, dizzying weakness took possession of her, and the illimitable horror of the vision before her caused her heart to rise in her throat....

The sound she had heard was the steady licking of a cat's tongue. The cat was crouching by the foot of the wardrobe, its head bent forward over a small tin tray that had been used to transport a mug of cocoa and some ginger biscuits into the bedroom.

In the tray was a large puddle of something red and sticky that was oozing in as fast as the cat could lap it up.

There was no movement from the body that lay on the other side of the tray. Just the gentle trickle of fluid from the broad, glistening breach in the back of the old man's head. The weapon, whatever it was, had been heavy and sharp. For around the wound, which was deep and raw, his skull had been all but excoriated and the bone that lay beneath shattered like an eggshell.

They had stolen £7.35 from his jacket pocket. So it had been well worth the effort.

When the police had completed their initial inquiries into the murder of Mr Albert Warris they were curious to learn that the victim had originally arranged for all his doors and windows to be secured that week by a firm of locksmiths. But that he had called the operation off at the last minute after deciding to use what was left of his savings 'for something more important'. Exactly what that 'something more important' was, and why it should cause him to part with all the money he had in the world will never be known. However it is interesting to note that a month later in Perth, Western Australia, four totally indestructible Bendy Dinosaurs received by a pair of children named Danny and Tracey failed signally to bend or twist in any shape or direction whatever, and after three and a half hours were lying dumped outside in the trash can, broken and battered beyond all repair.

It goes without saying that the first thing to snap was the neck of the brontosaurus.

CHAPTER NINE

Magic in the Air

It was a small parcel, enclosed in brown, coarse-grained wrapping paper. It sat on the desk of Angelica Kramer with a mischievous smirk, the way certain parcels do when you're dying to rip them open and only they know the disappointment that lies inside.

It was not, of course, addressed to Angelica Kramer by name. The writing on the front, which looked as if it had been executed by a felt-tip marker the size of a sequoia log, said simply: 'To the Head of Circulars.' And so, inevitably, to the office of the publishing company's Senior Director of Marketing and Promotions it had found its way.

There was a lot of other mail on Ms Kramer's desk that day, most of it early Christmas greetings from obsequious clients. But it was the parcel with the fat writing that intrigued her most.

The slimline lemon jacket by Jean Muir did not quite fit the swivel chair upon which she hung it, as the designer had not thought to include a vent at the back for height-adjustment handles. However, this went unnoticed by its owner as she began picking open her package until, presently, she was faced with a white cardboard box bearing the following words in spidery handwriting:

Congratulations! I am delighted to announce that YOU ... Head of Circulars for (here it named the well-known magazine for which she worked) *... are one of the lucky, lucky winners in my SPECIAL PRIZE DRAW! And you have already been selected to receive at least ONE of the following SENSATIONAL gifts ...*

One: *A pair of 24-carat diamond earrings, valued at over £20,000 ....*
Two: *A fabulous dream holiday for two in sun-kissed Waikiki ....*

Three: *A brand-new Ford Escort 16-valve cabriolet with high-performance fuel injection . . . .*
Four: *A dead rat.*

Open now to see which of these positively breath-taking gifts YOU have won!

Something told her the trepidation she felt about lifting the lid and looking inside would not prove to be groundless. And she was right.

Delicately swaddled in a pellicle of tissue paper it lay there with its long tail curled back upon itself: an object of such unspeakable atrocity it defies further description, except to say it was not a holiday in Waikiki. Wedged beneath its tiny hind legs lay another slip of paper which Ms Kramer managed to pluck free by skilfully employing a pair of manicurist's tweezers.

It read as follows:

Yes! This superb dead rat is just ONE of a special series of ROTTING RODENTS that are yours to examine, free of charge, in the privacy of your own office! To take advantage of this never-to-be-repeated offer, simply go on sending me all the usual crap about competitions, prize draws and personal lottery numbers that make my life a constant misery. It would also be appreciated if you could take a moment to complete the following form:

YES! I intend to go on shoving endless garbage through your letter-box whether you've asked for it or not, day in, day out, however much you loathe and detest the very sights of it. Please rush me a Decomposing Squirrel by return of post.

P.S. And for pity's sake, I have no desire whatever to own a hand-tooled Guide to the Empire of the Ancient Aztecs! Now in the name of God SOD OFF!

'Makes you wonder sometimes, doesn't it,' said Ms Kramer as her secretary Natasha swanned into the office at that moment with a cup of white cardboard coffee. 'What kind of deranged psychotics are actually out there . . . .'

Consult any edition of the *Shorter Oxford English Dictionary* and you will not find included the following definition:

Christmas *n.* **1. a.** a form of torture dating back to the Spanish Inquisition in which certain pop records from the 1970s by Slade and Wizzard are broadcast through concealed speakers in the ceiling to extract confessions of heresy. **b.** a similar device used by Boots the Chemist to shift gift-tokens. **2.** a serious brain disorder affecting members of the advertising industry, but harmless to humans, in which, oddly, most of the suffering is experienced by other people. **3.** *Archaic.* a national holiday characterised by one or two quite decent films on TV. *adj.* **1.** unwanted, hideous, serving no useful purpose. As in **Christmas present.** *Compare:* **haemorrhoid transplant, The Royal Family. 2.** shallow, superficial; ritualistic. As in **Christmas card, Christmas greeting.** *-interj.* **3.** *chiefly taxi drivers:* **Happy Christmas, sir.** Up yours, arsehole. [etym. uncertain, probably corrupt. of early Anglo-Saxon *Cristes Maesse* a period of approximately 120 days commencing in late summer during which it is impossible to get a new carpet delivered.]

. . . which confirmed Victor Meldrew's general contempt for dictionaries and the people who compiled them. One of these days, he promised himself, he would get round to penning a dictionary of his own that would set the record straight on everything from *abomination* (alternative spelling of *Observer Colour Supplement*) to *zombie* (a person employed to sell stamps in his local post-office).

It was December 17th, and Victor was on his way home from the hospital where he had just seen a number of bespectacled specialists about a number of unpleasant ailments which need not concern us here.

Since his car was still quarantined at the garage having its gears fixed he had been obliged to fall back on the horror of public transport. And although in the past thirty minutes he had moved just ten yards up the bus queue he took comfort in the knowledge that this was still fractionally faster than travelling on the bus.

Dangling above him from a lamp post was a strange two-dimensional mass of twisted fluorescent tubing which, when lit up, and with a lot of imagination on the part of the viewer, looked absolutely nothing like a team of reindeer pulling a sleigh. Indeed Victor, having stared at it for nearly half an hour, concluded finally that it was either several stapling-machines being chased by a packet of pitta bread, or six Freemasons hurling themselves into the path of a giant pancreas.

Victor hated Christmas.

He hated it almost as much as he hated those little white T-shaped bits of plastic that fell on the floor when you snipped the price-tag off a new shirt. He hated it for its glib celebration of the enterprise culture and the pressures it brought to bear on those already under siege from a charge-card society. In its bid to synthesise sincerity it merely stifled spontaneity. And just as the meaning and the message had become the inevitable casualties of commercial candy-floss, so the sweetness of the ideal had long since drowned in its own pervasive goo.

Just about the only cheer in store for Victor and Margaret this Christmas was the fact that it brought to an end twelve of the most calamitous months of their entire marriage. And if ever there was a time to look to the future and consign their recent woes to the pages of history that time was upon them now.

But then of course, the year was not quite over yet.

'This is just the stuff I've been trying to get for Chris,' said Mrs Warboys, fondling a brown smoked bottle she had inadvertently come across while snooping round Margaret's bathroom. 'He's just run *out* of hair-tonic....'

'Victor won't be needing it,' said Margaret. 'He's just run out of hair. And thanks for the card, I'll put it with the others.'

'So did you erm ... ask Victor about the ... you know,' said Mrs Warboys, anxiously trailing her friend into the other room.

'Oh,' said Margaret, wincing from a sudden ignition of guilt. 'Well not actually yet, as such. I was sort of hoping to wait till he's in a good mood.'

'We could all die first,' said Mrs Warboys. 'And I definitely need to know by tomorrow. Incidentally, did you decide what to get him this year, after all that? You were worrying yourself sick last time we spoke.'

Margaret unloosed a sigh that set her washing-line of Christmas cards briefly fluttering.

'Oh *I* don't know, Jean. *What* to do for the best. He could really do with a new watch, the one he's got's always slow. But he says he prefers it like that. Says time goes too fast as it is. He's never been the easiest person to buy for, I did think about getting him a nice bottle of sick all over the path outside our house again. They should get that dog seen to, if you ask m— Oh! You're back,' she said, pretending she had only just heard her husband return through the back door. 'How did it go? Did you get a chance to pop in Tesco?'

'*Don't*!' said Victor, pitching his cap frisbee-like onto the table. 'Twenty minutes I had to wait at that cash-till today, stuck behind that weirdo with the pimples again. Eleven frozen chickens and twenty-two bottles of Baby Bio he had in his trolley! I mean, is that normal? And it's always the same – always two bottles of Baby Bio to every frozen chicken, I've started checking it now. Oh, good morning Mrs Warboys,' he added, as he rounded the connecting archway to discover a toasted bap slowly departing this world behind a set of grinding teeth.

'Morning, Mr Meldrew,' said Mrs Warboys and the toasted bap in unison. 'How are you today?'

'Terrible,' said Victor. 'Never felt worse.'

'Oh dear,' said Mrs Warboys.

But then, deciding this would be as good a time as any, she hoovered up the remaining crumbs on the willow-patterned plate and went for it:

'Actually, Mr Meldrew, I was wondering if you'd like to do us a little favour. We're still looking for someone to play one of the key parts in the guild's Nativity production this weekend. I didn't know if you'd be interested at all.'

'Key part? What sort of key part?' Victor said, managing, by dint of the fact that he was not remotely interested, to sound as if he were not remotely interested.

'It's the back half of a cow,' said Mrs Warboys.

'I see,' said Victor. 'And how does the phrase *I should cocoa, matey* grab you?'

'Only, as I say, Mr Gosling from the chip shop was originally down to do it. But then, last week, he suddenly pulled out because he was afraid of looking stupid. And that was when I thought of you.'

'How uncommonly considerate of you, Mrs Warboys.'

'It's only for the one performance, and quite honestly I reckon you'd be a natural in the role. Especially after you were so good last year as the King of the Toadstools.'

'I don't *care*,' said Victor. 'I'm not spending two hours bending over with my head half way up someone else's b— King of the Toadstools? What are you *talking* about?'

'Last year,' said Mrs Warboys. 'When you played that giant toadstool in "Babes in the Wood".'

'Giant Toadst— I've *never* played a giant toadstool in my life!'

'What was it then, a giant mushroom?'

'It wasn't a giant mushroom, it wasn't any form of champion fungus of any kind! I wasn't *in* "Babes in the Wood", I didn't even *see* the bloody thing!'

'Well it definitely had your walk,' said Mrs Warboys, not to be deflected. 'And it's not often you see a toadstool that round-shouldered. Are you sure it wasn't you?'

'*Ohhhhhh* for God's sa—'

'You might as well save your breath,' interjected Margaret. 'You won't get anything out of him till after Christmas. It's a waste of time trying. He won't even have a *tree* in the house this year. Refuses point blank.'

If she had just learnt her friend's husband had contracted genital herpes from a camel Mrs Warboys could not have been more shocked.

'Mr Meldrew!' she gasped. 'You've got to have a *tree* in the house. For Christmas?'

'What for,' grumbled Victor. 'So I can hang chocolate rabbits on it and watch them melt under the fairy lights? So they can drip all over the carpet and dry up like miniature cow-pats?

'Not Christmas any more anyway. Just a four-month trade fair run by retailers and advertising agencies. Yes! What better way to celebrate the birth of Christ than by filling your intestines up with Newberry Fruits? Mmmm! I rather fancy having every bone in my body crushed to a pulp today – perhaps I'll go down W. H. Smith's and spend five minutes in the book department!'

Mrs Warboys scrutinised him with a long, hard look.

'So you don't want to then.'

'Don't want to what?'

'Play the back half of a cow. It's only for the one night, and you'll be able to swish your tail about with a concealed wire?'

Victor, as he turned to face her, could not fail to read the desperation in her pleading eyes, and it dawned on him, finally, that he was her last hope. So with a long, reluctant sigh of concession he broke into a friendly smile and said:

'*No!!!*'

Following which he stormed back to the kitchen to see if there were any baps left.

'Right. Well,' said Mrs Warboys, buttoning her coat and picking up her bag. 'I suppose I may as well be off. I'll give you a ring tomorrow, Margaret. And thanks for the hair tonic by the way. Might stimulate his roots a bit hopefully, I'll see you soon!'

'Yes, bye, Jean,' said Margaret, closing the front door behind her.

Returning to the kitchen she found Victor irritably fingering an empty swathe of cellophane on the bread-board.

'You have to wait long up the hospital?'

'What do *you* think,' said Victor. 'An hour and a half sitting there like a Toby Jug, only to find out in the end I'd *lost* the damn thing!'

'Lost it?'

'That urine sample they asked for. Must have fallen out of my pocket on the bus, is all I can surmise.'

'Perhaps someone'll find it and hand it in....'

'After all that time I spent last night, looking for something suitable....'

'I know....'

'Sterilising out that old hair-tonic bottle and everything – it's just typical. *Typical*. Tchhh, that wind sounds as if it's whipping up out there. Said in the paper we might be in for some storms later on.'

But Margaret was no longer listening to Victor or to the wind. She was too busy thinking about Mr Warboys' roots.

From the darkest corners of Billericay they came. Without warning and without mercy. They came close to lunchtime, and they came close to relieving Victor of the last shreds of sanity to which he could reasonably lay claim.

It was Margaret who answered the doorbell, and thus Margaret who first discovered them.

Hundreds of them.

They were on her front doorstep and they were on her front lawn. They were clustered together along her path and they were milling about in tight-knit groups on the pavement. Some of them were gathered conspiratorially in the garden next door and several of them were perched precariously on her front window sill.

All of them were smoking pipes.

For a moment Margaret thought she must be dreaming, and that she was, inexplicably, addressing a convention of circus midgets all played by Moore Marriott from the old Will Hay films. But then she realised that this was all far too bizarre for a dream and could only, therefore, be happening in real life.

Someone, for some reason, had packed every square inch of the horizon with garden gnomes. Indeed, it was hard to be sure there was a horizon there at all behind the vast phalanx of bewhiskered faces that winked toothlessly at her beneath their pink pointy hats: a crowd scene in concrete such as D. W. Griffith might have contrived had Fickle Fate but pointed his hand toward a cement-mixer instead of a cine-camera.

It is to be presumed that whoever it was that just rang the doorbell it was not one of the diminutive gentlemen now standing before her. More plausibly, that honour belonged to the driver of a large pick-up truck currently rattling away down the road at a rate of knots.

'*What in the name of Hell—??*'

Margaret was denied, at that moment, the dubious joy of communicating this turn of events to her husband by his sudden arrival at her shoulder, open-mouthed in the posture of a gargoyle.

'Wh – wh – wh – what *are* they?? Where the Hell did they *come* from???'

'What are you asking *me* for??' shrieked Margaret against the roaring wind that was now eddying round the garden, causing several individuals apparently to rock back and forth with mirth. '*You* were the one who sent off for the ruddy things!'

'I sent off for *one garden gnome* to put next to the front door!' barked Victor. 'Not a bloody population explosion!'

'Well you must have ordered them or why else would they have sent them?'

'I did *not* order them!'

'Well who *else* ordered them!'

'I don't *know*! But *I* didn't order them!!'

'You *must* have ordered them!'

'*I did NOT order them!!!*'

A brief glance at the delivery docket stuffed through the letter-box revealed that Victor had, in fact, ordered them.

'Well it was a mistake anyone could have made!' he grumbled five minutes later. 'I mean they must have *known* that 263 was the catalogue number!'

'Yesss! I'm sure they *would* have done if you hadn't written it in the wrong column!'

'Well it only takes a bit of common sense! What could I possibly want with two hundred and sixty-three sodding garden gnomes in the *first* place??!! What am I supposed to do with this lot now, take them down the local day nursery? Make them disappear with pixie dust?? It's like rush-hour in Munchkin Land out here!'

Two hours later, when Victor finally got through to the man who happened to be passing the office of the girl who was taking messages for the woman who wasn't in today who in any case didn't really deal with queries of this sort he was told he would have to fill in one of the company's returned-order chitties and send it back together with the goods, in mint condition, and any that were damaged would be charged for at the full retail price.

Kkkkhhhhhwwocrkkk-kkk-kk-kk!!!

Already one of the gnomes had crashed to the ground, a casualty of the gathering gale.

'We can't leave them out here, Victor!' wailed Margaret as the rains, at last, began to sheet across the darkening sky. 'The whole *lot* of them'll go for a Burton!'

Victor, who was not the most gregarious of mammals at the best of times, did not look favourably on the prospect of a Christmas shared with twenty dozen ossified goblins. But until he could find a way of returning them to their manufacturer he was forced to take them in, like so many wounded sparrows, and offer them sanctuary within his house. Here they were obliged to stand regimentally, in rank and file, around the walls of the sitting room, the dining room, the kitchen, the hall, the bedrooms and the upstairs landing, where they did not so much blend casually into the background as not blend casually into the background very much at all.

'Bloody *things*!!' he cursed that night, rolling over in bed to find himself eyeball to eyeball with a chubby face that leered at him over the duvet. 'It's like trying to sleep in Snow White's cottage! Put up with *this* lot for Christmas I *shall* go completely doo-lally!'

'Phone line's still off after the storm,' muttered Margaret, replacing the receiver by their bed and burrowing under the covers. 'Said on the news it was the worst hurricane on a Thursday afternoon before Christmas since records began. Said a lot of people might not get their electricity back till the New Year now.'

Victor, having floored the gnome that was grinning at him with a sharp uppercut, sucked his wounded knuckle and snuggled into the pillow with a grunt.

'Least they won't have to watch any television. Sit through all that festive tripe. Cilla Black! Can you imagine? Fate worse than death if ever there was one.'

'She's got a very infectious laugh.'

'So's a hyena with anthrax. Think I'll just rip the aerial out and get a few videos in. Thought I might give that new rental place a try tomorrow, see what they've got on offer. *Hohhhhhhh* ... Christmas, I'll be glad when it's all over, I will straight.'

Dismally, he launched a grave look at the ceiling that was, in reality, targeted far beyond the bounds of his own mortality. Outside he could hear the wind weeping against the window. And through the dark heart of the night Victor thought that the Eternal Answer To It All had never seemed more infinitely elusive.

'Sixty-one Christmases,' he sighed. 'Can't say *one* of them's ever really *reached* me inside. Given me anything to rejoice about ... wonder why it is. That all the miseries in the world always seem a hundred times worse this time of the year. Suppose it's always been the same. Don't suppose there ever was any "magic" in it, in reality. Only in old films with Jimmy Stewart. Never in real life.'

Sighing again he closed his eyes.

'Anyway,' he grunted, 'what do *you* want for Christmas this year?'

'A set of razor-blades, to slash my wrists with!' came the reply. 'God *Almighty*, you're in a bright mood all of a sudden! If it's that much of an ordeal you needn't bother, thank you very much.'

'Well I've told you before, you needn't go splashing out for *me*,' said Victor. 'Won't worry *me* if I don't get anything.'

167

'All right then! I *won't*,' said Margaret, angling the back of her head against the back of his.

'You remember what we said last year, it's only a ritual. If we both agree not to buy anything we'll avoid all the worry and there won't be any disappointments.'

'Fine by me!'

'Fine then.'

'*Right* then!'

'Right . . . .'

Ten minutes later the room had fallen silent, the stillness broken only by a gentle sibilance from beneath the murmuring bedclothes.

But only one of them was able to sleep that night.

The young woman in the video shop did not look at Victor when she spoke to him, presumably to save wear and tear on her eye muscles. Her face, which was moulded entirely from a rather sturdy flesh-coloured polymer, appeared to be one size too small for her head, so that her chin and her cheeks were, for the most part, roomily vacant. Of course this was nothing a nice big smile would not have put to rights. But like most people who are employed behind shop counters she had, I'm afraid, sir, no machinery for that sort of thing.

'Right then,' she said with the monotone of an electric tooth-brush, while flicking through pages of small print. 'I shall need from you three separate pieces of identification two containing your full name and address printed clearly plus an official document of some kind a driver's licence or current passport are both acceptable bearing your normal signature with a small deposit of approximately sixty pounds refundable should you cease membership at any time the rental charges are one pounds to two pounds fifty pence daily tapes to be returned by seven thirty p.m. we do close promptly at eight with a further two pounds payable thereafter plus an additional fifty pence surcharge should you or your family omit to rewind the tape.'

'*Right*,' said Victor calmly. 'Here is my birth certificate, duly witnessed as you'll see by Acker Bilk and his Paramount Jazz Band, here is a document containing my normal signature, here is a document containing an *abnormal* signature written while undergoing electro-convulsive torture in a Chilean prison cell, here is a cheque for the specified amount, and here is a pound of my flesh which I realise I may forfeit at any time should I happen to suck a spangle too loudly during the film.'

It was, in fact, a pound of raw stewing steak sitting in his bag below the counter, but the general effect of clawing up a handful for her inspection was sufficiently repulsive to drive the young woman into a cubby-hole to put Victor onto hard disk.

Bloody sales assistants, he grumbled to himself as he wandered off exploring the shelves. He'd never met one yet who seemed remotely human. He had entered the shop today in a perfectly cheerful frame of mind with a droll quip about the weather and what had he got for his trouble? Ten minutes of surliness from a fading bimbo with all the warmth of a rotting penguin.

But of course it wasn't just her, it was a British disease. Like these bloody video titles. Guts and gore as far as the eye could see. What *was* it with this generation's appetite for suppurating corpses reconstituting themselves in the attic and then ripping a young girl's brains out through her nose? Just about every shelf was infected with them, regardless of category. Vomit-covered mutants with snarling heads growing out of their bottoms ... screaming blondes dangling upside down in cellars with hooks through their hands ... freckle-faced cheerleaders with their right eyeballs skewered to the back door by a javelin ... and gross, slavering things with several sets of jaws, one inside the other, chomping on the intestines of a family of five from Wiscons— 'Ah! You *are* here, Margaret said you might be,' said Mr Prout, gate-crashing the paragraph at this point and slapping Victor on the back with a podgy paw. 'I could have called back later but I really need the details now. Just in case there are any alterations. If you get my drift.'

Victor didn't.

Instead he gazed blankly at his former neighbour and said:

'Oh! Yes. How are you today, Mr Prout.'

'Only, if it's not quite right Pam can always get on with it tonight, you see,' he continued. And then, flicking open a tape-measure from his back pocket he began, rather bafflingly, to grab Victor's neck and force his head down towards his knees.

'Whhh— Just a m— What're you pl—'

'It's all right, it won't take a couple of ticks,' said Mr Prout who, having man-handled Victor into the position of a young schoolboy waiting to be caned, was now jotting down various figures on the back of a dry-cleaning ticket.

'J— j— jjjjjjj!!!! What the Hell d'you think you're *doing*???' snapped Victor, angrily reverting to the vertical. 'What on Earth are you *talking* about??'

'We were a bit worried the costume might be too *loose* for you around the udder,' said Mr Prout, blinking at him behind a pair of fat spectacles. 'I always think there's nothing worse than spending all night with your teats dangling in a manger, don't you? So if I could just ask you to bend over again, to give me a rough idea of your—'

'Will you get *off* of me!' rasped Victor, pushing him away. 'I told Mrs Warboys the other night, I am *not* playing the back half of a cow! I don't know who told you I was, but I'm *not*!'

'Oh,' said Mr Prout, backing off at last. 'I er . . . we must have got our wires crossed somewhere. That's a shame that.'

'I daresay, but there it is.'

'Especially as you played such a blinder last year as the King of the Toadstools. The part could've been made for you.'

'Yes, well that's as may be, but you c— King of the T—?? I did not *play* the bloody King of the Toadstools, where do people keep getting this from? I have never, ever appeared in public as a Giant Toadstool! Ever!!'

'Oh,' said Mr Prout again. And although, staring at the man before him in his mushroom-coloured raincoat and broad floppy cap, he was tempted to say something he quickly thought better of it, and instead murmured an apologetic 'Merry Christmas' and was gone.

'Your card, Mr Meldrew.'

Victor turned to find a little plastic ticket being grudgingly tendered by the girl from the desk.

'*Thank you*,' he said. And then, adjusting his tongue to its razor-edged setting, he added: 'Can I ask, are these categories here supposed to *mean* anything at all? I mean, look at this one! Under "Family Viewing" you've got *The Cook, The Thief, His Wife and Her Lover* and *Lesbian Chain-Saw Lust*! I don't know what sort of family *you* belong to! And look at this shelf here, you've got *Santa Claus – The Movie* under "Horror' – which is fair enough I suppose – but then under "Children's Films" you've got *Evil Dead Two, Eraserhead*, and *Space Sluts in the Slammer*!'

The woman sighed, then spoke wearily to one of the light fittings above her head.

'It's how people put them back on the shelves, *I* haven't got the time to go round every single—'

'Oh I see. *Is* it! I suppose *your* little kiddies think it's jolly good fun, do they? Watching some mutilated cadaver suck women's blood out like a carton of Ribena? I suppose that's an ideal bedtime story in *your* house? Two hours of a bloke with a roasted face shredding people's heads up into fettucini? Well I'm afraid it's not *my* idea of whoopee! And another thing – if you want to *keep* your customers in this place you might try looking as if you're *interested* in them. Instead of treating everyone that comes in here as if they're something that's just crawled out the bottom of a pond!'

With which he made a sharp about-turn and departed, leaving the young woman to crumple the little yellow card in her hand, and stare after him with eyes that were strangely grieving.

There were days when God seriously reckoned that creating the world and everything in it was a mug's game.

You went to all the bother of devising something plausibly scientific so as to leave the divine foundations nicely understated, and ended up getting precious little thanks for Your trouble. These days, despite all the contradictions and paradoxes You had skilfully woven into the Laws of the Universe as a clue to its origin, most people wouldn't give You so much as a nod of acknowledgement, let alone the proper credit that was due for all Your inventiveness and hard work.

It was this irritating Free Will business that made things tricky. Policies of laissez-faire hadn't worked for the Conservative Government and they weren't working here now. Quite simply, people needed a guiding hand in life. They needed support and they needed encouragement and they needed – yes, He was not ashamed to say the word – *intervention*.

Because say what you like about the doctrine of Blind Faith and the principle of Absolute Conviction, you really couldn't whack a good Miracle.

The problem was that in a modern secular society You had to be so bloody subtle about it You were lucky if anyone ever noticed....

'Well, that seemed to go very well,' said Mrs Warboys on Saturday evening as she helped Victor step out of his cow-legs at the local church hall.

'Never, ever, *ever* again, as long as I have an ounce of breath in my body!' swore the perspiring figure before her. 'I *said* I wouldn't do the bloody thing, I *swore* I wouldn't do it!! The whole thing was nothing less than a complete and total humiliation – in front of five hundred cackling crones from the Women's Bright Hour! Nativity play? It was more like The Gospel According to the Marx Brothers! Swallow every last ounce of dignity to come here and dress up as the back half of a cow, and what do I find? The costume department have *lost the front half*!!! But not to worry! Mrs Prout was straight to the rescue with the top half of a giant *rabbit* left over from Easter! "With a bit of luck no one'll notice the difference" .... Ended up lumbering round the crib like the product of some horrific vivisection experiment!'

'Can you try and stand still please, Mr Meldrew, I think you've got a nipple caught in your flies ....'

'And *that* was a moving moment, wasn't it! When the Angel of the Lord came down and said "Bugger me! What the Hell's happened here?" You talk about a cheapskate production. The Three Wise Men were all cardboard cut-outs, it was pathetic beyond belief. Half the audience thought the stable was being invaded by the pirates from Captain Pugwash. And couldn't you at least have found a child's *doll* – or *something* – as the Baby Jesus, I mean that was the absolute limit! A *marrow* wrapped in swaddling clothes!'

Victor's impassioned soliloquy being interrupted at this point while two shepherds came in to use the urinal, he was obliged to reserve the rest of his comments for the car journey home.

'Well anyway, the committee were all very grateful for you giving up your time,' said Mrs Warboys after Victor had subsided into a sulk on the back seat. 'And at least you know the proceeds will go to a deserving cause, to help out poor Mrs Burridge and her son. Not that it'll bring him back of course, but still.'

Margaret looked blank.

'Mrs Burridge?'

'Didn't I tell you the story? It was the most dreadful tragedy. Young mother, barely thirty, got a little boy about five years old

172

.... Last Monday her husband left home to fly out to Munich on a business trip. He was going to be away seven days, and come back Christmas Eve so they could all go to Midnight Mass together. I'm afraid he never even got to the airport ... his car collided with a petrol tanker on the way there, and....'

'*Ohhhhh* my God....'

Mrs Warboys' voice sank to a reverential croak....

'... *he was burnt alive at the steering wheel.* A week before Christmas. I mean, there's nothing you can say, is there? Nothing at all.'

'And she goes to church, you say?'

'Of course I can't say I'm familiar with her myself ... perhaps *you* know her to speak to, Mr Meldrew? I gather she works in that new video shop on Hogarth Avenue ... that's your neck of the woods isn't it?'

M argaret could tell there was something preying on Victor's mind that night because he went to bed without kicking a single garden gnome in the testicles.

'I don't like the look of that oak tree outside Mrs Aylesbury's,' she said, coming away from the curtains. 'Wobbling about like mad in that wind now. I reckon it must've got very badly weakened in the gales. The children were all playing lumberjacks earlier on, trying to make it go through her upstairs window. Say they've rung the parks department five times but the phone lines are still all off apparently. Never known a Christmas like it.'

'No,' said Victor.

And indeed he hadn't.

As he lay awake in the chill December night his conscience reeled under the bombardment of memory and misgiving.

He had guessed, of course, even before Mrs Warboys had described her to him, that Mrs Burridge and the young woman he had brutally laid into about mutilated corpses and roasted faces were one and the same person. Upon leaving the shop that day he had congratulated himself on having made rather a nifty little speech. But with the catalyst of hindsight his sense of triumph had evaporated. Now all he could think of was how much his words must have wounded her. And, in retrospect, how commendably restrained she had been in the face of his oafish misconduct.

For an hour or more he lay there, surrendering to the twin tortures of grief and guilt.....

He thought of a young widow and her five-year-old son, and how their Christmas had become a Holiday in Hell. Of a cherished father, and the cruel vacuum that his death had left behind. He thought of a crabby old cretin in a cap blundering coarsely through someone's bereavement, with – as ever – his brain driven blindly by his mouth.

And he thought of Life.

And he thought of Death.

And, inevitably, he thought of Stuart.

Stuart Meldrew was born on Tuesday September 4th 1951. On Wednesday September 5th 1951 he went off with another woman.

Victor and Margaret were shocked to the core, and so were the doctors, and the police, and the authorities, and just about everyone who read of the affair in the local newspaper.

More accurately of course, another woman went off with Stuart. Baldly and brazenly. Just walked into the maternity wing while no one was looking, scooped him into her arms and then made off with him down the road in a London taxi cab.

Margaret, who had had a difficult pregnancy and an impossible birth, froze over with shock, while the father of the child was seen to gallop about like an ostrich, bellowing at the doctors to for God's sake get his son back.

Five days passed before the taxi driver came forward and led the police to the home of a poor, emotionally disturbed woman in Hertfordshire. Mercifully, the bemused infant was found alive and safe in a cat basket, and duly returned to his mother's arms. And never had the hospital witnessed such scenes of joy as those between the exultant parents and their gurgling, week-old child.

The doctors said there was no reason to believe that his death six days later was due in any way to the abduction. Subsequent examinations had sadly uncovered a hole in the baby's heart which under any circumstances would have limited his chance of survival.

Margaret was strongly cautioned against a second pregnancy, and for a while they had considered the possibilities of adoption. But they knew there was no way you can replace a memory. And ever after, when confronted with the suffering and despair which appear to be all that our time on this planet has to offer, Victor sought solace in the knowledge that his son would never know such pain; that he had been spared the torment of life in a twisted universe.

It was, of course, very scant solace indeed.

At certain times in his life Victor had seriously considered buying a cat so he could train it to be sick all over the Sunday papers. It was a truism to say there was nothing in them worth reading; just as it was to say there was nothing in a bottle of bleach worth drinking.

Nietzsche said a journalist was someone who vomited his bile and called it news. And if Victor had been there when he said it he would probably have given him a round of applause.

On the one hand you had the popular tabloids largely devoted, so far as one could tell, to the sexual fantasies of Dr Josef Goebbels. When they weren't publishing children's fiction under the banner of 'hard facts' their preoccupation seemed to be divided between the length of a certain soap star's penis, and those places where he had parked it during the last fifteen to twenty years. Prevented, for the moment at least, from showing male genitals in their newspapers, most editors did the next best thing by hiring them.

Then you had the so-called quality press, who were even worse. The phrase 'The slaughter of the innocent' seemed woefully inadequate to describe the relentless deforestation that went on so that lots of people who were jolly good at English could masturbate onto a word processor. Every Sunday it was the same. Vast plantations of plant life mercilessly branded like cattle with more specious opinion than anyone in their right mind could ever possibly need to read.

All of it commissioned with but one purpose: *to fill up space.*

To judge from most of their smugly posturing prose you might be fooled into believing newspapers had to be that size to cope with the sheer magnitude of essential reading. The reality, of course, was that the number of pages was entirely dictated by the volume of advertising. And it fell to the editorial staff to ensure there was plenty of nice dense copy to go around it. Rather like having to wall-paper the Grand Canyon really. And in the end just about as socially desirable.

And every Sunday morning, without fail, Victor went out and bought them all.

And she goes to the church, you say....

Deep within the biscuit barrel of his subconscious Margaret's words, uttered last night to Mrs Warboys in the car, continued to beckon him like a lone chocolate digestive.

Which may account for why, on his way back from the newsagent's that morning, he made a rather lengthy detour down Richelieu Terrace, across the recreation ground where a dog with an eye patch was having sex with a diseased elm tree, along the ash path that skirted the bowling green, and then down past the entrance to St Luke's Church.

Across the road the hunched figures of the congregation were dispersing through the lych gate and hastening homeward. Through the arched stone doorway a haunting undertone from the church organ melted into the wind. And high atop the spire the wrought-iron cross seemed to be swaying more precariously than usual: a flimsy antenna to God that was, perhaps, perilously close to disconnection.

Among the bobbing heads Victor identified the solemn features of Mrs Burridge, receiving commiseration from the cassocked priest. Sour and sullen just a few days before, it was – he could see now – a brave face in fact: crushed beyond endurance, yet emboldened by a fierce reserve of inner spirit. With what kind of fortitude, he wondered, would *he* have borne such a personal tragedy?

'Are you the postman?'

If Victor had possessed a pair of high-pitched talking knees – which he did not – he could be forgiven for thinking they were addressing him now. In fact the words had come from a fluorescent green shellsuit, in the centre of which nestled a young child with a drip on the end of his snub nose that was fast becoming an icicle. His hair was light and sandy, the way Victor's had once been, and danced in the breeze like a cornfield. And there was something in the subtle projection of his upper lip that instantly engaged Victor's sympathy, although for the life of him he couldn't work out why. Nor, for a second, could he grasp the reason for the toddler's question; or why he had just placed in

Victor's hand a crinkled blue envelope bearing the words 'To Father Christmas.'

'Sorry?'

He noticed, then, that he had stopped directly beside a pillar-box, which to the youngster he must have appeared to be guarding. He was about to correct this mistake and return the letter when a stern summons rang out from the lych gate across the road.

'Adam!'

Victor watched the boy scurry back to his mother and flinched at the acrid glare of recognition she flashed, briefly, in his direction

'Ummm.... Yyyy— I'm erm ... Mrs Burridge, about the other day in the shop ....' he began as he shuffled across the road towards them. 'The things I said ... at the time....'

But his attempt at reparation was doomed to expire upon the frosting air, for the young woman simply hooked the boy's hand in hers and led him away down the road.

Victor watched them go and sighed. With deep regret but without surprise. He had, after all, no right to expect her forgiveness or understanding.

He was about to continue on his way home when he found he was still holding the child's letter to Father Christmas. Idly he untucked the flap and removed a slip of paper which he unfolded and read.

'Dear Father Christmas,
Please I want my dad to come home for Christmas
Mum says he isnt so I am riting to you.
Love Adam.'

When he had read it Victor folded it up again, replaced it in the envelope, and slid it into the post-box.

It had not, it is fair to say, made him feel any better.

The weather men had predicted snow that Christmas Eve, and they had predicted a bitterly sharp frost with temperatures as low as minus eleven. What they had not predicted was that Victor Meldrew would be driving twenty-five old-age pensioners to a slap-up lunch at the local college, organised by Action for the Elderly. And no one, assuredly, can criticise them for that.

Mrs Warboys, as committee secretary, had been asked if she could think of anyone with a driver's licence who would be happy to give up their day for the old folk. She had immediately come up with thirteen people, all of whom said they would love to help but their sister's family were down that day from Pontefract and they only got to see them once a year, so there was sadly nothing they could do.

Next, she thought of asking Mr Meldrew if *he* would do it.

And after that she thought of asking a lump of granite to become a blood donor.

But then she stopped and thought again. Why *not*? After all, she had managed, in the end, to talk him into that Nativity play. What did she have to lose, apart from her head if he happened to be standing near a chain-saw?

So she had asked him.

And, to her complete astonishment, Victor had said yes.

Of course she had no way of knowing how much Victor's altruism was motivated by an emotional cocktail of guilt, frustration and desire for atonement. In his long and bitter life he had despised most things at one time or another, from self-assembly wardrobes to twin-ply toilet rolls where none of the perforations ever meet. But he had never, so far as he could remember, despised *himself* with the passion he did now.

If the last few days had taught him anything they had taught him that there were in this world far more questions than answers. And that arguably the most intelligent response you could make was to shrug your shoulders and say 'Pass'.

So it was that the morning before Christmas, wrapped up warmly in his best sackcloth and ashes, Victor left the house amid a light flurry of watery snow, and trudged down the road to his garage to get out the car.

He had barely reached the end of Rangoon Gardens when the clutch, which had been 'fixed' by the service department just a week before, began its old tricks by slipping about so erratically it was almost impossible to get out of first gear.

'Bloody car mechanics!' he grumbled. God knows where they recruited them from these days. The only qualification necessary, it seemed, was the ability to wipe your hands on a piece of rag while spitting phlegm all over the floor.

With much perseverance he finally arrived at the van rental centre in Inkerman Road to find Mrs Warboys waiting for him.

Together they collected the thirty-seater mini-bus in which they would ferry their guests to the College of Higher Education, where the authorities had provided all the necessary facilities for the occasion. Several committee members had gone in earlier to prepare the meal so it would be ready to serve when everyone arrived at one o'clock.

And so far everything had gone like clockwork. The problems only began when they reached their destination and were utterly unable to find the room allotted to them.

'Well it must be here *somewhere*,' groused Victor as he tramped round the maze of deserted corridors with a shuffling crocodile of pensioners at his rear. 'We've been past this notice board now *three* times to my certain knowledge. If I see that postcard offering to swap a yashmak for two Scriti Politi albums once more I shall go completely ga-ga.'

'Mrs Bithery definitely said the first floor,' said Mrs Warboys, doubtfully consulting a scrap of paper on which she had scribbled the directions. 'She said if we parked in the *north* car park and came in through the double doors on the *right*, then went up the main staircase and followed the signs to the refectory we couldn't miss it.'

'Yes well I feel compelled to point out we *have* missed it,' grumbled Victor. 'Place is a ruddy rabbit warren. And freezing into the bargain. The only time we've been remotely warm was when we accidentally wandered into the boiler room, I've a good mind to go back down there.'

'It'll be all right once we're there, everybody,' said Mrs Warboys, addressing the shivering herd behind her. 'Mr Killick said he'd make sure there was proper heating on in the room for us. And once you get stuck into your turkey you'll be as warm as toast. I'm sure it won't be long before we find it now.'

Twenty minutes later they were in the middle of a physics lab trying to revive old Mrs Althorp who had passed out from frost-bite.

'God preserve us,' said Victor, as he and Mrs Warboys each took a leg, like a wishbone, and began furiously rubbing to restore her circulation. 'I can't take much more of this. Thirty-five minutes traipsing round in circles with the cast of *Cocoon* inside a multi-storey igloo! Oh! Hang on, look, we're in luck! There's a hole in the toe of her stocking, we can all warm our hands round her chilblain.'

Mrs Warboys was not amused.

'Perhaps we should go back to the car park and start from scratch,' she said. 'It may be that we took a wrong turning earlier on.'

Since no one else had a better suggestion they made their way back to the mini-bus in order to consider the situation more carefully.

'*That's* where we made our mistake!' said Victor, pointing down another driveway to a parking area bounded by blocks of mouldering Sixties concrete. 'We were in the wrong car park to start with! Come on!'

Whereupon he strode off towards a different set of double doors which, it turned out, opened onto a major staircase that, sure enough, took them to a long corridor leading, as luck would have it, to the elusive room marked 'Refectory'.

'Thank God for that,' Victor said, opening the door upon tables lined with turkey portions and sausage rolls, potato salads and breaded drumsticks, and all manner of mouth-watering provender. 'Much longer getting here we'd have all been eating Easter eggs.'

At which everyone finally was able to laugh.

'Right everyone! If you want to hang your hats and coats up over there and sit yourselves down we can start to get cracking....'

Four miles away at the College of Further Education Mrs Bithery looked up from her sprouts as the door to the refectory opened and Mr Killick strode in.

'Any sign of them yet?'

'Nothing,' said Mr Killick. 'I rang the rental place, they said the bus was picked up two hours ago by a rather suspicious woman and a strange-looking man in a cap.'

'Well, that's them,' said Mrs Windle, re-sealing the turkey inside a vast tarpaulin of Baco-foil. 'I can't think what's holding them up, unless Mr Blackaby's artificial leg's got magnetised again. Once that's stuck to the side of a bus you can't budge it for love nor money.'

'It's going to be mashed potatoes if we have to wait much longer,' said Mrs Snetterton. 'And these carrots were past their best twenty minutes ago. Bottom of this saucepan already looks like something you'd use to tarmac the drive. Where in God's name have they *got* to?'

Back at the College of Higher Education things were now going with a swing. Victor had turned up all the convector heaters to full blast, and the musty refectory had quickly reached its normal operating temperature.

To begin with, Mrs Warboys thought it slightly odd that Mrs Bithery and Co. should decide to prepare a cold buffet instead of the more traditional turkey roast. But once they had warmed up the sausage rolls and the vegetable samozas and the pizza triangles in the ovens, and mulled several bottles of blackcurrant cordial in a saucepan, the spread had rapidly burgeoned into a positive banquet.

It was, Mrs Warboys reflected, a shame the committee members had hurried off home early. But then it *was* Christmas Eve and they all had their own lives to lead. Indeed she was herself due to leave at three to take her great-nephew to the zoo. So she could quite understand the pressures they were under.

'Who's for a mince pie?' said Victor, appearing with a large white carton he had discovered in one of the kitchen cupboards. 'Freshly home-made by the looks of them .... Mrs Warboys?'

'I don't think I could eat another thing,' said Mrs Warboys, unusually. Adding, as Victor was about to whip the box away again: 'But perhaps I'll take a couple for later. I'm sorry to have to leave you to it, Mr Meldrew, but I've been promising Toby this trip for ages, and it was the only time I could fit it in during the school holidays.'

'You run along, Mrs Warboys,' said Victor affably. 'We've got everything under control here, haven't we, Mr Blackaby?'

With these words he slapped Mr Blackaby on the back, causing the latter to plunge face-down onto the kitchen floor while his left leg remained upright on top of a drain grille.

'Right then. Well, thanks ever so much for your help and everything,' waffled Mrs Warboys, folding her black glossy coat about her. 'And I hope you both have a really lovely Christmas, and I'll see you soon.'

With a volley of assorted goodbyes she was then out of the door and beetling away down the corridor.

When she had gone, and cups of tea had been served, and

mince pies had been gleefully demolished all round, Victor suggested they might like to play a game.

'Who's for a spot of Pass the Parcel, or Blind Man's Buff?' he asked chirpily. 'Does that sound fun?'

'No, that sounds bloody awful,' said Mrs Althorp. 'What are we all – at kindergarten suddenly?'

'Well I just thought that – '

'Never mind what you thought. This is supposed to be a Christmas party. We're here to enjoy ourselves.'

'You just said it, Mr Parslow,' said old Mrs Webb who was now sitting cross-legged on top of a table, idly carving her initials into the cheese board. 'Let's do something that's *fun*. I know, why don't we see if we can call up Paul Robeson and ask him to sing *Ole Man River* ....'

'I thought Paul Robeson was dead,' said Mrs Croker.

'Of course he's dead,' said Mrs Webb. 'There's no point holding a seance to call up someone who's *alive*, is there? We could see if your Horace is up there as well while we're about it, and ask him where he put the guarantee for that Flymo.'

'*Horace?*' said Mrs Croker.

'Sorry?' said Mrs Webb.

'Who's Horace when he's at home?'

'How should I know?'

'You just said we should see if he was up there.'

'*Maurice* I said, have you gone deaf? Your old man as he was. Before that wasp got into his catheter.'

'You said *Horace*. Don't tell me you said Maurice when you said nothing of the kind.'

'She definitely said Maurice,' said Mrs Althorp, who had just threaded the lace of a surgical boot through her ear and was wearing it like a piece of jewellery. 'I heard her with my own eyes.'

'Look! Excuse me, everyone!' interposed Victor, who was starting to feel a bit like a wrestling referee. 'Can we have a bit of order please, or none of us'll be playing anything.'

'Who asked you to shove your nose in,' said Mrs Spivey in a laid-back drawl. 'Sour-faced old crab ....'

'I beg your pardon!'

But before Victor could frame a suitable reply her words were being echoed by several of her colleagues amid much fruity giggling and incoherent gibbering.

Victor frowned. Gradually he realised that a rather odd change was coming over the elderly party-goers. For certain they had not been as uninhibited as this an hour ago. Indeed, watching seventy-three-year-old Mr Dibley crash out on the floor while Mrs Trilling and Mrs Endicott took it in turns to click Hermesetas into his mouth he could almost swear they were getting drunk. Yet no one there had been issued with anything larger than a small glass of port. So how could *that* have happened?

At that moment, a sound rather like Dr Martin Luther King trying to deliver a speech while being rhythmically kicked in the spleen suddenly filled the room ... causing Victor to clap his hands over his ears, and everyone else to begin jerking about on the floor as if in the advanced stages of Parkinson's Disease. The source of this commotion was, it transpired, a twin-deck cassette-recorder someone had found, primed with a tape by someone – or something – called *Public Enemy*.

Oh well, reasoned Victor. It *was* Christmas. And if it gave them all a bit of pleasure who was he to argue? Squeezing his way through the bouncing throng, past Mrs Croker who was now laughing hysterically at a safety-pin, and old Mr Whittaker who, with strange grinning eyes, was twirling his bowler hat on one finger like a member of the Harlem Globe Trotters, Victor escaped into the kitchen where it was a bit quieter. Perhaps, he thought as he closed the door wearily, now would be a good time to try one of those rather nice mince pies....

M rs Warboys always enjoyed taking her nephew Toby round the zoo. It was vital that youngsters had a chance to observe these things at first hand, before they disappeared off the face of the earth forever. Zoos, after all, were a vanishing species. Faced with relentless persecution by Man, they were fast becoming extinct in many parts of the world. And it wouldn't be long before the only elephant-keeper you could see would be a stuffed one in the Natural History Museum.

'You can see the reasoning of course,' she said to him as they emerged from the parrot house, having just witnessed something uncannily similar to Prime Minister's Question Time. 'It *is* cruel to put animals in cages, if you stop and think about it. I mean, it's not natural. Apart from the tigers, obviously. You have to lock *them* up. Otherwise they'd be roaming round the streets mauling everyone to death. And the vultures. They're dangerous as well. You wouldn't want one of *them* perched on your clothes line, you'd be scared to let your cat out of doors.'

With much veneration Toby said 'Yes, Aunty Jean' and followed her across King Kong Boulevard to the monkey house.

The early puffs of snow had been mild and had not lasted very long. But in the waning light of winter's dusk there were signs that the weather was now getting its act together. Larger, fluffier flakes like cotton wool could be seen swirling in the glare of the street lamps, and the roads and rooftops were assuming a haunting, powdery glow.

'Please do not feed the animals' the notices said. But it was hard to resist the cupped hands the monkeys tendered through the bars of their cages. Before long Mrs Warboys and Toby were clean out of the nuts and dried fruits and bits of stale bread they had brought along with them.

'I'm afraid that's about it then,' said Mrs Warboys as they watched a pack of screeching chimpanzees fight it out over a Cloret breath-freshener. Then, noting the disappointed look on the boy's face, she added: 'Unless there's anything else I can find in my bag.'

It is no indiscretion to say that Victor Meldrew was not one of the world's great scat singers. Generally, his endeavours to thread more than three musical notes together without someone reporting a cat stuck up a chimney were doomed to failure. Yet for the last five minutes he had amazed everyone present – not least himself – with a rendition of *Mr Bo Jangles* that would have caused Sammy Davis Junior to sit down and weep with admiration. Ask not where he derived his sudden flair for rhythm and phrasing; or to what he owed his unlikely prowess as a tapdancer, shuffling and shimmying from table-top to table-top in a blistering display of improvised syncopation. The fact is that he did it. And, what is even stranger, that he had no idea why.

In the end he could only put it down to the festive spirit. Having emerged from the kitchen after his mince pie to find two dozen septuagenarians jitterbugging to a merry number by *Niggers Wid Attitude*, he decided it would be uncivil not to join in the fun.

For a full two hours thereafter the partying pensioners completely forgot where they were, they forgot what time it was, and they forgot how old they were. And strangest of all, they forgot what *colour* they were.

For the life of him Victor couldn't explain why he suddenly felt as if he had turned black. It was certainly not a sensation he had experienced before. But there was no denying that ethnic exhilaration that had come over him. It was as if the operating system in his brain had been switched from MS-DOS to Jive, causing every blood cell in his veins to swagger along to a hip-hop beat. And later that afternoon, when he found himself back at the wheel of the mini-bus, dropping the guests home one by one, there seemed nothing remotely odd about telling each wrinkled dude to give him some skin before they went inside to get down with their bad selves.

Because hey, it *was* Christmas after all.

Desmond was also feeling pretty black at that moment. And a very mellow feeling it was too. Of course Desmond *was* black, as most gorillas are. But like Victor and the others he had undergone a curious mood swing, causing him to view the world with a less jaundiced eye than usual.

Normally, sitting on a heap of straw all day long scratching your scrotum had precious little going for it, either in the way of job satisfaction or prospects for career advancement. It was for any animal – let alone one of the higher primates – a professional dead-end, and seriously damaging to your self-confidence. Especially when you heard that some floozie in the next block was up for another tea commercial, while you couldn't get so much as an audition for a singing telegram.

However, this afternoon all that had changed. Since he had been visited by that lady in the black fur coat the world had become a really neat place indeed. His bare stone cage, suddenly, was a seductive open-plan apartment, shrewdly styled as a hymn to minimalism. The hideous squawking racket in the corridor outside, which normally drove him batty, was now a symphonic poem of crucial ape-expression. Even that bad banana on the floor was a really *mean* bad banana; with something about its soggy, blackened appearance that whispered sexily to him the words: '*Smoke me.*'

Yes, the more he thought about that lady in the black fur coat the more agreeable it all became. He had always found big coats a turn-on. And hers had been exceptionally sleek, and bulged in all the right places for a gorilla. True, her face was a little on the 'human' side, but then no one was perfect.

Desmond growled. Deep within his copious breast he could feel a surge of primal emotion the like of which he had not known in years. Fired with a raw energy that appeared to begin somewhere between his stumpy legs and radiated outwards through every inch of his massive frame, he realised – to his surprise and delight – that something utterly delicious had happened to him.

He was *in love*.

And who would dare to suggest that this sudden ardour was in any way falsified, or associated with the two crumpled mince pies that the lady in the black fur coat had pitched into his yawning mouth for her nephew's amusement? Indeed, who would dare to speculate that those mince pies, and dozens more just like them, were part of a special consignment designed to enliven a student party that night at the local College of Higher Education? Or that those same mince pies might have been prepared using any ingredient stronger than a small dash of cooking sherry?

It would be futile, after all, to dwell on the shock and dismay exhibited by Mike, Steffi, Jools and Carla when they returned to the refectory that evening to discover the mouth-watering spread they had laid out earlier was now a mere sea of crumbs and chicken bones.

Such details would have held little interest for Desmond as he began to lollop backwards and forwards in his cage, his brain awash with torrid images from the gorilla equivalent of an art-house movie. And although Mr R. F. Dobkin didn't quite know what hit him when he stepped into the cage at feeding time, we can reveal it was the business end of Desmond's fist, sharply delivered to his keeper's jawbone with all the power you would expect from a sodding great gorilla who was high on mind-bending drugs.

Three seconds later, when the unconscious attendant was lying face down in something that you certainly wouldn't want to be *conscious* and lie face down in, Desmond leapt through the door and was soon bounding away down the corridor as fast as his knuckles would carry him.

What happened to Mrs Warboys on The Night Before Christmas was so unutterably horrific it made her pine for the relative haven of a mortuary drawer, or a five-hour session with her trusty old friend the stomach-pump.

It is all very well, with hindsight, to say that after putting Toby on the bus home she ought never to have slipped back into the zoo as they were locking up, to search for a mislaid glove. After all, the last thing you expect to see when you pop inside a Ladies rest room is a 400lb ape sitting on the lavatory in a state of obvious sexual arousal.

Mrs Warboys did what any sensible person would have done under the circumstances, and fainted. Which is probably just as well, as she would not have relished the experience of being heaved across the animal's shoulder and lugged back to its den through the darkly deserted zoo.

When, several minutes later, Mr R. F. Dobkin regained consciousness he was relieved to see that Desmond had not decided to abscond, but was still there in the corner, attempting to set fire to a banana that was loosely dangling from his lips. Pausing to snatch back his Bic lighter Mr Dobkin swiftly exited and secured the door behind him, paying little heed to a slight twitching movement in the pile of straw beneath Desmond's bottom.

'A bloody Merry Christmas,' he said, nursing his chin. 'I *don't* think.'

And as he vanished down the corridor, extinguishing every light and fastening every padlock, so vanished any hope that Mrs Warboys might be spared eighteen truly terrifying hours in the loving arms of her grisly new admirer.

Loving arms ... roving hands ... and ....

Well, let's be honest, it doesn't bear thinking about.

M argaret looked at the clock on the video recorder, which said 19.02, and sighed.

It was 21.41.

Where the *Hell* had Victor got to?

Indeed, where the Hell had he been all day, since it now appeared he had not arrived at the college as planned. According to Mrs Bithery she and her colleagues had waited two hours before deciding to put the dinner out of its misery into the pig-bins. After which they had shut up shop and gone home.

But here was the really strange thing ....

Victor and Mrs Warboys had definitely picked up the mini-bus that morning. And the pensioners had all been taken to lunch *somewhere*, for they were now back at home dribbling cake crumbs and coleslaw. Sadly, all efforts by friends and neighbours to question them had met with a stream of gibberish and, in one or two cases, a slurred rendition of *I Can Hear The Grass Grow*. Without doubt it was a mystery to rival that of the *Marie Celeste*.

For three hours Margaret had forced herself to believe there was a harmless explanation for it all; that at any moment her husband would come tramping through the door moaning about some new, mind-boggling outrage no one could possibly have foreseen. But as the minutes had ticked by her confidence had begun to ebb. And finally, with a deep breath, she lifted the phone and dialled the police.

There was, of course, a simple answer to the question, *Where was Victor Meldrew?* which was this:

Victor Meldrew was lost.

For the first couple of hours it had given him quite a buzz, driving round the streets going 'Brmmm brmmm brmmm!' and stopping at zebra crossings to let the Belisha beacons across – until gradually it had dawned on him that he hadn't the faintest idea where he was going.

Already the events of that afternoon had become no more than a faint splodge in his memory. He seemed to remember, at one point, being at a strange party where elderly women were attempting to limbo dance under a zimmer frame. But beyond that everything was sketchy. Oh yes, and he could vaguely recall careering around town in a mini-bus, wishing lots of people Merry Christmas as they opened the sliding door and fell head-first onto the pavement.

The next thing he knew he had been in a big yard with lots of vans in it, climbing back into his Hillman Avenger and setting off home. But that was three hours ago. Now here he was, cruising the streets, unable to make head nor tail of the perfectly legible road signs that loomed up at him in the night.

The snow was gusting fiercely now into the frozen cones of his headlight beams. On the paths it had crystallised into a layer of crunchy meringue, while on the bushes and the crooks of the branches it nested precariously in a marshmallow fashion, winking and sparkling with sequinned delight.

It was hard enough to steer a car in such conditions at the best of times – let alone when you were driving under the influence of a mince pie. To Victor's eyes the world appeared to be rippling and distorting into strange wave-patterns, like someone kicking the side of an aquarium. And the dark, raging blizzard that bayed at his car was a phantasmagoria of sinister shapes and images.

It should also be mentioned – if the next part of the story is to mean anything – that he was still having trouble with his clutch. For the last twenty minutes he had been creeping along in second gear at the piddling rate of 13 mph, searching anxiously for a familiar landmark in the gloom.

But by now he was way off the beaten track, flanked by rows of Victorian terraces that cowered behind flaking stucco walls. And as he crawled around the corner, his tyres crackling on the frozen mush, Victor spied ahead of him a young lady in a darkened doorway, stomping her feet on the paving stones to keep warm. She had clearly been caught out by the weather because she was remarkably under-dressed. Indeed from a distance it was hard to tell that she had a skirt on at all.

Seeing Victor's car purr slowly towards her she must have sensed he was about to ask directions, for she immediately clopped forward on her high heels and, skidding across an icy patch on the path, ended up clinging to a lamp post for support.

'Good evening, sir!' she called as Victor pulled up and wound down his window. 'You business?'

Since Victor had no idea what she meant by this he simply smiled and emitted an all-purpose grunting noise. His speech, when it came, was considerably muddied by a drunken slur:

'I wonder if you can give me a hand at all....'

'No problem,' said the young lady. 'Hand or head, I give either, it's you that's paying.'

Again Victor mustered a stupid grin before burbling:

'I think I've come the wrong way. You couldn't point me east could you?'

'I can point you anywhere you want, sir,' came the reply. 'We can use it as a sundial if you like. What are you, one of them Moslems or something?'

'I beg your pardon?'

'And in any case, who's to say there's a right way or a wrong way? Everybody's different, aren't they?'

Just as Victor had concluded the girl must be loopy and was about to move off he found, to his surprise, that she had opened the passenger door and climbed in beside him.

'Cold old night, isn't it?' she said, cupping her numbed fingers over his heater vent. 'Least it's Christmassy. I wouldn't normally be working tonight, but it's been a bad year.'

'I'm sorry?'

'Shall we go then?'

Victor sat blinking at her for several seconds, until slowly it dawned on him.

'Oh ... You're going to show me the way ... ?'

'That's right, sir. It's only a couple of minutes. You turn left at the end here.'

'Ohh. Right. Thank you.'

This was uncommonly generous of her, he thought as he set off again. There couldn't be many people who would personally accompany you to make sure you got back on the right road. But then, it was a pretty brutal night and she was probably glad to be in the warm.

She had a young face with old eyes. Her hair was bottle blonde and cropped hard against her head like a bathing cap. Her cheeks were raw and the skin washed out, like her voice. When she spoke to him she spoke directly to the night air, and her manner was oddly brisk.

'You live near here then?' mumbled Victor, trying to drum up conversation.

'Me? I live out of town. I've got a room in a house here I use. I just pay them a flat rent. They get their money they don't bother me. Watch this bend, cos it's very slippy ....'

As advice goes it was a little late, for Victor, whose head felt like a helium balloon that was about to pop at any moment, had already lost control of the vehicle and was bringing it shakily to a halt in the middle of someone's front garden. There was an excruciating crunch as his front wheel went over a broken Kronenberg bottle, followed by the slow sizzling noise of escaping air.

'*Shit*,' he said, and threw open his door to inspect the damage.

'I wouldn't worry, they're away,' said the girl, cocking a leg out and sinking her stiletto heel into the snow. 'Anyway, we're here now, come on.'

With which she threw her bag over her shoulder and began

carefully picking her way across the road to an old house guarded
by a rusting motor cycle and six overflowing dustbins.

Victor gazed down at his tyre and wept inwardly. Then he
wept outwardly, came over all woozy again, lost his footing, and
suddenly found himself flat on his stomach spitting out mouth-
fuls of slush.

'You OK?' the girl shouted from the porch, where she was
fumbling with her keys.

'I think I need to make a phone-call ....' gargled Victor
unintelligibly.

'You coming in or what?'

'Oh! Yes ... thank you very much, that's very kind....'

Groggily he hauled himself to his feet and staggered after her
into the house. The hallway was drably carpeted, with crusting
paintwork and what appeared to be a parking lot for push-chairs
in front of the kitchen. The door to the sitting room was open and
a family of Asians were seated reverentially in front of the television watching *Carry On At Your Convenience*. A line of chaser
lights blinked sluggishly round a threadbare Christmas tree on
the sideboard. And sprawled upon the floor was either a large
scrawny-looking Alsatian or someone's deceased grandmother,
Victor couldn't be sure which.

'Evening Mr Shastri, coming down really thick out there now!'
said the girl, kicking her shoes up and down on the doormat.

Within the room Mr Shastri, who was shaped like a small
bathysphere in horn-rimmed glasses, looked up with a cheery
wave.

'Evening Belinda. A merry Christmas to you.'

'Merry Christmas. Come on, sir, this way up.'

'Oh,' said Victor. 'Right.'

Pausing to give Mr Shastri and his family a friendly nod he
followed Belinda up the creaking staircase to a small room at the
end of the landing. Here, he presumed, he would be offered a
telephone so he could ring Margaret to let her know what was
happening.

But when they entered the room and Belinda closed the door
Victor couldn't see a telephone, or anything that resembled one.
The only things he *could* see were a rather spartan bed draped
with a grey blanket, a wardrobe that appeared to be in use as a
hostel for underprivileged woodworm, and on the floor a family
size box of Sainsbury's tissues.

Belinda plonked herself onto the bed, crossed her legs and leaned back on her hands.

'Let me just tell you the prices,' she said. 'It's twenty for straight, thirty if you want French, or extra for anything special. S and M and cozzies and stuff. Obviously it's up to you.'

'Hmmm?'

Victor was finding it hard to concentrate. This standing up business seemed to be taking it out of him, and he already felt fit to keel over again. His clothes were soaked and clinging to his skin like frozen leeches. In addition, he had badly gashed his knee on some broken glass and the blood was seeping through his trousers. He looked, and felt, a complete wreck.

'You hear me, sir?'

'Oh – sorry.' Dimly, Victor tried to recollect her words. Yes, twenty pence seemed about right for a phone call. Although why she imagined he would want to conduct it in French was a mystery. The main thing was to get his car operational again: he certainly wouldn't get very far with a flat tyre.

'Ummm . . . yes, that's fine,' he mumbled, swaying uncertainly from side to side. 'I may need a hand pumping the thing up . . . .'

'Don't worry, sir, that's *my* job. I can soon see to that.'

'Hhhhhhh! . . . I feel absolutely *filthy* . . . .'

'And why not, sir – it *is* Christmas. Just tell me what you had in mind.'

But again Victor had stopped listening, and was muttering drunkenly to himself as a prelude to being violently sick over the carpet.

'I don't know what's . . . hhhhhhappened to me today . . . I don't thing . . . I can sssssssssstand up . . . .'

'That's all right, no one expects you to,' said Belinda, sitting him down on the bed and threading her fingers inside his rain-coat. 'Let's get these clothes off shall we?'

'Wwwwwhat are you doing? I think . . . I'd like . . . a doctor . . . .'

'A doctor?'

Victor swallowed hard and nodded.

'Not sure I can manage one of those . . . I can do you a nurse if you like.'

'Nnnnnurse . . . yes . . . thank you . . . .'

'Oh no, I tell a lie! The uniform's still at the cleaners. What about a traffic warden?'

Victor gurgled dangerously as she levered his left foot through a sodden mass of blood-stained trouser. *A traffic warden?*

'Girl guide? Air stewardess?'

Victor's stomach felt distinctly like a pot of stew that was about to boil over.

'I'd bbbbetter go to the bathroom....'

'It's not as comfortable as the bed, sir....'

But he had already broken away from her now, and was lurching half-naked towards the door.

'Still, if you prefer it in there it's up to you .... Oh here's a thought, sir – what about a policewoman?'

Before he disappeared into the shadows Victor managed to blurt out the words:

'Policew – yesssss! Get the pppp— excuse me....'

A second later he had blundered into the bathroom and slammed the door.

'Policewoman,' said Belinda. 'Right....'

With cool professionalism she stepped out of her skirt and began unbuttoning her blouse.

A fter being sick in the toilet Victor seemed to remember climbing into the bath for a brief lie down. Which had, of course, been a fatal error, because the instant his head hit the enamel he fell into a turbulent sleep.

While he was asleep he had a terrible dream. What happened in the dream was that he was lying naked in a bath in a strange house when a policewoman strode into the room, forced both his wrists behind his head and handcuffed them to the shower pipe. Then, as he struggled to no avail, she knelt across his chest and proceeded to do things to him below the waist that he could not see, but which brought to mind the image of a demented beaver gnawing at a log of wood.

It was an obscene dream. It was a disgusting dream. And of course it was not a dream.

...as Victor discovered to his cost when his hand accidentally hit the tap and he was roused from his delirium by a faceful of freezing water.

The frantic gurgling noises this caused him to make were evidently interpreted by Belinda as a sign that she was doing something right. Thus encouraged, she increased the ferocity of her efforts, which only made Victor shriek all the more.

As he shrieked he became gradually conscious that he was becoming gradually conscious.

The emptying of his stomach, followed by his brief sleep followed by several minutes spent writhing under an ice-cold shower seemed finally to have done the trick. In a flash, the events of the afternoon came sharply into focus. The helium balloon popped inside his head. And for the first time in more than ten hours he was able to see straight again.

It was not a pretty sight.

Where the regulation black skirt had ridden up, inches from his eyes, a bulge of chubby white flesh could be seen above the quivering sheen of taut nylon. As she became more energetic and her bottom rose and fell in the air something on the other leg appeared to give way and Victor felt a small round button cannon sharply into his left eye. The stocking then shrivelled limply down her thigh and came to rest at the knee, which was half-resting in a puddle of water in the bottom of the bath.

In his mind's eye Victor could image the object of her attentions now resembling a half-chewed Topic bar. Indeed he was tempted to speculate that the woman was not, after all, carrying out the operation personally, but had engaged a specially trained crocodile to perform it on her behalf. Since she had her back to him he could only hazard a guess as to what horrors were going on down there in the name of sexual gratification.

All of which did not so much boost his masculinity as reduce it to a size where it would comfortably fit inside a pencil sharpener. Good God, he thought, did people in their right minds actually *pay* for this sort of thing?

'For mercy's sake,' he bellowed, 'will you get *off* of me!!!'

But Belinda did not get off of him. It was almost as if she was unable to hear, now that the strange, low buzzing noise had started up.

Buzzing noise?

For a moment Victor was seized with a panic that she was about to bring into play some form of battery-operated food whisker ... until he realised that the sound was in fact coming from the wash-basin. Looking round he discovered to his astonishment the owner of the house, Mr Shastri, calmly shaving with an electric razor in front of the bathroom mirror.

...while from downstairs, through the open doorway, came the sound of Kenneth Williams as W. C. Boggs uttering a priceless joke about cockles....

Victor was stunned into disbelief. Here he was lying manacled to a bath, shrieking to kingdom come while some uniformed bint used him for oboe practice, and two feet away the man was standing there in a dressing gown as merry as you please trimming away at his stubble. Presumably this sort of thing was perfectly normal in his household on Christmas Eve.

So distracted was he, for the moment, by the portly gentleman who was running a Ronson over his chin that Victor failed to notice the girl finally arise from him and clamber wearily back onto the bathroom floor.

'God, you talk about trying to raise the dead,' she said, flexing her jaw. 'I think I'm going to go and get a Strepsil, I'll be back in a sec.'

'Going to get a Streps— Look! Don't you g— No!! Come back!' yelled Victor as she limped, exhausted, towards the door. 'For God's sake, you stupid bl— *Will you take off these bloody handcuffs!*'

But Belinda was gone. And Mr Shastri, who had just completed his ablutions, turned from the sink preparing to follow her.

'Did you require the light left on, sir?' he asked, with one hand on the cord that dangled from the ceiling. 'Only I have to think of the electricity bills.'

'Require the light left on? I don't want *anything* except to get out of this sodding bath!!' shrieked Victor, rattling the pipes behind his head like a mad person. 'Do you think I'm lying here like this for *pleasure*??? Have you taken leave of your senses?? Look – the key's just there on the windowsill! For goodness sake undo these things so I can get out! *Please*!!'

To his astonishment Mr Shastri just stood and smiled at him with a look of benign understanding.

'They are very realistic,' he said. 'Your shouts and screams. And I know they are important for your pleasure. But could I ask you to moderate them slightly now as my youngest child is trying to sleep.'

Victor could only splutter his disbelief.

'Good night to you, sir!'

'Wait!!! Come back!!' he screamed as Mr Shastri left the room.

'It's all been a horrible *mistake*!! Will you for God's sake come *back* here!!'

'Downstairs Sid and Hattie and the gang were getting up to all manner of hilarious jinks, for he could hear the sound of doors being kicked in, followed by frantic scuffling noises and hysterical voices that were a bit on the shrill side, even for a *Carry On*. At which point Mr Shastri came racing back into the bathroom, puffing and gasping, snatched up the little key Belinda had left on the windowsill, and quickly released Victor from his bondage. Pausing only to toss the handcuffs out of the window he then scuttled out again.

Confused but relieved, Victor nursed his wrists and quickly retrieved his underpants from the back of the cistern. He was just groping his way nakedly across the darkened landing to look for the rest of his clothes when he found his way blocked by a police-woman's tunic. Determined that history should not be repeated, he lashed out fiercely with his elbow to send the poor girl rocketing through an open doorway, where she collided with a rickety old book shelf that proceeded to rain the complete works of Ruth Rendell down upon her head. Then he clapped his hands victoriously like cymbals and strode back into the bedroom where he found Belinda being questioned by two uniformed police constables.

'*A*rrested???' exclaimed Margaret down the mouthpiece of the phone. 'But— w— what's he supposed to have *done*?'

'Hohh! Now you're asking us,' said Detective Sergeant Gannis cheerily through a mouthful of wine gums. 'It's more a question of what he *hasn't* done.'

'But – *what*?? Is he all right? What's happened to him?'

'*He's* all right,' chirruped Sgt Gannis. 'Although I can't speak for the young WPC he brutally attacked half an hour ago. Doctors say she may never read a work of detective fiction again.'

'What on *earth* has been going on? Where is he now?'

'The last time I looked he was being physically restrained in one of our interrogation rooms, where his pleas of innocence were the source of great amusement to all and sundry. We take a video of these proceedings now as a matter of course, Mrs Meldrew, and the word is that this one could be a bestseller. If you fancy a bootleg copy just let me know. Though I should warn you it's not the sort of thing you'd show your granny.'

'For goodness sake will you tell me what he's been accused of?'

'Of course, Mrs Meldrew – you've got a few hours to spare have you? Ha ha, where would we be without a sense of humour? Now hang on, I've got the charge sheet in front of me here somewhere .... Yes, here we are. How does this little lot grab you? Assault on a police officer, indecent exposure, obscene language, damage to property, dangerous driving, illegal parking, kerb crawling, driving while under the influence of dangerous drugs, and armed robbery. Not bad for a night's work is it? As I say, we *were* hoping he'd refuse to give a blood sample as well – you know, to make it up to the round ten. But as he'd already cut his leg open it was just a matter of sticking a glass underneath and catching the drips.'

'I ... still don't understand,' stuttered Margaret, flopping backwards onto a dining room chair. 'When d— I mean how did all this happen?'

'How does it ever happen, Mrs Meldrew? Bloke with an unhappy marriage, a home life that's miserable and empty, a wife who can't satisfy him sexually any more? You tell me. What, I'm afraid, is undeniable fact is that your husband was observed at various points during the evening cruising slowly around an area of town notorious for prostitution.

'He was further observed picking up one of these prostitutes and driving her back to her flat, where he wilfully rammed his car into the front garden of a neighbour's home, causing inevitable damage to their property. By the time our lads moved in with the crowbars I gather your husband had been having a merry old time of it fettered to the cold water pipes with a pair of handcuffs. Handcuffs, I might add, that are believed to have been illegally acquired from a local police station. In fact it was only out of the kindness of our hearts we didn't do him for handling stolen goods as well.'

'And y— you said something about *an armed robbery?*'

'Oh yes, that was the fairy on top of the tree!' chuckled the officer at the other end, audibly crossing his legs on the desk. 'I mean we thought we'd already hit the jackpot as it was, but then blow me down if, when we took his fingerprints, we didn't find they were a perfect match with those taken at a local street market back in February ... bloke with a hand-gun who just bowled up to one of the stalls, as calm as you please, and made off with a brown tweed jacket. We've got the owner coming in shortly and we're pretty confident he'll make a positive identification. So yes, generally speaking it's really made our Christmas for us all down here.'

'Ohhhhhh my *Goddd* . . . .'

Margaret, not for the first time that evening, felt quite faint.

'Anyway!' added Sgt Gannis. 'I just thought you'd like to know. If you'll excuse me now, I've got to go and nick some carol singers for disturbing the peace. A Merry Christmas to you, Mrs Meldrew.'

A *Merry Christmas!*

Well, it is no idle speculation to say there was little that was merry about it for Victor Meldrew, incarcerated in a twin-bed police cell next to a man suspected of strangling a basketball team. On a merriness scale of one to ten it was also hard to imagine Mrs Warboys — struggling at that moment to work out the gorilla language for 'platonic relationship' — rating it much above *minus twenty*. Even Margaret Meldrew, sleeping on her own that night with just two hundred concrete gnomes for companionship, was bound to admit that she had known better Christmas Eves.

And what of the rest of us this Christmas?

Where, for any of us, is there comfort in the inevitability of tragedy? Where is there lasting joy in the ruthless passing of time? And where is there festivity in Man's futility?

Where is there Hope in Despair?

Such questions preyed heavily upon the mind of Mrs Linda Burridge as she stood before her bedroom window, watching the final minutes of the day slip softly into the black sleep of eternity.

Around her, all was silent. And in the stillness of the shadows she stood gazing upon the world, alone with her fears.

Her son was fast asleep in his room. Before she kissed him goodnight he had hung his pillow case on the bottom of the bed and asked what time his Dad was coming home tomorrow. And how much he was looking forward to seeing him, with all the presents he knew he would bring for them both. And inside her heart she had screamed. For how could she tell him?

Around her, all was silent.

Outside, the wind had faded finally and a frosting skin had begun to form upon the silken snow.

Snow, at Christmas! In truth it had no business being there, and should have remained where it belonged amid the fakery of films and supermarket commercials. Yet here it was, unseasonally in place, sugar-coating the skyline beneath a sea of stars, like a page from a story book.

Within seconds it would be Christmas Day. And bravely she steeled herself for the final, searing sadness that she knew this would bring.

Around her, all was s—

But no!

A sudden sound had caught her attention.

Not a loud sound.

But in the breathless hush of a still winter's night a sound that caused her pulse to quicken and a rush of terror to take possession of her soul.

Someone was coming up the stairs . . . .

The small cardboard label was in the shape of a grinning Christmas pudding, and bore the words: 'To Mr and Mrs Meldrew, with all our love from Mr and Mrs Burkett.'

It was attached by a length of red twine to a huge box swathed in Christmas wrapping paper. Around the wrapping paper jolly Dickensian gentlefolk could be seen driving horse-drawn coaches and laughing uncontrollably at the social deprivations of the Victorian under-class.

Margaret tore the wrapping paper off with her fingernails, opened the box and, lifting out the large concrete garden gnome, placed it in the sitting room with all the others. Since there were already 123 completely identical to it her husband would never notice it when he returned that afternoon from the police station.

It would be nice to report that, in the interests of a happy ending, the charges against Victor Meldrew had been dropped when the police realised it had all been a huge mistake resulting from a complex web of hilarious misunderstandings. And that, toasting his health with a small glass of ginger wine, the detectives had apologised for any inconvenience and wished him a Very Merry Christmas as they waved him on his way.

But this was real life.

In actuality Victor's release from jail at 2.17 p.m. on Christmas Day was due more to prison over-crowding than any admission of error by the authorities. In allowing him home, pending criminal proceedings in the New Year, the police were in truth responding to a plea by the serial killer in the next bed to for God's sake get rid of this bastard who keeps moaning all the time.

'Where did that other gnome come from?' said Victor as he entered the front room at half past three, having just trudged five and a half miles through rivers of melting slush.

'Mr and Mrs Burkett sent it,' said Margaret with a guilty flinch. 'I did tell them we wanted one, but of course that was before all the erm .... You ready for a cup of tea by now I expect?'

Victor threw down his cap and collapsed dismally onto the sofa.

'Yes, as I imagine we're out of strychnine it'll have to be P.G. Tips.'

Margaret filled the electric kettle and switched it on with a sigh. He would need more than P.G. Tips after all he had been through. At which point she suddenly remembered the herbal tea Pippa had given her a few weeks ago. What with all the traumas of the past month she had forgotten every word about it. But yes, there it was in its urn-shaped silver caddy, sitting on the top shelf where she'd left it ....

'There we are, drink that,' she said after she had prepared her husband a particularly strong brew to calm his nerves. 'It's a special herbal recipe, Pippa got it from the health food shop. Should help to soothe your nerves a bit, by all accounts.'

Victor drank it straight back and was sick for two hours in the bathroom.

'I'm never going to so much as *look* at a mince-pie ever *again*,' he groaned as he traipsed back into the sitting room that evening. 'Never did find out what was in the bloody things. Hohhhhhh *Goddd*. Christmas!! And you wonder why I never look forward to it?'

Margaret smiled a feeble smile.

'I yerrmm . . . .'

'What,' said Victor curtly.

'I know we said that ... you know, about not buying each other any presents this Christmas and everything, but . . . . So for goodness sake don't start moaning and groaning at me! All right? But ... well ... anyway. Happy Christmas.'

With a fond grin she thrust into his hands the gaily-packaged cube she had fished from the sideboard, and took one pace backwards to await his reaction.

'W— y— Ohhhhh ... For goodn—'

Removing first all the little red twirly bits and peeling back the crisp golden casing, Victor drew out a smart black box with a hinged lid which he snapped open.

'Tchhhh ... Ohhhhh – *thank you*. I don't know wh— What did you want to go buying me a new watch for?'

'Well at least you can throw that other thing out now and stop trying to guess what time it is.'

'Tchohhhhh ....' He took her in his arms then, with a smile of mock reproof, and in a moment of tender intimacy all the horrors of the past twelve months were momentarily forgotten.

'Well ...' he said, withdrawing with a mischievous sigh and heading for the bureau in the dining room. 'I suppose I may as well confess ....'

'What's that?' grinned Margaret.

'I'm afraid I did exactly the same thing ....'

He had returned to her now, clutching a small box of his own.

'Oh yes?'

'Yes,' he said. '*I* bought myself a new watch as well.'

Wincing with deep embarrassment he flicked the case open to reveal a similar timepiece on a bed of ruffled velvet. Margaret gazed at it through eyes of quenched anticipation, and tried to disguise the lumpy swallowing action in her throat by adjusting her collar.

'I'm sorry, Margaret ... but I mean we *did* both agree that – I mean ... didn't we?'

'Yes,' said Margaret, bravely. 'Yes we did. It's my own fault. I suppose I just didn't expect y— Well anyway. The damage is done now isn't it.'

Margaret's words had rarely proved more prophetic, for at that moment there was the most almighty explosion of crashing and smashing behind them, coupled with the sensation of a small earthquake erupting in the centre of the dining room. And through a swirl of dust and debris, to the sound of thudding timber and tinkling particles of glass, they turned, slowly, to behold a mass of branches poking through their front room window.

Mortally wounded by recent gales, the mighty oak across the road had, after due deliberation and taking all things carefully into account, decided finally upon the place where it should be laid to rest. And that place was not through Mrs Aylesbury's bedroom window. Which meant that Victor Meldrew – though all along he had set his heart against it – did, after all, have a tree in the house for Christmas.

In Victor's dream that night – as in so many dreams – the dead had risen from their graves. There in the living flesh before him was the husband of poor Mrs Burridge, alive and whole again, cheerfully carving the Christmas turkey with a handful of glinting blades like Freddy Kruger. But his face was not scorched or blistered or burned. For in his dream Mr Burridge had not, as he had in reality, died at the wheel of his car a week before Christmas. He had parked it at the airport and travelled abroad, all as planned. But the car had been stolen by a joy-rider who had been burned beyond recognition when he hit a petrol tanker. And because all the telephone lines were down after the storms Mr Burridge had been unable to call his wife from Germany, and had returned home on Christmas Eve knowing nothing of his family's grief. Which meant that they had all enjoyed the happiest Christmas of their lives.

In his dream, too, he saw his son Stuart who had not, as he had in life, died in a maternity hospital all those years ago. For he had been seized by an emotionally disturbed woman with a baby of her own that she knew would not live. Surrendering her own infant she had hidden Stuart away, and had tried to raise him until her untimely death when he had been taken into care and subsequently fostered and adopted.

And he had grown to manhood and had married and fathered a son of his own: a beaming, snub-nosed child with Victor's hair and Margaret's lips. Yes, Victor could see the toddler's face before him as if it were real.

But of course it was just a dream.

At 7.24 a.m. Victor Meldrew suddenly snorted very loudly and woke himself up to face another day.

Twenty-one point two per cent of the population were at that moment going to the lavatory.

Which was well in line with the seasonal average.

202